ISBN 978-1-330-36263-1
PIBN 10002777

FIVE YEARS

IN CHINA;

FROM 1842 TO 1847.

TH AN ACCOUNT OF THE OCCUPATION OF THE ISLANDS

OF

LABUAN AND BORNEO

BY HER MAJESTY'S FORCES.

BY LIEUT. F. E. FORBES, R.N.

COMMANDER OF H. M. S. BONETTA.

LONDON:

ICHARD BENTLEY, 8, NEW BURLINGTON STREET,

Publisher in Ordinary to Her Majesty;

1848.

104912

LONDON:
Printed by S. & J. BENTLEY, WILSON, and FLEY,
Bangor House, Shoe Lane.

CONTENTS.

CHAPTER I.

INTRODUCTION.

PAGE

CHAPTER II.

SHANGHAE.

CHAPTER III.

COINS.

CHAPTER IV.

AGRICULTURE.

CHAPTER V.

DIET AND DINNER IN A TAVERN.

CHAPTER VI.

EDUCATION.

CONTENTS.

CHAPTER VII.

CONFUCIUS.

CHAPTER VIII.

TAOUISM.

CHAPTER IX.

BUDDHISM.

CHAPTER X.

THE ISLE OF POO-TO.

CHAPTER XI.

CHRISTIANITY.

CHAPTER XII.

MILITARY.

CHAPTER XVI.

MISCELLANEOUS.

CHAPTER XVII.

THE TREATY AND TAKING POSSESSION OF LABUAN.

CHAPTER XVIII.

MASSACRE OF BRUNÉ.

CHAPTER XIX.

MANNERS AND CUSTOMS OF THE BORNEO MALAYS.

APPENDIX.

ILLUSTRATIONS.

CHINA AND LABUAN.

CHAPTER I.

INTRODUCTION.

Object of the Author's Journey in China.—Fallacious ideas respecting the Chinese Character.—Improbability of Renewal of Hostilities.—Official Rank.—Impartiality of the Emperor.—Government.—Character and Death of Mr. Thom and Captain Gordon.—Sources of Information.

It having been my lot during the last five years to cruise about the country where the quaint figures that are familiar to us on porcelain have a real existence, and man appears under such an extraordinary aspect as to have led some writers to doubt whether Noah might not have settled in China with a fourth post-diluvian born son, and with the prospect of a long sea voyage before me, I thought I might beguile the tedium of it by arranging the following few notices of what I saw and heard in China,

B

together with such of the affairs of Borneo as occurred while I was on the spot.

I was present at most of the late hostilities in China, but being recently arrived I should suppose that they must long ago have found an abler chronicler than me, so I confine myself to what I was able to learn of the manners, customs, and peculiarities of the country and its inhabitants.

The object of my different journeys when on land was principally to form a collection of coins, of which I shall in due time give merely a passing notice, as the subject generally, and my collection, are in the hands of a learned Chinese scholar, who will shortly be commenting upon them. But to that object I directed a great deal of attention, and travelled over a vast tract of country; and mixed, as much as circumstances would allow me, in pure native society of all ranks, from the Governor-general of the province to the poor tenant of the humblest cottage. And here I feel bound to say that I laid aside a mass of preconceived ideas prejudicial to the Chinese.

I had formed something like an estimate of Canton from the accounts I had previously read— of true local descriptions I admit; but as regards the nation at large nothing can be more fallacious than the ideas conveyed by them. After the first blow of hostilities, and a little irritation consequent on defeat, which an Englishman can well afford to make allowances for, I found my-self in the midst of as amiable, kind, and hos-pitable a population as any on the face of the globe, as far a-head of us in some things as behind us in others.

No one could think of searching the back streets of Chatham, or the purlieus of Wapping, for a fair criterion of British society, or specimens of the yeomanry of merry England; yet from data such as these we have hitherto drawn our ideas of Chinese morality and civilization, but, as the country opens, and we become better acquainted, I trust that both parties will find that they are not the barbarians they have hitherto mutually believed each other to be.

As to any renewal of hostilities I have not the slightest idea of any such being likely to take place: the treaty on the part of their government has been most religiously observed. The emperor would willingly have paid the 21,000,000 of dollars down in one year, but as it was preferred in instalments he was never behind-hand for a day. The only in-terruption that British commerce is likely to meet with is from the detestable rabble of Canton, and the Meaow-tse, or men of the hills, the gallant but wild remnant of unconquered Chinese who have never bent to a Tartar yoke, over both of whom the government has little or no control, and a good thrashing now and then administered to either or both would not cause much sensation at the court of his Imperial Majesty Taow Quan.

It is not so easy to gain the *entrée* into the higher orders of society. The spirit of aristocracy is high and exclusive. I know nothing of hereditary rank, further than the fact of its existence, but official rank removes the bearer from all communion with his kindred. The great object of every father is to give one at least of his children such an education as may qualify him for government office, which is almost sure to be the lot of any who passes the requisite examinations. But the *employé* is seldom or never appointed to any situation in his own province, nor can he be on terms of intimacy with any one of much less rank than himself.

Traders of any sort or description he can never reckon amongst the number of his acquaintance, poor relations he cannot acknowledge in public; but, if after his resignation of office he retires to his own native province, he again returns to the bosom of his family, and becomes the acknowledged head of it by purchasing the patrimonial estate.

Great impartiality between Chinese and Tartar is shewn in the appointment of officers; the imperial patronage is most equally divided between the two races, which may be sound policy on the part of the emperor, as there is little chance of fusion between them. They never intermarry, except that the emperor now and then takes a Chinese wife, but the mother of his heir must be a Tartar.

In all other ranks that I have seen, but little jealousy is shewn; the Chinaman unemployed by government is as ready to give as to ask for information, and however poor he may be, will vacate the best, or if he has but one, the only chair in his house, and bring out the best fare that his establishment can afford on the entrance of strangers.

Under the despotic sway of the Son of Heaven, the subject enjoys a fair portion of liberty, and more happiness than falls to the lot of most nations. The empire is as one family, and if the Imperial Father sometimes visits severely the error of a member of it, yet is he slow to exercise his authority; and though death be the penalty that the law awards for many offences, capital punishments are extremely rare; and the bent of the legislation aims at providing against the ills of humanity, by relieving its wants, and preventing rather than punishing crime. For this purpose education is general, arts are encouraged, gigantic undertakings are completed for facilitating trade, agriculture is held in honour, and every possible means adopted for feeding the people and preventing or alleviating famines, which, without some such regulations would perhaps oftener occur.

The whole system of government from its antiquity is necessarily most elaborate, the constitution has lasted almost entire from times when the rest of the world was barbarous, and has had the advantage of centuries of peace to consolidate itself.

The history of the country presents an extraordinary number of different dynasties; but their revolutions have done little more than to put a new monarch on the throne, who has found it his interest to leave the great body of the people to pursue the even tenor of their way much as before. And if a report reaches our ears of some case of hardship, we must make allowances for the immense machine that the executive has to direct; and under what government will not individual cases of hardship arise?

Mandarins have been subjected to unmerited degradation, and the people have been oppressed by mandarins; but, on the truth appearing, the government never fails to amend an error and redress a wrong. As for the honesty of the people, "Let us speak of a man as we find him;" and though comparisons are odious, yet rather costly experience compels me to say that my own property suffered more from actual robbery in landing and passing the English frontier, than during my whole sojourn in China.

But besides the opportunities I enjoyed of seeing for myself, it was my good fortune while at Ningpo to make the acquaintance of a gentleman who was always ready in the kindest manner to render me any assistance that lay in his power—I mean the late Mr. Thom. He was in every respect a remarkable man, holding a high situation in a great mercantile establishment at a liberal salary, and with every expense provided for him, he was on the way towards making a very large and rapid fortune; but on the breaking out of hostilities, it was absolutely necessary to procure an interpreter—a post for which his extensive knowledge of the language and people thoroughly qualified him. From a mere sense of duty to his country, (it would not be easy to point out many parallel instances) he left his employment, and took the interpretership on much less advantageous terms than he had previously enjoyed, and rendered himself highly useful throughout the war; and at its conclusion became Her Majesty's Consul at Ningpo, at a moderate salary, with the disadvantage of having to keep almost open house to any and every stranger whom chance or duty took to Ningpo.

The assiduity with which Mr. Thom discharged his functions, heightened an illness under which he had been for some time suffering, and when leave of absence for the benefit of his health was granted, his high zeal for his country forbade his availing himself of it until the arrival of a successor, who arrived just in time to bury him, leaving a family very poorly provided for. His death deprived Her Majesty's Government of a faithful and experienced servant, and me of a valuable friend.

I had also for some part of the time the advantage of serving under Captain James Alexander Gordon, who took great pleasure in accompanying me in my rambles, and whose hearty *bonhomie*, urbanity of manner, and kindliness of disposition, ensured us a welcome wherever we went. I have to lament his falling the first British victim to the climate of Labuan, where I had the melancholy satisfaction of seeing him properly interred, soon after our taking possession of the island.

In cases where I have felt myself at a loss to understand many things that came under my notice, I have freely to acknowledge myself under obligation to a periodical, published at Hong Kong, under the title of the Chinese Repository, a valuable cyclopedia of local information, which I much wonder has not found its way more into the libraries of Europe. I have also copied from Sir George

Staunton, such of the laws as I thought I could throw any light upon from personal information. With such advantages, perhaps, these few gleanings may yet appear but scanty; but I have endeavoured to avoid dilating on whatever I supposed might be known to the mass of English readers, and shall feel very happy if the only fault that can be found with me be that of omission.

CHAPTER II.

SHANGHAE.

Division of Provinces.—Vessels in the Harbour.—Superiority of Shanghae for Foreigners as contrasted with Canton.—Description of the City.—City Gates.—Bridges.—Charitable Institutions.—Police Regulations.—Salt.—Forestallers of Rice.—The Customs.—Local Officers.—Travelling.—Want of Fire-places.—Streets and Shops.—Bazaars.—Itinerant Traders.—Dentists.—Fortune-Tellers. — Quacks and Jugglers. — Punch and other Shows.—Baths.—Fire-engines.—Fu-kien Thieves.—Encounter with them.—The "Sons of the Soil," or "Wolfmen."—The Salt Treaty.—"Society of the United Three."—Chinese Beggars, numerous.—Their Mode of Exaction.

THE cities of China and their inhabitants, with the exception of those of Canton, are mostly very similar to each other, and as I consider Shanghae, for reasons presently to be stated, to be the most important for Europeans to have some information about, I have selected it to describe as the best means of giving an insight into Chinese town life.

Every province is divided into a certain number

of districts, called a Fŭ, Ting, Chow, and Hëen. A Fŭ is a large portion or department of a province under the general control of a civil officer, immediately subordinate to the head of the provincial government.

A Ting, a smaller division than, and sometimes a portion of, a Fŭ, when separate it is governed as a Fŭ, and called a Chŭh-le.

A Chow is similar to a Ting, as also a Hëen, but each is a smaller division; each Fŭ, Ting, Chow, or Hëen, has one or more towns, or walled cities, under its guidance, one of which takes its name and rank as Kwang-Chow-Fŭ and Shang-Hae-Hëen, which latter, although of that subordinate rank, is the largest maritime city in the empire, and the greatest resort of the native ships or junks.

I could not, from the jealousy of the government officials, ascertain the number of craft that enter the harbour, but should say that from three to four thousand, of large dimensions, ride at anchor there, at the close of the South-west Monsoon. The whole would seem to be under the direction of a very able harbour-master, moored head and stern in tiers of from fifteen to twenty. The harbour, which is formed by a bend of the river, is in every way commodious, and adapted for an extensive trade.

The imports in native bottoms consist mostly of

Straits produce, i. e.. from Sincapore, Malacca, and Penang. Sugar, tobacco, and rice, from the Luconias and other islands of the eastern archipelago, while a considerable number of smaller craft are employed in the coasting trade to the various maritime provinces.

From its central position, as an emporium on the banks of a river, tributary to the Yang-Tse-Kiang, near the Imperial Canal, and midway between Pekin and Canton, I should not be at all surprised if, in a few years, Shanghae became the only port of real trade with foreigners.

The disturbances continually arising in Canton, causing inconvenience, to say the least of it, to the merchants there, together with the additional expenses arising from its distance from the tea and silk countries, must soon go far to lessen the trade of that port.

Amoy is almost drained to supply its tributary, Formosa, and imports almost all necessaries from the native trade, in junks, with the Straits and the Luconias; besides, being far from either the tea or silk countries, it does not offer a convenient market to foreign enterprise.

Foo-choo-Fŭ, from the jealousy entertained towards foreigners by the Tartar inhabitants, who form a majority of its population, labours under a like disadvantage. While Ningpo, from its difficulty of access and vicinity to the far superior port of Shanghae, has not as yet been found of sufficient importance for the establishment of a single branch-house.

Thus nearly all trade with foreigners is sustained, at present, by the ports of Canton and Shanghae; and the convenience of the position of the latter, together with the liberal hospitality of its inhabitants, must soon, in my opinion, increase its importance, and secure its monopoly.

The English merchant at Canton is almost a prisoner in his house; he has only a few streets open to him for the required recreation, even for the benefit of exercise, and then with the probability of insult. Experience has taught him that even his own house may be a very unsafe refuge from a furious and ignorant mob; any excitement, from whatever cause it originates, is sure to vent itself on the unfortunate foreigners, and, perhaps, bring the building about his ears with very small chance of redress. On the other hand at Shaughae, he is surrounded by a peaceable and hospitable community, where crime is a matter of such rare occurrence, that His Excellency Kung Mŭkiŭ, the civil governor, said in my presence that, during his government of so large a pcpulation, which had lasted, I believe, nine years, one execution only had taken place, and that for *crim. con.* and murder of the injured husband; this may serve as an illustration not only of the morality of a people, whom I have read somewhere termed a nation without morals or truth, but of the general mildness of the government.

But, besides the absence of crime in Shanghae, the city is always open to the foreigner equally with the native; and I have had several years' experience to ground my statement on, that insults or annoyances, of every kind, are less frequent to strangers than in any part of the world.

The above may be considered but light reasons for the decline of trade in one port, and its accession in another; but want of land in the one, and the easy acquirement of it in the other may be conceived more weighty. It is not very long since, that the mandarins threatened the destruction of a garden recovered from the river in front of the foreign factories at Canton: nor has the effect of the war induced the provincial government to yield any portion of land for foreigners' uses, except to build their actual houses of business on. But at Shanghae, several acres of ground are already the property of individual merchants. I feel no doubt that, in the course of a few years, country villas will be owned by partners in the larger houses at convenient distances from the city.

But in one particular Canton has the advantage—in the greater salubrity of its position; between the mast-head and the horizon around Shanghae, not a single rise of ground is visible—the whole expanse is a country something like Holland or Belgium, with its rich cultivation, and numerous canals, teeming with wealth, beauty, and ague.

The city, that is to say, the walled city or citadel, is by no means extensive, for China, being less than four miles in circumference (that of Nankin is thirty); but it is surrounded on all sides by very large suburbs, making the area of its dependencies of an enormous extent.

It is entered by four principal and two smaller gates, the north, south, east, and west, and the little south and east gates; besides these are three water gates, by which the different canals (having made the circuit of the walls,) pass through the city into the river, carrying with them all the offal, and affording the means for the transportation of merchandize.

The streets are narrow and dirty, and the houses low. Nearly all the government-offices are within the citadel; and her majesty's consul has a large residence in the centre. Among the principal institutions are the college, a fine building with stone edifices, and ornamental temples surrounding; a

highly elegant grotto garden, varied with lakes,
bridges, hills, and trees.

The Temple of Confucius is a handsome structure, covering about three acres of ground. Near
the centre of the city are the public gardens with
lakes and islands, in and around, which are pictu-
rosque overhanging temples fitted as tea-houses.

In various parts of the gardens are temples for
the deities, playhouses, and grottoes, surmounted
with exotics arranged with great taste, while in
the area in front of the principal tea-houses, are
the tents of astrologers, doctors, dentists, necromancers, booksellers, almost all itinerant trades,
peep-shows, dancers on the tight-ropes, and Punch;
although this place is generally thronged with visitors no disturbances or annoyances ever take place.
In the houses adjoining are every kind of shop,
among which are numbers of dealers in antiquities
and curiosities.

The mandarins' offices are among the most showy
buildings, being generally painted with bright colours, and approached through large court-yards in
which are huge carved representations of dragons,
lions, or other animals, each of which is emblematic, as the figures in our heraldry : on the left-
hand side is mostly an orchestra for a band of
music; and on the right the saluting guns. The
house is in three distinct buildings, a court-yard

separating each; the first is that of ceremony, consisting of a large hall, with a smaller apartment on each side; the next, the receiving rooms for visitors; and the third, private apartments.

Several very large Buddhist temples ornament the city, these are nearly always painted red; on the city walls are some large temples, commanding fine views; among these near the north gate is the Temple of Spring, in which are fine apartments open on all sides, where the ladies meet in the month of May to watch the progress of Spring, and deck their raven black hair with the early flowers.

The bridges which mostly consist of one high arch with stone stairs, are in many instances highly carved, and each ornamented with a painted lantern. In the principal streets are high triumphal gateways of elegant structure in splendid alto-relievo, to commemorate some important event, or hand down the name of some great officer — some of these are very magnificent.

The Hall of United Benevolence is the principal charity: it comprises a general society for assisting the poor; when I visited it there were at least fifty coffins in store numbered; and one number was something past three thousand, besides coffins for the poor; it bestows medicines, supports a free hospital, and is in every sense a noble insti-

c

tution, and well worthy its name. A branch of it, the Foundling Hospital, is supported by voluntary subscriptions; and if of equivocal benefit elsewhere, is not misplaced in China, where the practice of female infanticide has had the sanction of the law. From inquiries made on the spot, and a report published and translated into English, for a copy of which I am indebted to the kindness of Captain Balfour, her majesty's consul, I am enabled to give the following particulars. It was founded, together with some other charitable institutions, in the forty-ninth year of the Emperor Kanghe, A.D. 1710, by imperial order. It is indebted to a benevolent individual, Sir-chin-chang by name, for the garden in which it stands, and is under the management of a board of directors, represented by two who reside in the establishment. On the left hand side of the entrance is a perforated drawer, inscribed with the two characters "Show ying," or reception of infants.

A sound on a gong, or a knock at the door, gives notice of the arrival of a new inmate, which is immediately removed into the interior, if not more than three years of age, after which it is inadmissible. It is then carefully examined, and a register is kept of its age, date of admission, appearance, the lines and fashion of its fingers, whether the five senses and four limbs be perfect or not, whether there be any sores or scars about it, whether it be fat or thin, and what clothes it had on when admitted, all which particulars are most minutely recorded, after which one of the wet nurses is assigned to it by lot to prevent dispute and partiality.

The qualifications of the wet nurses are rigidly inquired into and ascertained, and the children are maintained and educated for a period not exceeding ten years, when, or before, they may be adopted by any body who, in the case of boys, will legitimate them into some family, or, in the case of girls, will besides give security for their future well treatment and proper employment. The report for the twenty-first year of Taou Kwang (A.D. 1841) gives the following list :—

Old inmates . . 23	Deceased . . . 30
New inmates . . . 114	Returned to Sunkiang-fu . 8
New inmates received	Deceased before Registry . 48
from Sunkiang-fu . 34	Present inmates . . 35
Transferred by adoption . 50	

For the twenty-second year of Taou Kwang, or 1842 :—

Old inmates . . 35	Deceased before registry . 33
New inmates . . . 91	Returned to Sungkiang-fu 1
Deceased . . . 25	Present inmates . . 42
Transferred by adoption . 25	

I am very glad to find that the funds of the institution are in a flourishing state.

The General Free Hospital which is immediately

under the city walls, between the Temple of Spring and the north gate, is in good order, and during the five years that I from time to time visited it, it was always full. It is visited by three medical officers from the Hall of Medicine—a branch of the Hall of United Benevolence.

In front of the chief magistrate's office stands the prison, farmed out to private speculators, but under military inspection. On one side of the entrance is a common room for the soldiers, on the opposite another for the officers, whose chief duty would seem to consist in drinking tea, smoking, and playing at chess. The rooms or cells are not uncomfortable for a prison, but strongly barred. · I have visited them when occupied by British merchant seamen (delinquents locked up at the consul's request); their time was not so disagreeably spent, as numbers of visitors came daily to see the Fankwei or foreigners, and each had something to give. This is not a singular instance: some English prisoners in Formosa, during the war, derived many comforts from the curiosity and benevolence of Chinese visitors. The lounger spends most of his time in the public gardens, witnessing feats of strength or jugglery, smoking, drinking tea, or eating dried pips of the water-melon; and the innumerable priests of all orders and different colours, the French grey predominating, roaming about the streets, with now and then a few nuns, bring one's ideas back to the Catholic cities of Europe.

The duties of the police are in the hands of a body much resembling our churchwardens and parish beadles; their office, besides being attendants on the mandarins, consists in the settlement of minor disputes about boundaries, and other lighter cases of property, as well as in keeping regularity and order amongst the inhabitants; they may be, and mostly are, natives of the place in which they reside; but other appointments of command, of whatever degree, in town or country, are from the emperor, and very rarely is a man employed in his own province in any capacity under government.

Every father is responsible for the well behaviour of his family or household, every oldest inhabitant for that of some decimal number, varying from a hundred to a thousand, over whom he has control.

Sometimes each house, but invariably each street, has its watchman, who patrols all night beating a small drum, and in many cases the neighbours bind themselves to assist one another, by entering into an agreement to repay a certain amount of the loss any of them may sustain by fire or robbery, in other words, a species of private insurance; besides this, most of the by-streets have at each end a gate

barred and locked at nine o'clock, and the key
kept by the watchman, so that if a thief should
succeed in gaining an entry, his exit is by no means
so sure.

Salt is brought to Shanghae by land from Ningpo; transporting it by water is prohibited. As in
some other countries, the trade in this is a government monopoly, farmed out to private speculators, under the direction of a salt commissioner
(Yen-yun-sze) and a board of subordinate officers;
the penalties for contraband trade in it are high
but very often evaded. Not so always: while I
was at the place, a vessel arrived with a cargo of
salt from Liverpool, but failed in selling it. The
government offered to buy at very low prices, but
the people could not make an offer, so the
owners were obliged to seek a market for it at
Manilla.

Another board is that of the Leang-choo-taou,
or commissioner of grain, one-tenth of which becomes the property of the emperor. Each department has its granary for storing a portion of it, by
which means famines are provided against. By the
public sale of government grain a tariff is arranged, and fluctuation in price and speculation is
discountenanced, as the subjoined will shew.

"AN EDICT AGAINST FORESTALLERS OF RICE.

"Keying of the imperial house, Governor-general of Kwank-tung and Kwang-si, a director of the board of war, vice-high-chancellor and guardian of the heir apparent, minister and commissioner extraordinary, &c., issues a severe prohibition against storing rice, from fear of famine. Whereas, it is important that rice should be in the market, to stop it, is against the law. The population of Kwang-tung is great, and its produce is too little, and the support of the people always depends upon the rice of Kwang-si, which the merchants bring. But now the price of rice, in Canton, rises every day, and it has been found out that there are some villains and dissolute persons stirring up the people, and saying that in the year Ping-woo and Ting-wi, in the reign of Kien-lung, there was a famine, and now this year is Ping-woo again, and we shall keep our rice for a good market. These villains hinder the rice boats from coming, and squeeze them in every way according to their wishes, and the merchants stop their trade; and this causes the want of rice among the people. But those men surely do not know the rainy season of the last year Yih-sye, came exactly in time, and it enriched the earth very much, and when compared with the Yih-sye year, in the reign of Kien-lung, it is very different, and, I believe, when the spring comes we shall have fine rains. If those villains still dare to keep back the rice, seeking profit, the law cannot suffer them, and their policy must be thwarted, so that the merchants may trade again, and the people have food. Besides commanding the Governor of Kwang-si to renew his former edict, I will command all the officers of the districts through which the merchants of Kwang-tung, must pass in trading with Kwang-si, to issue proclamations so as to let all people know, that after this, no man should store up rice for the fear of famine. If any merchants from Kwang-tung go to Kwang-si to buy rice, they should buy their rice freely, and bring it to Kwang-tung to sell, and there should be no secret hindrance of buying and selling rice, so as to raise the value of rice, and cause all sorts of difficulties to the poor.

" If, after this second edict, any of the villains dare to store up their rice, seeking profit, and send boats along the entrances of the province to hinder and squeeze the merchants, the officers of their districts shall seize them, and bring them to trial, and punish them with heavy penalties, and shall not set them at liberty. Do not disobey this edict. First month, 21st day." (*Feby.* 16*th*, 1840.)

The remainder of the grain is annually shipped to Pekin. And one of the prettiest maritime scenes in China, I ever beheld, was the arrival of the grain-junks at Shanghae; they range alongside the government wharf, in tiers, of from ten to twenty, a huge temporary bridge runs over the tier immediately over the hold, and thus they are promptly loaded.

The customs are under an officer called the Hae Kwan, whose functions vary in most of the provinces according to local circumstances: as for instance, the Hoppo of Canton is at the head of maritime customs only, and the custom-houses of inland trade are not under his control. Each of the five ports has a Hae Kwan for foreign trade. The superintendents have secretaries, called Keng Ching, and they appoint Wei Yuen, or deputies, to important places under their charge, and Keayui, or domestics, to inferior places; to collect duties and prevent smuggling. In cases where there are no superintendents these duties are collected by officers acting under the local magistrates.

The jealousy of the government entirely precluded the possibility of my arriving at any satisfactory estimate of the amount derived from the custom duties, paid by natives, on either home or foreign importations. Considerable contraband trade must be carried on by bribery, as I have seen opium landed in Shanghae at mid-day, although expressly against the law. A Spanish government officer endeavoured through bribery to arrive at the extent of the native trade and amount of duties received, but when his object appeared nearly obtained, he was given to understand that the Hae Kwan had discovered the intrigue, and that it must be discontinued.

The principal local officers are the Foo-yuen or Prefect, military intendant of circuit of Su-chan-fŭ, Sung Kwang-fŭ, Sai-tzang-chau and Shanghae-hëen, — the Tsan-fŭ, or sub-colonel, — the che-hëen, or chief magistrate—and the Tinig-che, or sub-prefect of the coast guard.

The mandarin, in his sedan chair, is surrounded by attendants, who clear the way for him in no very civil manner; as should any luckless countryman's curiosity tempt him to stand and gape on the great man's equipage, as it passes, an attendant very soon gives him to understand, by a blow from a bamboo, that his attentions are not wanted; this ceremony answers to the "move on" of our policemen.

According to his rank, he has one or more horsemen in his train, with the invariable state umbrella of crimson silk, trimmed with vermilion or yellow. High colours and tawdry dress disguise a considerable quantity of filth, sometimes about the attendants. Should the object of his visit require more attendants than belong to the dignity of his situation, bystanders in the street are seized upon, pressed into service, and made followers for the hour. The number of his sedan-bearers varies from two to six, according to his dignity; but a merchant cannot have more than two bearers, and a single follower, to carry his visiting cards, &c.

The travelling is mostly by water, but when a canal will not serve, and a land journey must be undertaken, the mandarin travels in his sedan, and his lady in a species of palanquin, or litter. Subordinates content themselves with a kind of wheelbarrow, propelled by two coolees, the body of which holds the luggage, and a seat on each side of the wheel, (which is cased over,) the two passengers, the whole being balanced with great nicety, so as to require little more labour than that of propulsion by the coolees. A poor man, who cannot afford this mode, slings a pole across one shoulder, with a basket hanging from each end, which may contain a child, or luggage, as the case may be, the poor wife making the best of her way, that her cramped feet will allow, behind him, carrying a basket in each hand.

There is a remarkable omission in each room, the kitchen excepted, of every house, which is the want of a fire-place. The climate of Shanghae varies according to the season, from tropical heat to frost, sufficient to allow skating, and yet a fire, for the purpose of warming a very slight-built house, is a luxury unknown. The only approach to it that I saw, was now and then a little pan, like the French " Chaufferette," which a Chinaman would use for either feet or hands. There is no standing round a fire, or stove, in a tea-house, or wine-shop, as with us. The dress is varied with the season. Should the morning be cold, huge gowns are put on, lined with fur, if on a rich wearer, stuffed with cotton, if a poor one, in number as the necessity requires. If the weather gets warmer towards mid-day, one or more are shed, but resumed for the afternoon, if required, and by this means a man is enabled to weather the coldest winter without a fire.

The principal streets have a brilliant appearance. All the shops are open, and set off in the gayest manner possible. Red and gold are the predominant colours, and the stock arranged so as to shew off to the best advantage. The thoroughfares being narrow, are frequently covered in with an awning, and have thus the appearance of a bazaar, or arcade. The shopmen are dressed according to the pretensions of the establishment, and attend with the utmost civility, shewing at the same time great ingenuity in making the purchaser and his money part good friends.

The richest shops, both in appearance and reality,

are the silk-shops, although their attraction, in some towns, is denied to the street, from their standing much in the rear. They are entered by a plain gateway, illuminated by several gaudy lanterns, and the sign alone directs attention, such as Chaw-twan-foo, silk and satin shop. Passing through this gateway, you enter a paved courtyard, fitted *en grotte* with several large vases of gold fish, and many exotics, often covered in with trellis work and vines, hung with numbers of cages, containing singing and other birds, the most famous of which is the Soo-chow mocking bird, a species of lark, which mocks all sounds.

Facing the entrance are three apartments, hung with variegated lanterns, supported by splendidly carved pillars, &c., generally of polished wood; the centre apartment is fitted as a receiving room, with handsome furniture, and here one of the partners attends, to whom the customer's wants are explained, and by whom a seat and tea are offered; the various articles are brought from the other two apartments, divided from you and the courtyard only by rectangular counters. The general contents of the shops are blazoned forth in gold letters, on varnished black boards, or painted characters, on light-coloured boards, such as "Pekin satins and Canton crapes," "Hang-chow reeled silks and Hoo-chow crapes," "Hoo-chow cottons and

Ningpo senshaws," "Gauzes, lawns, pongees, and satins."

The display of embroidery is magnificent. The satins are the richest, the colours the most brilliant, and the work well worthy of such beautiful materials: the patterns for sale are mostly worked by men whose wages vary from two mace (eightpence) to a rupee (one shilling and elevenpence) per day, one mace being the rate of wages of labour in general. The ladies embroider for their own use, but the wives of the poorer order are more employed about the household duties and attendance on their families. In no one of the silk shops that I entered did I see a single female employed.

Having made your selection you leave every thing to be made up into parcels at the store, and giving your direction pay on the receipt of the article at your residence to the master or one of the partners, who hands you a receipt for the money, which it may be necessary to ascertain has the seal not of any individual member of the house, but of the house itself, as it is said that they do not mind doing a little private bit of roguery on their own account, but dare not trifle with the fair fame of the firm.

Vying in colours and appearance with the silk warehouses, are the fruit shops, in which rich and poor can luxuriate on delicious fruits from the two oceans; the former on grapes and the fruits not in season, which sell for high prices; but an iced slice of pine apple or melon can be obtained by the latter, in the hottest part of the year, for a few cash, or something less than a farthing.

The next, perhaps, in size, are the cloth ware-houses Sih-poophoo. In them are great varie-ties of woollens, puffed off as "all kinds of woven stuffs, selected and picked," "we neither spare pains nor money," &c.

The tea-dealer has his establishment surrounded with metal vases in which are the samples; boiling water is always at hand for the purchaser to try the taste, but is not so often resorted to as the shorter process of laying a small quantity in the palm of the hand, and on application to the nose, judging by the aroma; the portion ordered is packed in a leaden box of the required size. The sign may be Song-min-cha, "famous teas from every province," or the names of some of the most valuable growths, as Singlo-Woohe, i, e., Singlo and Bohea.

The chandlers' establishment, Chuh-yuen, is often an extensive one, inasmuch as he is a general dealer, besides selling candles of different descrip-tions as "poured over and made for sending as pre-sents and offerings:" these are of the tallow-tree, with an ornamented coating of wax, many of them very gaudy, both in colour and decoration, and are

described in the signs as " small wick candles made
heavy with wax, and increased by other materials."

On all sides are inscriptions eulogistic of these
costly lights: such as " in the evenings in the celestial palace they hand down the order;" "late at
night in the snow gallery they study the books;"
but should the shop have a view only into a back
street a more modest sign suffices, as Chuh-haow-
shwang hac se sin chu chub, "candle warehouse,
double dips and small wicks, superior candles." Hams,
sugar, rice, cakes, flour, bacon, dried fruits, and
every kind of grocery, may frequently be found in
these establishments, whose granaries, bakehouses,
and other offices, are very extensive. Smokers and
snuff-takers are seduced by romances, such as the following: " we issue and sell Hang Chow tobacco, the
name and fame of which has galloped to the north
of Ke-chow; and the flavour has pervaded Keangnan in the south;" "famous tobacco from the Shih-
ma district;" "original importers of the Fokeen
Chappoo and Hong Chow tobaccos." The pipes are
arranged often with a great deal of taste, like
swords in an armoury, and snuffs of various qualities,
some of them very highly scented, are taken out of
bottles, with a small spoon attached to the stopper.
Cigars are unknown, and the weed, in spite of its
galloping fame, is but indifferent.*

* " Fokien, orange-flavoured, and female chastity wines dis.

A sufficient introduction to the dainties of a tavern might be supposed to exist in the grand display of the various dishes, stews, soups, and *entrées*, exposed to view, without additional allurements, as Leang-shih Hang, " rateable and provision warehouse ;" " six kinds of eatables' warehouse ;" " Tartar and Chinese tables spread according to the seasons, bowls of vegetables, meats, puddings, soups, cakes, aromatic and simple vegetables, and common rice bowls." Through the four seasons bowls of vegetables, with Tartar and Chinese, complete dinners, one of which I have attempted a description of below.

Tea-houses are fitted up in a fairy-like style, and in situations over water, or high above the tops of other houses, to catch the air in summer time, and when convenient have gardens, Cha-yuen, attached. In them you can have a private apartment lightly and elegantly fitted up, generally with bamboo furniture, or seat yourself at one of the many tables in the public rooms, with a pipe, cup of tea, and a few

tilled from the grain, and brewed in our own coppers." " Famous liquor from over the ocean," reads very tempting in an expensively arranged shop filled with shining metal vessels, containing these liquors, that if the man speak true who makes them, and ought to know most about them, might meet the approval of a teetotaller. Some of the vessels are placed on a heated metal plate, beneath which is a slow fire, and contain very tolerable samshoo, of all strengths, from brandy to sherry.

D

dried melon pips, all for one penny. The walls are hung with various pictures in rolls and inscriptions, such as "fruits of all kinds brought from the north and south, with aromatic and plain tea cakes;" "flag and lance, shaped with sparrow-tongued teas;" "Prince's eyebrow and Oldman's eyebrow teas;" "according to your wishes a small cup of tea."

These houses are generally well filled, and are the haunts of jugglers, fortune-tellers, and other idle vagabonds, and itinerant dealers of all kinds; women are seldom seen in them, except dancing and singing girls. But the drug shop, Yo-tsan-choo, is, perhaps, the most showy establishment in some towns: besides highly-ornamented drawers, there are all sorts of porcelain jars and vases, containing the specifics.

It is said that the physician is not a well-paid man; however that may be, the apothecary is, and he generally combines the two professions. Surgeons and surgical instruments are unknown; nearly all the common European medicines are in use, but instead of essences, extracts, and tinctures, the native preparations are very simple decoctions, although these as well as plaisters are on a very extensive scale, for *malades imaginaires* abound. In cases of severe pain an opposite part is punctured, with the forefinger and thumb, as a counter-irritant. Actual cautery is not unusual, especially in cases of rheumatism.

A portrait-painter of note at Canton told me that for the outside, *i. e.* wounds, an English practitioner was to be preferred, but for the inside the Chinese was more to be relied upon. On the latter we certainly differed. They have medicinal works, and illustrations of them are hung on scrolls round the shop, and inscriptions, such as "fragrant materials and decoctions accurately prepared;" "pills, powders, ointments, and extracts carefully made up."

Not being of the faculty myself, I am afraid of saying more than, may Heaven preserve me from a Chinese doctor !

A dying-shop, Ten-fang, recommends itself thus, "green double dye, black as ink, in skill we rival celestial workmanship." An encomium rather more qualified might not be misplaced, their dyes are indeed splendid.

Bazaars are very handsome and extensive, well filled with articles "for sending as presents, antique curiosities, ornaments for setting out tables, and presenting as dowries;" "crystal for young and old eye-glasses." The spectacles are as large as teacups, set in heavy tortoiseshell frames and slung round the ears with two strings, their odd appearance may be imagined.

Besides these signs, and many more different kinds
not enumerated, each house has its carved sign: thus
a doctor's shop will be ornamented with a patriarch
leaning on a crook, and by his side a deer or a
stork, the stork being the emblem of longevity,
which, as is well known, at least in China, pul-
verised dried deer's flesh affords the surest means
of attaining.

A tea-house is known by huge vases almost
surrounding it in all directions, filled with the
water of Heaven, *i. e.*, rain water, which is preferred, and in private houses is often kept for
upwards of a year to acquire considerable imaginary
powers of extracting the flavour of the tea.   It is
in such celebrity, that the Son of Heaven himself,
the, literary Emperor Kang-He composed an ode
on the propriety of keeping the waters of heaven,
and the celestial mode of making tea, which may
be read on many of the small Chinese tea-cups,
that is to say, if you can translate it.

A huge Tartar boot crowns the shop of a dealer
in that line, with a carving of some kind or
another, as is the case with most shops: notice is
given sometimes in this manner: "All here measured by one rule, when favoured by merchants
who bestow their regards on us, please to notice
our sign of the Double Phœnix on a board, as
a mark, then it will be all right."   I would merely

add that the motto of *caveat emptor* would not be much out of place in any of them.

The pawnbroker and the banker are often synonymous terms with the Chinese. They are called three per cent per month shops, that being the rate at which they advance money on any kind of goods whatever, beyond which they are not allowed to charge upon pain of receiving sixty blows. These shops, as may well be believed, from the rate of interest, are often immensely rich. About four feet from the ground, a strongly barred opening appears, through which the goods or security are passed, and if accepted, the money is handed out, and a ticket corresponding to the one placed on the article given, redeemable in three months if required.

Using false weights is punished with sixty blows: there are houses appointed by government to direct these weights and inspect them, called Keaou-Chun-Keoan-Ch'hin, " comparers and determiners of government weights."

In addition to the shops, the frequented streets and populous villages are supplied with travelling trades of every kind besides; the tea-gardens and squares are filled with astrologers, necromancers, fortune-tellers, peep-shows, jugglers, Punch, dentists, quacks, in short, all the drags on the purse to be found in other countries. The most useful of these is the walking *restaurateur*. His apparatus is of the most compact order, all lightly balanced on his back with one hand, while with the other he teazes a fire, and goes from place to place crying his various prepared dishes, until his progress be arrested by some hungry traveller. His whole apparatus, which may be six feet high by nine feet long, is almost entirely made of bamboo. Besides the one in which he walks, there are two perpendicular divisions; on the top of that before him are the basins, plates, &c.; then the supply of wood, below which is the fire-place and kitchen, consisting of an iron-pan, covered over by a wooden tub, and let into light plaster-work upon the fire; thus he boils, stews, or fries according to the taste of the customer; in the other division are the meats, vegetables, &c., besides a quantity of gaudy Chinaware, containing the dried herbs, peppers, &c. required; for a very trifling sum the labourer can here procure a hearty meal without leaving his work, as the *restaurateur* hovers about all places where most needed.

Besides the above are tea-stalls of the same kind, in which are kept hot and ready the various kinds of Bohea for public convenience.

The itinerant barber's apparatus is complete, the water always boiling on a fire over his head, while in his rear on a pole, balanced over his shoulder, are water, basin, razors, towels, &c.; if he be in requisition he picks out a convenient spot, shaves the head, cleans the ears and eyes, cracks the joints, and shampoos the body, in an incredibly short space of time. Hair is only worn on the crown of the head in shape of a queue. The shaving is a matter of necessity to the mandarin and gentleman, while scarcely a labourer goes more than three or four days unshorn. This trade is in constant exercise, but the death of an emperor is a sure holiday to the barber, shaving and mourning being inconsistent with each other.

Tinker, tailor, and shoemaker, each has his pack, and basking in a sunny spot plies his trade, finishes off one job and utters his peculiar cry for another.

The dentist no sooner pitches his tent on arriving, than he unfolds to the admiring crowd a huge scroll, on which, at the left side, are set forth his home, place of birth, &c. ; the rest of the scroll speaks of his fame and skill in cleaning, curing, and extracting teeth, and knowledge of the mouth in general ; if this fail to obtain a customer, he opens box after box, producing hundreds of human teeth, on which he lectures, declaring each large and more decayed tooth to have belonged to a prince, duke, or high mandarin, who honoured him with his patronage, and saved himself from the most terrific tortures. Should a bystander at last be attracted and offer his mouth for inspection, the instruments are produced, and if extraction be required it is done with much expertness ; he shews the instrument to the crowd, describes its use and power, and, as an illustration of it, draws the tooth, while the sufferer imagines he is merely going to shew how he would do it ; if cleaning is required he exhibits his instruments one by one, and using each, keeps up a chaunt and lecture alternately ; after the operation is performed he recommends his powders ; I tried several, and detected a strong mixture of camphor in all. Thus he continues, until having remained a short space without a customer, he packs up and moves to another convenient spot.

The fortune-teller is a cunning, mysterious looking rascal ; he is seated at a table under an awning, before him his magic mirror, books, pencils, ink, &c. So intent is he on his studies, that the vociferations of a country looking bumpkin, which have attracted a crowd of gazers, have failed to awaken him. Slowly he rouses himself from the trance of his meditations, and with a mysterious shudder and start he excuses himself hastily, shuts his book with an air, talks of the spirits having deceived him in causing him to believe that a poor man, destined to fill a high office, humbly awaited him at the gate of celestial bliss ; is much surprised when his clownish customer calls upon him to unfold his prophetic powers, and relate what heaven may have in store for him. Having asked him if he is sure they have not met before, which question confirms the bumpkin in the opinion that he must have been the cause of this extraordinary vision, he places a stool for him opposite, and then commences the divination of futurity. After asking a few questions, he places his mirror so as to reflect the heavens, and inscribes thereon certain mystic signs, these he continually changes (having referred to a number of books and talking all the time aloud), writing now and then on a slip of paper; he at last fills up all he requires, and hands it to the delighted and deluded simpleton; then falling into a reverie awaits the arrival of another, who is not slow in arriving : one fool makes many, and the trade is a good one.

The craniologist unfolds his plates, and, if no one will come forward, lectures on them at great length. One of these plates I bought immediately after a lecture as a curiosity. It is a representation of a face, with a head-dress that has not been in use for some centuries, inscribed all over with characters; every feature bears some development or other. The ears speak volumes; the forehead is almost an encyclopædia of organs, some denoting the qualities of the mind, others emblematic of the destiny of the individual. Some of the characters are in circles, surrounded by numbers and professional terms. From the fore-head to the nose are seven. "Heaven's Centre, or Zenith;" "Heaven's Hall;" "The Lord of the Firmament;" "Just the Centre" (between the brows); "The Seal Hall;" "The foot of the Hill's Years" (between the eyes); "Old Age" (the bridge of the nose). Two kinds of eyes are given, the one Ming-he, or "clear opening," the other Yen-he, or "observed opening;" the lid intruding on the pupil in the latter. The interpretations do not exactly tally with those of our phrenologists, and when doctors differ, I cannot decide a point on which one is as likely to be right as another, with the chances, if any, leaning in favour of the Chinese, who have studied the matter for centuries before it was dreamed of in Europe.

In a quiet little nook, perfectly apart from the noise of the street or garden, sits under a tree or awning, the chess-player, he either teaches the art or offers to play, and has much custom in both; the principles of the game are much the same as with us, though the board differs materially, and the men are in shape like draughtsmen, bearing the characters indicating the rank of the piece thus,—Ma, a horse, answers to a knight, and Ping, a soldier, to a pawn, &c.

The quack! How this gentleman travels has often puzzled me, and I have met the same man at

a distance of more than a hundred miles; I presume
he must always keep to the canal country. His
paraphernalia occupy a large space; he is peculiar
in many things; he wears no tail, but makes up
for it with the dirt he carries. The whole fraternity
have the same idiotic look which characterises the
Buddhist priest, whom they much resemble in appearance. He displays the jaws and bones of the
tiger, elephant, shark, whale, in short of almost all
animals; diseased livers, tumours, &c.; sea-weeds,
gigantic funguses, in short everything that is horrible
and disagreeable. If he succeed in decoying a patient, he, besides supplying medicines, punctures or
inserts hot needles into the diseased parts, or burns
moxa upon it, chaunting all the time amid the
fumes of incense and candles. Before leaving he
loads the patient with medicines of a very harmless
nature for a trifling sum, and pays the most profound respect and attention to all suggestions or
questions from the crowd.

The juggler's art is not so well displayed as
either in England or India. Among the night-
scenes I have seen with these are the following:
two of the performers dressed as mandarins in the
height of fashion, enter into conversation, during
which they from time to time lift each arm and
leg, apparently with an intention of displaying
that there is nothing hid; presently a discus-

sion takes place, and each produces, one after the other, two enormous porcelain vases filled with flowers, the height of which are from five to six feet; the vases are real, about two and a-half feet high — the flowers sliding one inside the other; this is a good trick. There was another very well executed, viz.:—balancing a basin, which appeared in all parts of the apartment. Now it would rise to the ceiling, make a descent to within a foot of the floor, rise mid-air, dance, curvet, and cross the room, &c., all to the tune of a gong, which was kept constantly beaten; the gong-man no doubt directed the movements. Gymnastic exercises and feats of strength are displayed in almost every street.

Punch is all in his glory, native and to the customs born, though his birth-place, like that of Homer, may be a subject of controversy. Yet I am afraid that to China alone belongs the glory of having produced Pun-tse, that is, the son of an inch; from thence it seems he found his way into Italy under the name of polichinello, but resumed his old appellation on his further travels.

As soon as the effects of the war were over and the trades began to recollect, Punches in numbers flocked in and were great favorites among the sailors. Gong and triangle answered the purposes of drum and pan-pipes. The twang of voice,

" roity toity," was the same that I have often heard on Ascot Heath ; Judy, mad with the same harsh usage from her loving lord—Toby, too, was there ; but the devil introducing a huge green dragon to devour him, bones and all, was the only innovation of importance.

Immediately under a huge highly-painted scene of a battle, stands a fellow with inflated cheeks, trying to out-sound a gong which he is beating with all his might ; under the picture are small holes for ocular demonstrations of the mysteries within, and the bended form of some juveniles shews that all his wind and noise is not expended for nothing, which may mean, " look a little farther, and you will see the discomfiture of the barbarian eye, by the son of heaven's general his excellency How-now, master general of ceremonies, director of the Gabel, and tamer of the sons of the western ocean."

But the most novel travelling trade that I met with, was that of the circulating librarian, with a box filled with little pamphlets of dramas, tales, and romances. He goes the circuit of the town, and leaves, brings away, or exchanges his books as the case may be, bringing information and tittle-tattle home to every man's door. His trade is not a bad one, as his stock costs very little, and is in some demand.

Every cry almost to be met with in London, or

other cities, may find its equivalent in China. Dancing on the tight-rope, travelling players, gambling, cakes, oranges, &c., in short, every species of out-of-door mode of extracting money from the unwary.

In every city and town, there are several public baths; and no village is without one or more, in which the million may have baths for the small sum of five Le, or the twentieth part of four pence halfpenny,—these houses need no sign: from every aperture issues steam in vapours and volumes, their very vicinity is moist. Nor is cleanliness the only benefit conferred by them on the poorer classes of a people, whose almost sole beverage is a decoction of tea, and it is a great convenience to be enabled to purchase from their enormous reservoirs, as much boiling water for a Le as would nearly supply a family in drinking for a day. Fuel being scarce in the winter time, this is a great boon, and much taken advantage of, and might well be copied in cities nearer home.

Within are two kinds of baths, hot water, and steam baths; the former are large rooms with about five feet depth of water, around which are small closets for the convenience of dressing; these rooms are in number proportionate to the demand. There are also private rooms with baths in them of small dimensions, for the *exclusive*.

Into the large baths are placed sometimes as many and more than twenty bathers, whose entrance and exit often takes place without a word, although they are at times as closely wedged as possible. The water is constantly shifted and renewed. The vapour baths are very long, and about six feet broad, with convenience on each side for dressing; boards are laid across at a distance of about a foot or eighteen inches one from another, and each board forms a bath, provided with towels; although the sum paid is small, these must be lucrative establishments as the ingress and egress is continual, particularly in the spring, summer, and autumn seasons.

While I was at Shanghae, taking a stroll, about three o'clock on the last day of the Chinese year, in the immediate neighbourhood of the custom-house, for collecting the Fukien dues, this building took fire, and, together with some houses adjoining, was burnt; I was much surprised at the alacrity and excellent order with which the engines were brought to the spot.

Every division or, as we should say, parish of the town has its engine, and every engine company its separate dress. I suppose, on this occasion, there must have been nearly twenty engines on the spot in less than half an hour, made like large tubs, with two cylinders each, worked by two

men, and throwing the water very well through
a leather hose.

A fire is a grand occasion for a certain class
of the emperor's lieges, who come by water from
Fu-kien, and take advantage of the confusion to
plunder, and, in this instance, were suspected of
being the incendiaries. As the fire increased, the
inhabitants began to transport their goods. Two
or three men might be seen laden with boxes,
preceded by a man, as their advanced guard, armed
with a sword, or a large knife, in each hand, brand-
ishing his weapons about as if he would never be
taken alive: but, notwithstanding, when the procession came to a turning, two or three Fu-kien
men would dart forward, seize one of the boxes,
form a guard round it, and carry it off in triumph
to their junks; and all this in broad daylight, and
in the very teeth of the mandarins, who were all
on the spot endeavouring to keep order.

I spoiled the fun of two parties, having in my
hand a big stick, of that kind of cane that grows to
a good thickness in Malacca, and goes by the name
of "Penang lawyer," from its being the arbiter
of many quarrels. I brought it to bear with effect
on the rascals' heads, but found next day that it was
a dangerous game, for an English merchant had
tried the same thing, but without the assistance of
such able counsel as I was guided by; he was sur-

rounded and set upon by the villains, desperately wounded, and almost murdered.

The Taou-tai, or intendant, gave 3000 taels, or nearly 1000*l.*, to the sufferers, a magnificent act, but I trust he did not lose by it, for this kind of thing gets his name up for benevolence, highly desirable at all times in China, but especially when, as in the case of a custom-house being burnt, the whole affair is likely to reach the ears of the emperor.

The men of the sea, from Fu-kien, are not the only dangerous class that disturb the tranquillity of the central government; perhaps a more formidable body are the Meaow-tse, "Sons of the soil," called also Yaou Jin, "Wolfmen," the mountaineers inhabiting the inaccessible highlands of the Leang, Kwang, and Fu-kien provinces.

These Chinese repealers have never acknowledged the Tartar dynasty, and are said to have amongst them the scions of royalty of the genuine old native stock of the Ta-Ming-Chaw. They are an organized body, divided into eight leading tribes, subdivided into twenty-four, and again into fifty smaller branches. They are in many respects peculiar; they wear their hair all over the head, tied into a knot at the top, and ornamented with pheasants' feathers and beads.

They marry and intermarry amongst each other, and choose their wives by their powers of singing,

E

and the marriage ceremony consists merely of taking the measure of each other's waists, when the couple are declared man and wife.

They are a brave, hardy, active, fierce, and quarrelsome race, inured to deeds of blood; their weapons are bows and arrows, spears, and swords, with which they are quite able to make their independence respected by the constituted authorities. The only control that the government has ever been able to exercise over them, is the advantage taken, when once, every three years, they come down to Canton to buy salt, a necessary that they cannot otherwise procure, and, as it is a government monopoly, the mandarins refuse to supply them with any until they have entered into a treaty to be of good behaviour for the space of three years, and on this occasion only are they to be seen by foreigners. A very respectable and well known native of Canton is my authority for the particulars of the salt treaty.

Besides these open and declared enemies, there is a mysterious freemasonry (no offence to the brethren) spread all over China and its dependencies, together with Java, Singapore, Malacca, and Penang, called the San-hoh-burie, or "Society of the United Three," known to Europeans as the "Triad Society," originally formed for purposes of mutual benevolence, but now a very dangerous institution. The "three" are heaven, earth, and man.

The late Dr. Milne made the following researches into this difficult subject. The members of it, calling themselves brethren, are the most depraved of the dregs of the people, the idlers, gamblers, opium smokers, and such like vermin; their objects are, at home, mutual assistance, theft, robbery, overthrow of regular government, and aim at political power. Abroad, plunder, mutual concealment of crime, and defence against established authority. Their government is a Triumvirate of elder brethren, who have a larger share of the plunder than the rest. They are bound together by oaths and certain initiatory rites, and make themselves known to each other by secret signs. The society has a common seal, in shape an equilateral pentagon, with a double lined octagon, within inscribed with the characters of some of the planets, and mottoes susceptible of different meanings. The government are alive to the danger of this association, and severe penalties are denounced against any member of this or any other society. Sir J. F. Davis has issued an ordinance, passed by the legislative council of Hong Kong, for its suppression in that island, declaring all convicted of being members of it, guilty of felony.

There are many other illegal associations; among

them formerly was reckoned the Portuguese Roman
Catholic Religion, or Tien-chu-kian—Christianity,
as taught by the Catholics, which has been sometimes rigorously persecuted in consequence, but
Christianity, of whatever denomination, is now to
be tolerated in the five ports.

I have heard it remarked, that there are no beggars in China, but personal experience in the
country has given me rather a different opinion.
In the city of Shanghae, there are more beggars
than, I was near saying, in Naples, but certainly than
in Lisbon; and for impertinence, loquacity, and
filth, would beat all I ever witnessed. Their name
is legion, and a formidable legion they are, completely organized, and possessing great power; no
respectable shopkeeper is free from the presence
of one or more of them, nearly the whole day, unless
he pays a tribute, or, in other words, compounds,
with the king of the beggars; and, odd as it may
appear, this filthy horde are represented by a chief,
who is, in his own person, responsible for his gang,
in case of any extraordinary enormity being committed. As a mark of their independence, they
wear no tails; they either encamp in the outskirts, or
inhabit a deserted joss, or other house, or barn, or
ice-house, in summer time; their dress is sackcloth
and dirt.

Scenes of misery, that would scarcely be believed,

are witnessed daily in the streets, in winter, with these unfortunates; they are certainly enthusiastic in their profession, and not to be pitied; they will not work, but, to excite charity and commiseration, cut and maim themselves to an extent hardly credible. It is no uncommon sight to see men dying, and even dead, half buried in snow, and almost naked, in the middle of a populous city, and yet they are constantly receiving alms, which is immediately spent in all kinds of debauchery.

The most usual mode of exaction, is as follows :— the beggar either covers himself with the most loathsome filth, or ornaments his person with flowers, sometimes a red tallow lighted candle is stuck in his hair, and with a small gong, drum, or two pieces of wood in his hands, he enters a shop, where either the smell or the noise the rascal kicks up, soon teaches the unfortunate shop-keeper the value of peace and quiet, opens him to conviction, and brings him to terms to get rid of the nuisance. So he goes on through street. after street, no attempt is ever made to turn him out, though he be filled with vermin, some of which, he not unfrequently leaves in exchange for the alms he receives, They are said to recruit from the people by stealing their offspring; however that may be, child-stealing is a common crime in China, as the numerous placards and warnings from bereaved parents may prove in any city; (there are bill-stickers in China as elsewhere.) Besides the above, there are some real objects of charity, who, from inundations of rivers, banks, fires, &c., are rendered houseless, these have frequently, as in England, begging-letters, calling on the charitable to assist them, and not in vain, as the Chinese are a benevolent people, and not one of any respectability, will pass an object really deserving of his charity without relieving his wants. "Are there widows? compassionate them; are there aged? support them; are there sick? dispense medicine to them; are there starved and cold? give clothing to them," are the words of a Buddhist, from which some Christians might take a useful hint

CHAPTER III.

COINS.

Early Emperors had no Coined Money.—Antiquity of their Coinage.—Has undergone no material change from the Time of our Saviour, or thereabouts.—Coinage decimally arranged.—Cowrieshells served as Money, according to Monsieur Hager.—Tortoiseshell anciently used as Money.—Weight Money.—Bronze Money—its first appearance in the Time of the Founder of the Chou Dynasty, B. C. 1105.—Round Money, its several kinds.—Metals of the Coinage various.—Sycee Silver and Gold in Ingots.—Origin of the term Sycee.—Classes of Sycee Silver.—Copper Money.—Medals.—Origin of the Bank Note.—Banking in China.

THE early Emperors of China, according to some native historians, had no coined money; shells, precious stones, gold, and other metals, in ingots, were used in barter.

Again, others attribute the moneys of the various figures called the Ho-paou and Kin-taou-tseen, to the genius of a very distant period. However this may be, from the time of our Saviour, or thereabouts, the coinage of China has undergone no material change, save only in the reintroduction, at various

periods, of the coins of their ancestors. These innovations generally occur in the formation of new
dynasties, or during an interregnum, or the assumption of some powerful usurper. The coinage is decimally arranged, being strung in thousands, divided into hundreds of Le.

10 le make   .   . =1 candareen or fun.
10 candaren, 100 le . =1 mace, or Yih-pih, yih-tseen (4d.)
10 mace, or 1,000 le . =1 tael or leang, or above
                30 per cent. on the ounce of silver.

These coins are all the same size, or nearly so, and
viewed carelessly, would appear of the same die.
They are round, pierced in the centre with a square
hole, with a character stamped at each side of the
square, two of which, either from top to bottom,
or obliquely from the top to the right, are the emperor's name, the other two are either Thung-paou
or Yuen-paou, sterling and precious or original and
precious. Thus, the coins of the present emperor,
bear, top and bottom, Taou Kwan, his name, and
right and left, Thung-paou, that of He-ning, the emperor, A. D. 1048. He-ning, top and right, Thung-
paou, bottom and left.

According to Mons. Hager, in his " Numismati-
ques Chinoises," cowrie shells served the ancients as
money, but I am inclined to believe he has made a
slight, but important mistake, in his translation of
the Emperor Kang-he's quotation of Ko-tchi-ho.

poei (from his majesty, Kang-He's dictionary); as Mr. Medhurst thus translates the character, poei, viz., the shell of a tortoise, the above passage would translate, "In ancient times the money was of tortoise-shell." The cowrie-shell is a stranger in China, not so the tortoise, but it is looked upon with great veneration, from the diagrams taken from the back of a tortoise, by Fuhhe, who, contemporaneously with Noah, (or perhaps Noah himself,) is said to have invented the arts of fishing and grazing; to his reign, (the exact period of which, has puzzled all the historians of the flowery land, who now stand divided, between 3300 and 2850 years B. C.,) is ascribed the invention of that diagram, called the Luh-shoo, or odd and even digits, placed so as to make ten each way. Kangbe adds that chou-shells remained in use as money, to the time of the Tsin dynasty, which ended B. C. 201, when they were totally abolished.

It is asserted by some historians that metal coins graced the reigns of the three divine patriarchs, Fuh-He, Shin-nung, and Hwangte. Agriculture commenced with Shin-nung; and Hwang-te, in a reign of a hundred years, adopted the calendar between twenty-six and twenty-seven hundred years B. C.; but, says Dr. Morrison, (and I am not disposed to doubt him,) this is a period of much obscurity, one of the coins assigned to this period, is described as being round without, to represent the heavens, and square within, to represent the earth.

Mons. Hager discovers that the successors of Yaou and Shun (the Hea dynasty commencing 2140 ending 1786 B. C.,) ordered, that criminals might ransom the punishment to be inflicted for certain faults, with metal; and again in an era which answers to B. C. 1000, that Lo Leang, or six taels of metal would ransom the criminal from either the punishment of amputation of the feet, branding, or other mutilation.

Thus it would appear, that the currency of metals among the ancients, was arranged by weights, and this is borne out by one of the earliest of the Ta Tseen, or large coins, having the characters of Pwan-leang, or half-ounce, engraved on it, which coins are said to have been current between the time of King Wang, B. C. 612, and the Kin dynasty, which was concluded B. C. 201.

Du Halde states that the emperor Kang-He, whose reign concluded in 1722, had a cabinet of medals and coins, the most ancient of which, were represented to be of the time of Yaou, B. C. 2250, and that the money of the first dynasties was round, without inscription; this early coinage, if it existed, must have been of iron.

The Emperor, Kang-He, himself, records that bronze money first appeared in the time of the founder of the Chou dynasty, B. C. 1105, when Tae-Koung, the minister of Woo Wang, introduced round money, with a square hole in the centre. In this dynasty flourished Leaowtze, Confucius, and Mencius, and it is also supposed to be the period of the first appearance on earth of Buddha.

Notwithstanding that the first round money is supposed to be the time of Woo Wang, by the Emperor, Kang-He; those who make Hwang-te, B. C. 2600, the originator of coined metal, state that it was in the form of a cutlass, and was called the Kin-taou-tseen, or money of the metal knife. And Kang-He assigns to the Kin-taou, a place among the earliest of the coinage.

Of the Kin-taou coins, there are several kinds, varying in length from three to seven inches, some of the larger bear the characters, Yih-taou and Ping-woo-neen, *i. e.*, one knife worth five thousand (Le) of the smaller; there are several kinds, one of which, having the characters Yih and Taou, inlaid of gold, have the value of five thousand. Another Fang-tsin-tsbech-Ho-paou, Woo-Pih, Fang, Tsin, precious valuable, worth five hundred, the others have the characters, Yih Taon Ping Woo Pih, knife coin worth five hundred.

Others date the Kin-Taon in the dynasty of Chou (commenced B.C. 1112, and ended B.C. 243); in this dynasty Chou, the philosopher, invented the

seal or signet character. Thornton relates that the
usurper Ouang-mang, who overthrew the throne
of Yuen Che, A. D. 9, among other innovations as-
similated the coinage to that of Chou, whose
coins were called Taou-tscen, " knife coins ; " this is
the last mention of them.

The coins termed. Ho-pou, have the same obscurity of history attached to them as the Taou,
these are in seven orders ; they also were reintro-
duced by Wang-Mang ; in order to procure metal,
caused the tombs to be despoiled of coins which
ancient customs had caused to be buried with the
dead.   These and the Taon are of copper and
bronze.   There are several classes of symbolic coins
of various shapes and dimensions, whose origins are
equally obscure.

The round moneys after the Pwau-leang, or
weight money, came the Woo-choo, or pieces of five
Choo, having simply the two characters Woo and
Choo on the right and left of the central square
in the seal character.   The first coins extant bearing
the name of an emperor, are those of Ho-King,
who was deposed A. D. 465, and from that time
all moneys have been inscribed with the Kwo-
Haoua of Life, title of the emperor.

All dates are either arranged in the date of
the cycle, or of the emperor's reign, thus a reference
must be made to the comparison of the cycle,

or the corresponding year in the chronology of China, whereby not infrequently great trouble is entailed. As the chronologies hitherto translated materially differ the one from the other. 1847 is the forty-fourth year of the seventy-fifth cycle of sixty, being the twenty-seventh year of Taou-Kwang.

That the metals were various is decided by the annals of the Leang dynasty, in which it is related that in the twelfth moon of the fifty-fifth cycle, or the fourth year of the Emperor Tsin Thung, A. D. 500, in winter, (which may mean in a scarcity) of other metals, the use of money of iron was revived. Bronze, copper, and brass, had hitherto been in use for some time.

SYCEE SILVER AND GOLD IN INGOTS.

Sycee silver in Chinese Wan-yin, is the only approach to a silver currency among the Chinese. In it the government taxes and duties, and the salaries of officers are all paid; and it is also current among merchants in general. The term Sycee is derived from two Chinese words—Se-sye, "fine floss silk," which expression is synonymous with the signification of the term Wan. The silver is formed into ingots (by the Chinese called shoes), which are stamped with the mark of the office that issues them, and the date of their being issued.

The ingots are of various weights, most commonly of ten taels each.

Sycee silver is divided into several classes, according to its fineness and freedom from alloy. The kinds most current are the five following :—

1. Kwan-Leang, the Hoppo's duties, or the silver which is forwarded to the imperial treasury at Pekin. This is of ninety-seven to ninety-nine touch, that is ninety-seven to ninety-nine one hundredths are pure silver, and not above three hundredths alloy. On all the imperial duties a certain per-centage is levied, for the purpose of turning them into Sycee of this high-standard, and of conveying them to Pekin without any loss in the full amount. The Hoppo-koeen in all probability increases the per centage far above what is requisite, that he may be enabled to retain the remainder for himself and his dependants.

2. Fan-koo or Fan-foo, the treasurer's receipts, or that in which the land tax is paid. This is also of a high standard, but inferior to that of the Hoppo duties, and being intended for use in the province, not for conveyance to Pekin, no per-centage is levied on the taxes for it.

3. Yuen-paou, or Yuen-po, literally, chief in value. This kind is usually imported from Soochow, in large pieces of fifty taels each. It does not

appear to belong to any particular government
tax.

4. Yen, or Eem-leang, salt duties. It is difficult
to account for these being of so low a standard, the
salt trade being entirely a government monopoly.
This class is inferior only to

5. Mut-tae a Wuh-tae, the name of which sig-
nifying uncleaned or unpurified, designates it as the
worst of all. It is seldom used, except for the
purpose of plating, or rather washing baser metals.

Copper money of a nominal value has in times of
scarcity been made to represent a certain amount of
rice or grain, payable at the granaries.

At various periods the companies of merchants
have issued local coin in different shapes, and with
indicative inscriptions, as for instance on one of
Hang-chou-foo (the ancient name of which was Lin-
an-foo). "In the shops of Lin-an-foo this passes
for 300 Cash or Le."

The vanity of many emperors has been gratified
by the assumption of a different name on the occasion of a victory, or any other great event ; and to
such an extent has this been carried that in one reign,
Kaow Tsung takes thirteen names : this causes much
trouble in arranging a collection, where the best chro-
nologers give only five or six, and money has been
coined in all; thus, the Emperor King-Tsing (so
called after death by his Meaon Haou, or " death

name ") took at various times the following, Kwo
Haon, or " life names."

1. Keen-chung-tsing-Kwo. 2. Tsung-ning. 3.
Ta Kwan. 4. Ching-Ho. 5. Chung-Ho. 6.
E-Ho. Of these I collected the coins of five.
The " life name" appears first on record B. C. 189,
before that the Meaow Haow, or "death name,"
alone was used.

Besides the number of names belonging to each
actual reigning sovereign, the empire, although
having an acknowledged sovereign, has been subdivided into petty principalities, the names of the
kings of which do not appear in the chronologies.
Thus, in the reign of Woo-Wang, the founder of the
Chou dynasty, China was divided into one hundred
and twenty-three different states. From the circumstance that China has often been divided into
petty principalities, the separate rulers of which
under many different titles have coined their own
money, an idea of the difficulties of settling their
chronology by numismatics may be imagined.

MEDALS.

Napoleon's absurdity of stamping *Frappé à
Londres* on a medal found its equal in China. When
the city of Amoy was taken by storm in 1841, silver medals were discovered commemorating its defence and the discomfiture of the barbarians. Many

medals of considerable antiquity are still extant, mostly of bronze and copper, commemorating military exploits, long reigns, seasons of abundance, extraordinary literary genius, &c., as well as in honour of the gods of antiquity and the Buddhist religion.

On military medals is generally a horse, and reverse a mandarin in *alto relievo*, such are those in honour of the eight famous horses of the Hou dynasty also called the dragons, thus one was struck in honour of Sha-pao, a military mandarin who owned one of the eight horses, and another called the Hwa-Ha, the name of one of the eight horses themselves. Medals of long and prosperous reigns are thus inscribed, that of Këen-Lung, the grandfather of the present emperor, with "peace and plenty;" "Tae-ping," others with "plenty and profit," &c. Others have such inscriptions as "avoid what is depraved that happiness may follow," "united we are happy," &c.

At this day coining of money is farmed by the government to private speculation, and at the opening of a new mint it is requisite to produce a specimen die: these are often of large dimensions and inscribed with the ancient or modern character according to the taste of the artist. One I collected had in ancient characters the following inscriptions Lëen-shin-Wang-Chung, and reverse, Tsheih-Nëen-Woo-Choo, and it would appear that in the firm of

F

Lëen-Shin and Wang-Chung this coin was made; and the reverse states it to be of the nominal value of seven thousand times five Choo pieces (Choo is another name for Le).

The medals are for the most part well executed, with a decided decline of the art in those of later years. This is especially observable in the coins of Taow-Kwang (the present emperor), which are far inferior in die to those of many of his ancestors. Mr. Thom, her majesty's late consul at Ningpo, honoured me with his opinion of my collection, in which he states,—"During a residence of twelve years in China I have seen no collection of Chinese coins, so varied, so full, and so complete as that which you shewed me on board H.M.S. Wolf; and I may add, that though my official position has made me acquainted with some mandarins of high rank, yet I honestly believe not one of them, nor all of them conjointly, could produce the coins which you have in your collection."

ORIGIN OF THE TCHHAO, OR BANK NOTE.

About one hundred years before Christ, the Emperor King-te reigned over China. He was one of the great house of Han, whose dynasty was so famous for the encouragement of wisdom, that to this day the Chinese term themselves the Han-Jin, or "men of Han." It became a matter of uneasiness to the great emperor, that, owing to the scarcity of metal, the expenses of the state far exceeded the finances. It cannot be wondered at, amidst so much wisdom as then surrounded the throne, that an expedient was soon thought of. The prime minister caused the skins of certain white stags, that were fed in the imperial park, to be cut into pieces a foot square, each valued at 40,000 cash, and issued as a currency, which is, perhaps, the earliest instance on record of a paper currency.

From scarcity of metal, the Emperor Hëen-Tsung, of the Tang dynasty, again had recourse to paper currency, A.D. 800, calling upon all wealthy people to deposit their metal money in the public coffers, and receive therefrom paper-money of a nominal value, which it became imperative on the subjects to receive in exchange, or, as we should say, to take as a legal tender,—the penalty of refusal being death. In the time of Chin-Tsung, of the Leang dynasty, A.D. 1000, metal being scarce, merchants on depositing merchandize in the public coffers, received therefrom paper-money for the value of deposit.

These bank notes continued to be issued from time to time, being renewed at presentation if damaged, and charged for renewal three per cent., with little or no alteration up to the time of the

F 2

Ming, or Chinese dynasty, which overthrew the Mongols in 1366, until about the middle of the fifteenth century, when, notwithstanding great exertions on the part of the Emperor Kingtae and his predecessors, it fell into disuse.

Banks take their origin in China from the time of the Emperor Jin Tsung, A.D. 1020, or more than two hundred years before, who, in order the better to regulate the arrangement of the paper currency, deputed twelve rich merchants to different parts of his empire to superintend the payment of the cheques, which then became payable every three years from its date. Hence arose a regular banking system.

Since the conquest by the Mongols, banking has become a private arrangement, although, for better safety, under government control, and each bank, as in Europe, issues its cheques and bank notes. A more perfect system now exists than formerly, on which the following specimen may throw some light.

BANKING IN CHINA.

In my trip to Ningpo in the early part of 1846, an English merchant from Shanghae formed one of our party. Not wishing to be encumbered with some hundreds of dollars, which it was his intention to spend there, he had obtained from a bank in Shanghae, called the Keen San, an order for the amount on a corresponding house in Ningpo.

I gladly availed myself of the opportunity to accompany him to the banker's, whose house we found with little difficulty in a street of banks (every particular trade is confined in a great measure to its own street), situated in the suburb of the Tungmun or east gate. We were kindly received by one of the partners of the establishment, and after the usual ceremonies, peculiar to the entry to a Chinese dwelling, viz., obliging the guests to be seated and serving them with tea, my friend immediately produced the bank check. The corresponding part of the bank book had been sent overland, and was no sooner produced than being proved to be satisfactory, the money was offered in exchange.

My friend did not ask in vain to be allowed to take only one hundred dollars at a time, the sum taken being each time marked on the order. As soon as he had specified the quantity required, four men took positions at a small table near a huge iron-studded strong box, which was no sooner opened, than, for a minute or two, each had his employment; one counted, a second cleaned off all old marks, a third renewed, with an Indian ink stamp, the seal of the bank, while a fourth, with blotting paper, dried it. The object of stamping was, in the case of any being spurious on being presented with the house-stamp thereon, for them to be changed;

of course this never happened: while, on the other hand, it deterred any artful person from bringing bad money to the bank on pretence that it had been drawn therefrom.

Ningpo is said to be the greatest banking city in the empire, but establishments of the kind are found in all, both large and small. A considerable excitement was apparent among a party of well-dressed people, who stood at the doors of those banks in the centre of the street; we were told that this was the mode of arranging, among the bankers, the value of the dollar and other money in the market; it fluctuates in the dollar from 1100 to 1400, and is a matter of much annoyance to the poor; in particular in those districts where, from distance to the capital, and the ground producing nothing worthy of being sent to his imperial majesty as tribute, or land-money, specie is demanded. In many cases the tael of silver, which formerly could be bought for 1000 cash, now cannot be purchased under 15 or 16,000; increasing the burden of the tax some 50 or 60 per cent. This demand, if rigorously insisted on by the presiding mandarin, frequently causes an insurrection; when, as a *douceur* to his people, the imperial father beheads his servant, who, had he not so acted, would at the least have lost his place, and perhaps ended his days in some Chinese Siberia; his too fondly served master confiscating his wealth, and that of his family and connections, to a more distant connexion than even Scotch cousinship,—to his own coffers.

Banking is so generally in use in China, that, as in Europe, people travel with their blank bank cheque-books, which can be filled up to any amount. On returning to Shanghae, I requested, and obtained a specimen. My friend being about to purchase a considerable quantity of raw silk, and other articles on sale, in the neighbourhood of the ancient city of Soo-chow-Foo, (one of the most antique in the empire, and a considerable emporium for manufactured silks, carpets, &c., besides being the greatest seat of luxury in China,) obtained from the Keen-san, bank; a note of which the following is a true translation :—

" No. 132.

"This order is to pay Wang-Ting-Yang, by the 17th of June, the sum of 20,000 dollars exactly; application to be made at Soo-chow, to Koo-Tsye-Sing, in the Hang-ke store, or bank, who will pay it accordingly.

" Pingwoo,* fifth moon, eigh-
teenth day of the twenty-sixth
year of Taou Kwan.

* Name of the district in Shanghae in which the Keen-san is situated.

This corresponds to the 11th of June, 1846, and was duly cashed.

These banks are under the superintendance of government, and into these, in the five ports, all government dues are deposited.

CULTIVATION OF RICE (PLOUGHING).

CHAPTER IV.

AGRICULTURE.

Beautiful Economy of Chinese Agriculture.—Mortgages.—Waste Land.—Quit-rent.—The Emperor a Patron of Agriculture.— Irrigation. — Manure. — Chinese Farm. — Agricultural Implements.—Chinese Industry.—Number of Crops.—Highroads.— Bamboo.—Cattle-feeding.—Contentment of the Chinese.

IF there be one thing that the genius of this extraordinary people has brought nearer to perfection than another, it is the cultivation of the soil. The economy of their agriculture is beautiful, the whole country presents the appearance of one continued garden; no large commons starving a few miserable horses, nor parks and chases laid

waste for the special purpose of breeding rabbits
are to be met with; the land is meant to feed and
clothe the people, and to that use its powers are
directed. Not an inch of soil is lost that can
be made useful by the most laborious and apparently unpromising industry, save only such parts as
are set aside for burial grounds. Swamps are drained by canals, which carry the superfluous waters
where they are turned to profitable account in en-
riching land that otherwise would not be productive.
Hills are terraced to the summits, and the banks
of rivers and shores of the sea recede and leave
flourishing farms to reward the enterprise of man.
I know nothing that would be likely to be more
valuable from this country than the report of an
experienced and scientific farmer, could such be
induced to bestow a short time in travelling to
China and making its agriculture his study.

The whole country may be said to be one vast
estate or manor, of which the Emperor is the lord,
with pretty large power over his tenants, which
he is not slow sometimes in exercising. Omitting
to enter lands in the public register for taxation,
entering less than the real quantity, or evading payment of taxes, incur a forfeiture, as likewise does
neglect of cultivation where cultivation is feasible;
and in case of invasion, as of old by the Japanese,
and more recently by Koshinga, with the gallant

remnant of unconquered Chinese, all lands for a certain number of miles from the coast were, by Imperial edict, vacated and laid waste to stop the prosecution of invasion, by establishing a dense population on the frontier of a desert. But practically the Emperor is a good landlord, and though the occupying tenant may be rejected at will, yet, except in cases such as the invasions above mentioned, when once registered and in lawful possession, he continues so during good behaviour, and most frequently transmits the same estate to his family for many generations, with the value of all his improvements guaranteed, and if he has more land in hand than he can conveniently cultivate, he may lease it out at a rent payable either in money or in kind.

Mortages are not uncommon, except in military tenancies, inasmuch as land is assigned to the soldiers when off duty, in lieu of a part of their pay, and continued to their families if they die in possession.

Waste and uncultivated land may be appropriated by any applicant on proof of his competency in capital and skill to cultivate it, by which means enormous tracts have been recovered from the sea, when the water shoals; and it would really appear that miles upon miles of the Kiang-tsu province have in this way been added to the country. I myself have witnessed, at a distance of nearly a hundred miles, from the month of the Yang-tse-Kiang river, on the lower base of a hill, which has the appearance of having been, at no distant date, an island, the perforations on the rock, which could only have been worn by the sea,—this, it is true, may also be accounted for by the water receding naturally; but having seen the like effects in other parts on a scale of less magnitude which I know to be artificial, and considering the stupendous efforts the Chinese are capable of, I am inclined to ascribe this also to the labour of man.   In Chusan, in the lower Chi-ou Valley, there are three boundary ramparts in succession, at a quarter of a mile distance from one another, each of which occupies a site formerly under water.

The tax or quit-rent, by which land is held of the Emperor, consists invariably of one-tenth of the gross produce of grain, mostly paid in kind, but in times of dearth reduced partially or totally as the case may require.

The Emperor, as is well known, is a great patron of agriculture, and condescends once a year, with his own royal hands, to guide a richly-ornamented plough, specially kept for the purpose. His Majesty first turns a stated number of furrows (I believe three), then the royal kindred, and afterwards the ministers; the land so ploughed is then sown with grain, the produce of which, on its arriving at maturity, is eagerly bought at a high figure by the pliant courtiers.

It has often been the custom for Emperors, whose reigns have been marked with peace and plenty, to compose odes and songs in honour of the labours of husbandry. Thus, the second Emperor of the present, *i. e.* Ta-Tsing dynasty, Yung-Ching remarks, "Of old the Emperors ploughed and the Empress cultivated the mulberry tree, though supremely honourable they disdained not to labour, in order that by their example they might excite the millions of the people to lay due stress on the radical principles of political economy.

"Suffer not a barren spot to remain a wilderness, or an idle person to abide in a city, then the farmer will not lay aside the plough and hoe, or the wife her silkworm or her weaving. Even the productions of hills and marshes, orchards, and vegetable gardens, and the propagation of the breed of poultry, dogs, and swine, will all be regularly cherished and used in their seasons to supply the deficiencies of agriculture."

In the sacred edict of Kang-He, the first Emperor of the present dynasty, author of a Chinese dictionary and an ode on the process of preparing and making tea, is the following clause, "Give the chief place to husbandry, and the cultivation of the mulberry tree, in order to procure adequate supplies of food and raiment."

Although each sovereign, or at least some of each dynasty have promulgated their own laws, still models are to be found of them in the ancient works, and, in point of fact, they are similar in the present day to the laws which governed the husbandman in the days of Confucius,—"Give the chief place to husbandry," is a maxim universally received.

To obtain the largest supply in the most economical manner from the smallest space is the desideratum of the Chinese agriculturist, which, beyond all other nations, he has been successful in arriving at. Nature has given him a favourable climate in most parts, a good soil, and numerous and splendid rivers on which art and labour have been most unsparingly lavished in making them subservient to the purposes of irrigation, which may be said to be universal.

Besides the canals and navigable rivers, which no part of China is far distant from, every field is partially bounded by water, which in the low countries is easily made to inundate the fields, and cleared off at convenience by means of flood-gates. In Kiang-tsn, and all parts having canals, it is raised by means of chain-pumps of the rudest materials, worked either by hand, feet, or bullocks, according to the size of the machine; that by hand can only be worked by two men, that by foot by as many as four, but only one bullock at a time is yoked. In Fuhkien, and where springs are constantly met, wells are dug, and over each an upright pole of large dimensions is raised, at the upper end of which is slung a cross-piece, and to one end is attached the bucket with length of rope sufficient to reach the water, to the other a stone of sufficient weight to over-balance it, and thus a single man can draw hundreds of tons daily; these wells are sometimes found at each corner of the paddy or rice-field.

But irrigation is not confined to the low countries, but on the highest terraces, the smallest mountain stream, the veriest drippling of a spring, is carried by convenient channels from one level to another, with as little waste as possible, till, having gone through each in succession, it is conducted into a deep reservoir, to be ready for service again; but on those high grounds, where springs and streams are not at hand, the water has to be raised from a lower level. In Quang-tung, where the hilly country sometimes requires the water to be considerably raised, reservoirs are established on ledges, twenty or thirty feet above each other; at every reservoir stand, one on each side, two men; between whom is slung a bucket or pail, of large proportions; the ropes being relaxed, the bucket fills, when it is drawn up, the rope being horizontally tightened; and by a peculiar swing or jerk every drop is received into the reservoir above, and so on till it reaches the highest point desired.

For manure almost everything not edible is preserved, and this becomes the more necessary from the comparatively small quantity of stock kept. Nothing in town or country is wasted; the refuse of the drain is not left to pollute the rivers, but is carefully collected; all remnants of animal and vegetable matter, even to the wiping of a barber's razor, are sought for and duly appreciated.

Water, when it can be spared, is drawn off from the canals for the sake of the deposit it may leave behind; the small canals are cleared out for this purpose nearly every year. Large vessels are everywhere seen, and, in place of the legends of commination which adorn our walls, the smallest contribution is invited and thankfully received, ay, even paid for.

There being no farm-horses or vehicles of any sort for them to draw, the "olla podrida" is removed by means of band-pails and applied, after dilution by water or liquid manure, as required or convenient.

The farm, however small, is not so much the estate of an individual proprietor as the home of a family or seat of a clan, many generations of which, under one acknowledged head or patriarch, are often congregated in the same dwelling. As the farm-houses in general differ but little from each other except in size, I will endeavour to give the reader a description of one.

In a small island, formed by a moat for the supply of water and the rearing of ducks and geese, well sheltered by bamboos and other trees, and nearly hid from view, stands the house, consisting of one floor only, built, when possible, of stone, in other cases of brick (of so superior a quality as to become an article of commerce with this country, and to find its way to Liverpool), or of wood. In the centre is a large hall called the " Hall of Ancestors" common to all the family. In it are arranged the household gods, (among which are invariably the Taouist divinities presiding over hearing and sight,) and relics, such as an ancestral picture, in the most conspicuous part of the wall, on each side of which is an aphorism of Confucius, and in front a table bearing incense burners and fruits as offerings, and ornamental porcelain vases, &c. The hall also serves for a drying room for their seeds, and a depository for the smaller implements of husbandry. It is the scene of their entertainments, many of their festivals, and the adoration of the gods, but never used for culinary purposes. This forms the nucleus of the building, around it are the dwelling rooms of the different divisions of the tribe; and as often as a marriage takes place an apartment is added for the newly-wedded couple, and, in time, the whole presents rather the appearance of a village than a single dwelling-house. The furniture of each family consists of a bed highly ornamented, in many cases carved and richly inlaid with ivory; a few high-backed chairs, often of bamboo; a plain polished round table; washing utensils of brass; and, in one corner of the room, cooking utensils consisting of a block fire-place, in which a few round pans are set with masonry, though in the larger establishments the kitchen is a separate building: around the room are several red varnished cabinets, and in these apartments the females are employed in the household duties of needlework, spinning, &c., a spinning wheel and loom forming necessary appendages to each farm-house in those parts where cotton is grown. Nearly everything for the use of the family is home-made—agricultural instruments are home-made and repaired; cotton is grown, and spun, and made into clothes; silk-worms are reared, and all the process of winding and weaving done by the family; flour is ground, cakes are baked, and sam shoo is distilled from rice, and as much as required stored, the rest, and whatever other produce not wanted for home consumption, is either exchanged for other necessaries amongst the neighbours, or sent to some town in the vicinity to find a market. In Kiang-tsu, where that species of cloth better known under the name of nankin is made, the drapers, who are proprietors of large houses in the cities, hire stalls outside the walls and meet the farmers on the road and buy their cloth, paying in bills drawn on their own houses.

The live-stock consists of a liberal supply of fowls, ducks, geese, goats, and pigs, and a dog or two, (scarcely any family, however poor, is without one or more of the latter two,) together with one or two bullocks and buffalos according to the labour required. The buffalo is almost an amphibious animal, being constantly in the water.

The implements are very simple and primitive—I may almost say barbarous. The Le, or plough, has no coulter, and but one handle, and, with the exception of the share, is entirely of wood. It is drawn by a single bullock or buffalo, by means of a trace passing before the breast with a strap over the shoulders. The Pa (harrow), drawn in the same manner as the plough, is of two kinds, one perpendicular, and the other horizontal; the former consists of a row of iron spikes, like a comb, with a handle on the back of it, on which the labourer leans his whole weight to break the clods; the latter is a parallelogram of wood, armed with iron or hard wooden knives, and is used after the former to level the ground; the driver adds his weight, standing with one foot on each cross-beam. The spade, for the purpose of working the ground, is entirely superseded by the Cha (hoe); it is of use, however, as a shovel in widening ditches, clearing canals, &c. The hoe is used to break the heavy sods as well as the harrow, and, although a simple looking implement, in the hands of a stout farmer is rendered very available, the women use it also in weeding and hoeing out the stubble, &c.

Pa, the rake, (the same pronunciation with Pa, the harrow, but a different character in writing;) of these there are three kinds, the first, entirely of bamboo, which is generally used to rake in grain (the curved end of the bamboo almost meeting), and collect offal, dirt, &c., in the streets; the second, which is much like the English rake in proportions as well as use; and the third, which is more in the shape of a brush, with hard wooden teeth, and is used to loosen the ground about the roots of the paddy crop. Lien (bill-hook) may also be termed a sickle, being used as well for the one as the other, it is mostly serrated, and cuts grass, rushes, hedges, &c. Taow (the knife) belongs as much to the house of the artisan as the farmer. It is well known that in China chop-sticks are in use instead of knives and forks, hence the great want of those articles universally found in a European establishment; a large chopper-looking instrument is used for almost the minutest requisitions for a knife of even the smallest dimensions.

There are four modes of threshing; first, with the Leen-kea, or flail, as with us, except that the instrument is smaller than ours and the handle is of bamboo; secondly, treading out by oxen when the quantity is large; thirdly, over a table made in frame and filled in with pieces of bamboo just far enough apart to allow the grain alone to escape; fourthly,—and the most general—by placing a large tub conveniently in the field, round three parts of which is a mat to defend it from the wind,—the labourer taking the sheaf in hand, batters it against the sides of the tub until the grains are out, when he lays that aside, &c. Winnowing is either performed by a machine like that in Europe, or by the primitive mode of raising the grain in a flat basket, from one mat, as high as a person can reach; then suddenly jerking it out, the grain alone reaches another mat laid to receive it, the chaff being scattered away. Husking is equally primitively done so far as the mills are concerned; they are generally of two kinds, the first is a circular stone ledge let into the ground, in which traverses, round a pole on its own axis, a large stone-wheel, propelled by a bullock, a man constantly supplying the grain until it is requisite to replenish, when the ledge is cleared; the second is a kind of wooden mill. The most primitive

CULTIVATION OF RICE (HUSKING).

mode of grinding is pounding the rice or corn in a mortar by a stone pestle; this is usually performed as a species of treadmill, jumping up, weighing down, and jumping off, to assist which the hands are slung at convenient heights.

It will readily be believed that with such poor mechanical assistance the Chinaman does not eat the bread of idleness. From sunrise to sunset, with the exception of meal-times, the whole family work hard; the meals are three per day, the first as soon after rising as the pot can be boiled, the second at noon, the third about an hour before sunset, consisting of tea invariably, rice the staple food of the country, vegetables, fish salted or dried, pork, goat, mutton, fowl or duck sometimes, but the animal

CULTIVATION OF RICE (SOWING).

food in small quantities, now and then seasoned with a drop of samshoo, after which it is time for rest.

The principal crop cultivated, in the parts that I visited, is rice. A small part of a field is first of all prepared and sown as thickly as possible, after which the rest is inundated, and while still under water is ploughed and harrowed with the harrow No. 2 described before, which, in clayey soils, is a work of great labour; after this the water is run off, and the sods are broken with the hoe, when another harrowing follows if required, the manure is then laid on in a moist state, the ground is now ready for the rice which is transplanted in small clusters in rows, the entire length of the field. Water is again run on, but not in sufficient quantities to cover the plant,

CULTIVATION OF RICE (TRANSPLANTING).

and from time to time the workmen proceed down the rows with rake No. 3 above described, and loosen the soil about the plant, and thus allow the moisture to sink down to the roots; the manuring is continued from time to time, according to the strength of the plant, until it has attained the height of a foot or fourteen inches, when the field is allowed to dry as it may, which generally is the case by reaping-time. The land, being highly manured, yields two crops per year; but it was observable in the year 1845 in the north and east valleys in Chusan, three crops were taken from most of the fields. During the growth all weeds are culled, and anything that might obstruct the crop or unnecessarily draw the land, carefully removed.

Corn and vegetable lands are usually productive

CULTIVATION OF RICE (REAPING).

of three crops, as the following :—The corn seed is sown in rows, between every two of which is a row of cotton, beans or other vegetable, (the cotton is an annual.) At harvest-time the corn is reaped, and the field, all yellow to-day, is beautifully green to-morrow, the cotton being about six or eight inches high; the minutest portion of stubble is removed by women and stored up for manure, and the field weeded; the cotton on coming to maturity is plucked, the tree ploughed in for manure, and the field prepared for the third crop of clover, vegetables, or a kind of sesame; if clover, only a part is cut, and the rest ploughed in for manure. Fallows are unknown, and, from the constant manuring, the land is enabled to produce at the above rate with little variation without becoming exhausted.

In tea plantations and orchards of all kinds the land is equally worked.

In each province there is generally a paved high-road from one Foo to another, and sometimes, but not often, to a Hëen; these roads are in good order and about six feet broad, besides these there are the foot-paths, which skirt the fields as boundaries, but are sometimes very inconvenient to the traveller from the tortuous courses they take, as sometimes you start off at right angles from the object of your journey; besides these and the canals, a stone often divides two properties. In this way the country is perfectly open, save where here and there dotted with picturesque farm-houses, joss-houses, and bosquets of bamboo.

The bamboo here deserves a passing mention, as I know no plant so useful for so many purposes as the Chinese make it. There is scarcely a trade or manufacture amongst them that is not more or less assisted by it, while its early shoots form one of the choicest edibles as a vegetable preserve and pickle. The Bambusa Arundinalis is of two kinds— the black and the yellow—the former very scarce and valuable, the latter most in use; it is indigenous to many, and found in most parts of China. Its height varies with the climate that it is grown in, but averages about forty or fifty feet, but very sel-dom passes seventy, with a diameter in proportion to its height averaging about eight inches. When it is cultivated, the less promising young roots are sent to market as an article of food, but the most healthy are transplanted for growth; the grove is one of the most picturesque and graceful sights imaginable, waving to the slightest air, and forming a delightfully cool and shady retreat to those fond of retirement, but the care required in rearing and cultivating it is in proportion to its profit. During the first years the suckers and the tops of the shoots must be removed very tenderly, and the wounds filled up with sulphur, but its varied utility repays the care bestowed upon it. In early times, before books were compiled, all records were carved on slips of bamboo. The most elegant household furniture, chairs, sofas, tables, beds, and even the pillars, to support the house itself, are made of it. The curiosity-maker, the toy-maker, the carpenter, the agriculturist, are indebted to it. The masts of boats and small ships, besides a long list of other marine paraphernalia, are from its wood, clothing from its fibre, and lampwicks from its pith; the soldier and sailor, the clerk and civilian, carry it as pike-handles, and arrows, and pencils. I have in my own possession a jacket, for an under-garment, made of it, like net-work, to be worn next the skin in hot weather. The housebreaker finds it an assistant of his crime in his own hands and his repentance in those of the executioner.

I have made no mention of pastures, and I saw

none; the cattle are fed by the sides of the roads or in stalls on the different productions of the farm, and, amongst others, oil-cake, which is in great abundance; it is the refuse of the sesame and cotton-seeds after the oil has been expressed.

In the northern provinces sheep are reared on lands that would not pay for other cultivation. They are a long-tailed, long-legged breed, like the sheep at the Cape. At Shanghae they sell for about four dollars a head; at Canton from ten to twelve. The price of labour is a mace or fourpence a day.

It is forbidden to plough, feed cattle, or cut wood in the places where emperors, kings, princes, saints, sages, faithful ministers, and other illustrious worthies are buried. Now, as it is apt to please each and every farmer and others to vote his or their immediate predecessors "the illustrious dead," the actual farm is sometimes diminished by the frequency of these ancestral monuments. But I do not know that we should grudge them that whim when they make so good a use of the rest of the land; and if some of the above particulars may not square with European notions of economy, amongst their fruits may be mentioned the most contented, good-humoured, well-fed, industrious, and happy population that, in the course of sixteen years of service in the navy, and rambles in most parts of the globe, I have ever met with.

CHAPTER V.

DIET AND DINNER IN A TAVERN.

Chinese Bill of Fare.—Its Constituents.—Ducks—Their remarkable Discipline.—Regular Tavern Dinner.—Waiter.—Pipe-bearer. —Courses and Dishes.—Reckoning.

The Chinese bill of fare may be said to include everything animal and vegetable that nature will digest, together with some few items of minerals, with the exception of milk and its preparations. It is only for the use of foreigners that cows and goats are ever milked, but otherwise no part of the animal is lost; but when one is killed the blood is carefully collected, the hair is removed, and the skin, and offal, apportioned in lots and sold.

Poultry, game, and fish, all kinds of grains, vegetables, fruits, are to be had in the different parts of the empire, abundant in quantity and excellent in quality. Some, together with the dishes made from them, were new to me; such, for instance, was the King of Cabbages, indigenous to the Shang-

tung province, which would form a splendid ac-
quisition in England to the cattle grazier; it is a
thick-set cabbage, perfectly white, and so close that
when required to be kept, removing an outside
leaf or two about once a week, will make it last
for many months; it has found its way I hear to
Paris, where it is known as the "Chou de Nankin."
It is used as a simple vegetable cooked or "au naturel,"
or in winter a most excellent mild salad, and the
Chinese salt and pickle both this and other cabbages, and make a kind of sour krout. It frequently
weighs twenty pounds. In the south is a species
of orange called the Kin-kengh, or Kum-kwat,
very small and of very high flavour; in size and
shape it resembles a pigeon's egg, it is eaten, skin
and all, and when preserved makes a very fine
marmalade. In the Fu-kien province is the hand
citron somewhat resembling a hand, with a multitude
of fingers. The Loquat, a yellow fruit, with a most
velvet skin, has four or more stones, and a most
peculiar flavour which an acquired taste only can
admire. The Liche is a most delicious melting
mouthful, the outside shell must be burst first, it
grows in clusters, and is not unlike a strawberry in
appearance but in nothing else. Most European and
tropical fruits flourish in different parts of the
country, according to the climate, and a large trade
in fruits is carried on by means of junks, these are

mostly preserved in different modes, moist and dry, whole and in shreds, with vinegar or sugar, which latter, in the province of Fo-kien, and the island of Formosa, is grown and manufactured in high perfection, but is never used to sweeten tea. Honey is abundant, oils are extracted from the olive, sesame, cotton-seed, several kinds of cabbage, pork-fat, and fish, which, together with the castor-oil, are all used for culinary purposes; the use of the latter for any purpose other than a medicine, is, I should suppose, peculiar to the Chinese; it is expressed through a cullender, and when fresh has not the aroma that it afterwards acquires. Ducks'-eggs are in great requisition, and in order to meet the demand for them great numbers are kept on all the navigable rivers and canals, in floating poultry houses. They are under very remarkable discipline, they go out to feed, and return home with wonderful expedition, and at a word from their masters will do almost anything that can be required of them; he stands meanwhile at the entrance, and flogs the straggler, and rewards the foremost. They are never allowed to hatch their own eggs, almost all towns having ovens for that purpose. The eggs of all birds are used, but those of the ducks are salted in the shells, as is the flesh also, for sea stores. Considerable quantities of fish are salted and dried; the collared eel is very fine, but none are thrown away, blubber even is eaten, as are water snakes, frogs, toads, shell-fish of every species, tortoises, snails, gelatinous worms, and lizards.

The various grains are used in making unleavened bread, not unlike a muffin in appearance, cooked on the side of a portable oven, and generally by steam, together with pastry of divers sorts, among which are some very similar to European, as wafers, sponge-cakes, &c., which would be palatable enough were it not for the introduction of a lump of pork-fat, discoverable only by the uninitiated, at a most disagreeable period. The introduction of pork-fat into these articles of Chinese gastronomy is universal and disgusting.

Imported are Ginseng, a kind of liquorice, which was formerly a royal monopoly, and could only be grown on the Emperor's property in the north, but has latterly been introduced from Canada, and some parts of the United States; and birds'-nests of the sea-swallow, a transparent substance, in appearance somewhat resembling a gum, reckoned a great delicacy, and sold at very high prices. I have seen four or five when very clear, weighing only three or four ounces each, sell for thirty dollars. They are brought from the islands of the Eastern Archipelago, as likewise are Bêches-de-mer, or sea-slugs, brown looking snails about six or seven inches long. They are an expensive luxury as are the exotic dainties of roes, sounds, tripe, fins, and tails of sharks. In fact, a Chinaman will eat everything but his own father. Great art is shewn in dressing all these delicacies; the cookery is perhaps a little richer than most English palates would relish, but some of the stews, soups, and made dishes are excellent, and a good dinner may be eaten and relished if no questions be asked.

Returning one day from Tien T'hung, a party of five of us agreed, as a matter of curiosity, to sit down to a regular tavern dinner. By great good luck one of the party happened to be the consular interpreter, who induced his linguist and teacher to take the chair: to him, a fine old Chinese gentleman of convivial habits, and great information, we left the entire management, stipulating only that the dinner should be the best that the first tavern in Ningpo could produce. He promised to take us to one in the principal street which he himself frequented. He was to direct us in the most accomplished way of dining *à la Chinoise*, and to illustrate the courses, in order that our repast should be perfectly *à la mode*. I have unfortunately forgotten the beautiful collection of monosyllables that composed his name. In the lobby of our hôtel was a tempting display of, to us, very novel delicacies, illustrative of mine host's proficiency in his calling, together with a cloud of

H

steam and a most variegated odour. Calling the
waiter, our *major domo* ordered that every dish
the house could provide should be served as soon as
possible, at the same time requiring a private apartment.   The waiter (whose dress was not calculated
to impede his movements much, consisting merely
of a pair of short unmentionables, it being the
height of summer) led the way up stairs, through
a large apartment, in which at small tables, one
or two at each, sat respectably dressed Chinese,
taking their afternoon meal, or conversing over a
cup of hot sam-shoo, into a neatly furnished small
apartment.   No sooner had we entered than a pipe-
bearer, with necessary paraphernalia, introduced a
pipe (technically a bubble-bubble) into the mouth of
one of the party, who, being told by our preceptor
that it was *selon le règle*, drew a whiff or two and
passed it on to another, and so on all round.   After
a few moments' delay tea was served, succeeded
by six small saucers, containing separately sugar-
candy, cherries, dried pips of melons, walnuts,
ground-nuts, and brown sugar; these, we were informed, were for our amusement, while the landlord prepared a dinner worthy the reputation of
his establishment; our Chinese friend beguiling the
time with anecdotes of heroes who had distinguished
themselves in the convivial line, and heroes with
a vengeance they must have been, if these stories

of their mighty appetite, and grand exploits of gormandising had any foundation in fact. Soon the advanced guard made its appearance, consisting of several small basins, filled with soups and stews of birds'-nests, bêche-de-mer, sea-slugs, and other light and stimulating delicacies, patties of shrimps, &c., fried in pork-fat, salted and boiled eggs, and boiled and stewed vegetables (salt, pepper, soy, and oil, in smaller saucers, were in every part of the table.) These, we were given to understand, were mere provocatives of appetite, intended as a foundation for more substantial fare, they were ranged in a line round the table, leaving an open square in the centre. The best wines were now produced, warm, in small metal pots (not unlike coffee-pots) and poured into very small China cups; from our *maître de cérémonie*, we took our queue, and, seizing the diminutive vessel in both hands, we half rose, and reaching across in direction of the person whom we wished to honour until both vessels met, when, each making a profound bow, and Chin-chin, we reseated ourselves, and emptied the cup, which was no sooner empty than refilled by our officious Ganymede.

Before each of us were two or three small basins to serve as plates, and a pair of chop-sticks. The repast might be said now to have commenced in

earnest, with the appearance of a large bowl of
stewed mutton, by no means bad, which was placed
at an angle of the square, at which each pecked
with chop-sticks, and the more finished example
was set by our accomplished friend, breaking a
piece with his own chop-sticks, giving us at the
same time to understand that it was highly com-
plimentary, and handing it over to me. After an
interval of ten minutes, viz-a-viz to the stewed
mutton, appeared a corresponding bowl with the
tripes of a rare fish, found on the coast of Coro-
mandel. Our Chinese friend was an epicure, and
this a favourite dish with him, and he was now in
his glory, and did full justice to it in no equivocal
manner. The other angles, at equal intervals, were
occupied by stewed fowl and puff-puddings; and
these four surmounted by a dish of salted blubber.
The pile of five dishes being complete, so was the
course, followed by other piles of five dishes, consisting of stews of fowls, ducks, puddings stewed
in gravies, kabobs, sweetmeats, gelatinous soups
and vegetables, to the number of thirty, in fact,
every variety of fish, fowl, and pastry, when it was
agreed we should move that the repast be brought
to an end, upon which everything was removed but
the salt, &c., when, all of a sudden, a stewed duck
with some peculiar sauce appeared. We had all,

with the exception of the Chinaman, long cried, " Hold, enough:" but when that worthy, after many vain attempts to cheer us up, told us of an extensive friend of his, who, having dined, topped up with six ducks out of compliment to him as host; we could not do otherwise than make an effort to help him out of his difficulty, and managed the one before us: a bowl of rice for each concluded the feast. Our officious waiter now appoared with warm water, and a very dark coloured and uninviting towel, which, to his astonishment, we rejected, when offered to us as a general finger-glass and napkin.

On calling for the reckoning we were whisperingly instructed by our friend to fee the waiter and pipe-bearer who would stand our friend with the landlord; they received a rupee each; presently they re-appeared with a long account which, when totaled, amounted to five dollars, or altogether a most extensive feast for about twenty-five shillings in all for six. The above, one might imagine, would have been a feast for the lord-mayor, aldermen, and all the civic dignitaries of Ningpo (if such had any existence), but it was served up extemporaucously; the dinner was on the table within a quarter of an hour of our ordering it; the waiter apologized, and said if more time were given a grander entertainment would be provided. The price of a good tavern dinner, consisting of fish, flesh, fowl, and entrées, would be about a shilling of our money; a common club dinner a mace, or fourpence.

CHAPTER VI.

EDUCATION.

Learning the Key to Civil Offices.—Open to all without distinction.—Three classes only excluded, viz., Boatmen, Coolees, and Actors.—No civil Appointment can be held without a literary qualification.—Village School.—Is generally attached to the Joss-house.—Meaning of Joss-house.—Mode of learning at village Schools.—Four Degrees of Literary Honours.—Different Classes of Teachers.—Edict regarding Literary Honours.—Great care taken to prevent any unfair practice.—Subjects of Examination.—Fraud sometimes used in obtaining a Degree.—Hall of Examination.

LEARNING assumes its proper position in the flowery land, and is the key to all the civil offices under the crown; the highest *employé* is the best scholar without regard to birth. Sons of peasants contend in the race for preferment with members of the imperial family; and no one who can pass the requisite examinations with the exception of the three excluded classes of boatmen, coolees, and actors, need despair of promotion; but no civil appointment can be held without a literary qualification. "A stone uncut forms no gem; a man unlearned knows not good principles." If the clever and intelligent do not study, they will become empty, frothy, weak, and evasive : the stupid and dull without learning, still more will be impeded by obstinacy, inadequacy, violence, and perverseness.   Every province is as it were an university of itself, of which the inhabitants are born members; and many a scholar finishes a long life before his education is complete.   On entering some of the poorest establishments, very often a little fellow may be seen sitting on a high stool behind the counter, reading to himself most intently and aloud.   He is the child of parents whose poverty compels them, for want of an assistant, to keep their sons alternately at home for a day to mind the shop.   Having served the customers, who have perhaps had to bawl pretty loudly in his ear to engage his attention, with as little loss of time as possible; he remembers the proverb his mother has so often dinned into his ear, that " It is better to be a fowl's back than a cow's tail " and sets to work again in the hope of keeping pace with his brother, whose time for staying at home comes to-morrow.   The village-school is generally attached to the joss-house, (once for all as the word is likely to recur, the word joss means a god, and joss-house a temple,) and is supported partly by government and partly by the fathers of the pupils, consisting of a master, often a very superior man, and twenty or thirty boys, each of whom has his separate chair, table, books, and a piece of wood, painted white to serve as a slate, on which he writes with a camel's hair brush and Indian ink; while learning his lesson, he reads aloud. The din of so many voices at once, on my entering a school, often reminded me of my experience of the Bell system in England in days of yore; every youngster, on the approach of a stranger, straining his throat to the loudest pitch. Near the door in awful dignity, with spectacles on his nose, sits the dominie behind a table, bearing the very unacademical pipe and tea-tray, with some future mandarin swinging his body to and fro like a mast in a storm, stumbling over a saying of Confucius that he has just learnt by heart, and trying to make himself heard amid the confused howling of the rest.

"To bring up a child without education is a crime in the father, to educate without due severity betrays sloth in a teacher," a charge not often brought home to the latter worthy, whose cane has by no means a sinecure of it. The first idea of writing is gained by placing thin transparent paper over the characters and so copying them; after that the tablet above-mentioned is used with Indian ink, easily washed out with a little water.

The appearance of the young dog is the same everywhere. "The whining school-boy, with his satchel, and shining morning face, creeping like a snail unwillingly to school," if he meet another boy on the road, causes himself a flogging for being detained by a game of hop-scotch, which is as popular amongst the rising generation of China as of England. From about eight to ten is the age of tendance at the village-schools. The salaries of the masters are, I am afraid, small; they are very courteous, and respectable men; but their domestic establishments are very humble.

After gaining the rudiments of education at school, or from his father, or some professor his friend, the aspirant may, at his leisure, it would seem, next look to becoming a candidate for the first of the four degrees of literary honours. These are under the superintendance of an officer called the Heo-Ching, or literary chancellor of the province, who deputes the duties of preparing and bringing forward the candidates to four different classes of teachers. Their titles are, 1st, Kean-Chow, "giver of learning;" 2nd, Chow-Heoching, "corrector of learning;" 3rd, Heaou-Yu, "teacher of the commands;" and 4thly, Heau-Taow; ranking according as the city, they are appointed to stand in the different classes of Fŭ, Ting, Chow, and Hëen. The Chancellor himself makes an annual tour of the province, and assists at the third and last examination for the first degree of Sew-tsae, or "flowering talent" the graduate in which becomes exempt from corporal punishment at the sentence of any but the Emperor himself, or his representative, the Tsung-tuh, or governor-general of the province. The degree is not complete until enrolled in the office of the chancellor of the province in which the scholar's family have been resident for three generations; and all particulars of name, age, and personal appearance lodged with the Foo-Yuen, or lieutenant-governor. A false entry incurs a penalty of degradation, and exclusion from all literary honours, and as a necessary consequence, all hope of holding civil office. The number of candidates for this degree is often enormous (in the province of Canton, upwards of twenty thousand in one year,) consisting sometimes of men of all ages, from the stripling of fifteen to the grandfather of seventy. The Che-foo, whose functions correspond in some measure with those of our mayor, in the absence of the governor-general, appoints the days and order of the examinations. The following edict, copied from the columns of the Hong Kong Gazette newspaper, may throw some light on the proceeding.

" EDICT REGARDING LITERARY HONOURS.

"Keying, Vice-Guardian of the Crown Prince, Governor-General of the two Kwang, &c., &c., &c. Kwang, Lieutenant-Governor of Kwang-tung, in reference to the examination for admission into the Literary Halls, hereby proclaims:—

" Whereas the examination for admission into the Colleges of Yuesan and Yuchwa, has hitherto taken place in the early spring. As the season for opening the session now approaches, we, the governor-general, lieutenant-governor, and literary chancellor, have appointed that it be this year held on the 20th day of the present month : and now publicly notify the same for the information of all graduates, and others who would be candidates throughout the province. Let those who now come up to the trial for the first time, proceed at an early period to the city, and with papers setting forth their names, ages, and a description of their personal appearance, repair to the superintendents of the college to whom they must report themselves for registration, procuring from them sealed certificates, which they must present for inspection. On the day appointed they must assemble in the Examination Hall waiting until their names are called out by an officer; when the graduates and others, ranged in order east and west, will receive their themes, and the doors being shut, the examination will proceed. Those who produce any thing really worthy of notice, though they may hitherto not have been successful, shall yet be admitted, and as for those the style of whose present essays does not surpass mediocrity, but whose compositions may on previous occasions have been superior, their former merit shall be taken into account on determining their deserts. Impartiality will guide the decisions of the lieutenant-governor, who hopes that all may succeed. Let the candidates exert to the utmost their powers for one day in making an exhibition of their long-cherished sentiments.

"Every essay must be delivered in at the specified hour in the afternoon of the day fixed, and be collected together to be presented. There must be no borrowing and echoing of each other's expressions: nor may the assistance of other parties be procured; nor yet may the papers be taken abroad. Those guilty of such disorderly practices, shall be ever after refused permission to enter themselves for examination. Let all be reverently obedient, and not oppose this special edict.

"Taonkwang, 26th year 1st month, 13th day. (8th *February* 1846)."

Great care is taken to prevent any unfair practice. The candidates enter the hall the day before, and do not leave it until the day after each of the three examinations, which take place at intervals of three days between each. On entrance their persons are searched, and their names entered, and papers being found concealed, or a wrong name given, incur degradation; so likewise does assisting, or asking assistance from another candidate.

The subjects are the themes from the works of Confucius, and his disciples and Mencius, history, poetry, and political economy, the successful candidate may consider that he has entered upon a new era of his life, and is now eligible for preferment. This first degree may, under some circumstances, be purchased. The examinations for the second degree of Kew-jin, or " promoted men," three in number, each at an interval of three days, take place once in three years before a board consisting of the Heo-Ching, and the Chow-kaow, or "master of the examinations," and all the principal authorities of the province, together with an officer from Pekin specially sent for the purpose, and presided over by the governor-general. The themes are from the same works as those proposed to the candidates for the former degree, but the subjects required to be gone into much deeper, and elegance of penmanship is not overlooked by the masters in estimating the several performances. Many fail during the first two days, but after the third the hall is closed for fifteen days to allow time to the examiners to read over the papers, and assign each his rank according to his merit. Some few of the best papers are kept for publication and a catalogue of the graduates is printed. The Kew-jin elect are now entitled to wear boots, and a button on their caps, with some significant badge on the breast of their gowns. The visible anxiety on the countenances of so many people during the time that the examination lasts tell truly the importance of success.

Notwithstanding the care that is taken to make merit the only means of getting a degree, the vigilance of the authorities is not always successful. Last year seventy-two candidates were proclaimed Kew-jin elect, in Canton; but amongst them it was discovered one had passed his examination by proxy; he had agreed with an old man, whom age and poverty had prevented from making an effort on his own account, to give a large sum of money if the old man would enter in his name and pass for him the requisite ordeal; but a dispute between them concerning the payment of the money disclosed the whole transaction, and put the authorities in a desperate dilemma. The successful candidates were loud for inquiry; the examiners, having a delicate sense of the position they were in, and a lively apprehension of the punishment consequent upon their negligence, were as eager to hush it up; but it afterwards appeared that the would-be

Kew-jin could not write even the most ordinary essay, having bought his first degree, as is sometimes done. But the second, unless by express favour of the emperor, is conferred only on talent. How the matter ended I never heard.

The Hall of Examination is generally the finest building in each city, covering a large area, surrounded by several temples, also used for examinations, and dedicated to the different branches of literature, which are announced over the doors; in each there are large rooms filled with separate tables and chairs. An image of the presiding deity faces the entrance, and the sayings and maxims of Confucius, on wood and paper scrolls, adorn the walls; a few bronzes holding burning scented sticks, and a few fruit-offerings, complete the furniture. Without, are gardens tastefully laid out with grottoes; numberless bridges crossing ponds filled with lotus plant and gold-fish; lofty trees shading rustic seats; while isolated temples, inviting the retirement of the studious, are planted on the pinnacles of artificial rocks, so high as to catch every breath of air clear of the city walls, and surmounted by the figure of a stork, or other bird, as large as life. Nothing can exceed the care and attention paid to these temples and gardens, the carved work about the former is in profusion, and of the highest order, while the most rare and beautiful plants and flowers grace the latter. They appear to be open to all who have any connexion with the examinations, and strangers enter without the slightest molestation or question; they seem to have no idea of any one thinking of doing any damage; I have passed whole mornings in that at Shanghae with a book, unnoticed and undisturbed; everybody who enters appears to do so with some object in view, and to have no time to interfere with anybody's business but his own. Tea and pipes are procurable in the establishment for a few Le (under a penny), the latter, *à la Chinoise*, was a very favourite beverage with me when I became accustomed to it.

Besides the large rooms above enumerated, there are several small rooms, or closets, in which the candidates are locked up. The Hall of Examination at Canton has seven thousand five hundred of them.

The third degree of Tsin-tse, or "introduced scholars," is confined solely at Pekin, in the college, and before the president of the Han Lin once every three years. The subjects for examination are much the same as required for the two former, only more deeply gone into; and lest poverty should prove an obstruction to merit, the Emperor, as great father of his people, defrays a part or the whole of the expense, according to the means or exigencies of the aspirant. The Tsin-tse elect are presented to his majesty, who, in person, rewards three of them, who are adjudged to have passed the best examinations. The last and highest of all is that of Han Lin, "ascended to the top of the tree," also conferred at Pekin. The examination takes place before the most learned men that can be selected throughout the empire, in the hall of the imperial palace, before Son of Heaven himself, who with his own hands liberally rewards all that are elected.

CHAPTER VII.

CONFUCIUS.

Chinese Deities.—Sacrificial Officers.—Aim of the Studies of Confucius.—His Birth, Parentage, Character, and Personal Appearance.—Respect for his Mother.—His Descendants, Tenets, and Temples.—Religious Procession at Amoy.—Mencius.—His Education, Character, and Descendants.

THE Emperor, as great father of the nation, is the high priest of the ancient state religion of China, and permits no one but the mandarins, his representatives, to officiate at the sacred rites performed in honour of the following deities.

1. Teen, "The heaven," or Hwang-kung-yu, "The imperial concave expanse," under which title adoration is paid to the visible azure skies, and not the Maker of them.

2. Te, "The earth." The worship of the earth is much the same as that of the heaven; the strongest expression of an assurance of fact, is "heaven and earth can see it." Thus the following maxim, (I believe of Mentze,)—"Men may be fallible, Heaven cannot be deceived; things may be hid from

man, they are open to heaven. When the heart of man conceives a thought, heaven and earth know it fully."

3. Tae-meaw, "The great temple of ancestors;" including all tablets in them dedicated to the names of deceased emperors of the present dynasty. Of equal rank with Teen and Te.

4. Shay-tseih, "Gods of land and grain."

5. Teih, "The sun;" or Ta-ming, "Great light." .

6. Yue, "The moon;" or Yue-ming, "Night light."

7. Tseeu-tae-te, "Names of emperors and kings of former ages and dynasties."

8. Seen-tse Kung-foo-tse, "Confucius the ancient master."

9. Seen-ming, "Ancient patron of agriculture."

10. Seen-tsan, "Ancient patron of manufacture of silk."

11. Teen-shin, "Gods of heaven."

12. Te-he, "Gods of earth."

13. Tae-suy, "God of the current year."

14. Seen-e, "The ancient patron of medicine; together with innumerable of the illustrious dead."

15. Sing-shin, "Stars."

16. Yun, "Clouds."

17. Yu, "Rain."

18. Fung, "Wind."

19. Suy, " Thunder."

20. Woo-yo, " Five great mountains."

21. Sye-hae, " Four seas."

22. Sye-tuh, " Four rivers."

23. Ming-shan, " Famous hills."

24. Ta-chuen, " Great streams of water."

25. Ke-tuh, " Military flags or banners."

26. Paow-loo-che-shun, " God of a road where an army is passing."

27. Ho-paow-che-shin, " God of cannon."

28. Mun-shin, " Gods of the gates."

29. How-too-che-shin, " Queen goddess of the ground."

30. Pih-keih, " North pole."

When his majesty the high priest worships in the Temple of Heaven he wears robes of azure, the colour of the sky; when the earth, yellow, the colour of day; the sun, red; the moon, pale white; the assistant mandarins and officers of the court wear their full court dresses; the altar of heaven is round, that of the earth square, to represent their shapes according to the Chinese notions of them. The Chub-pan, or tablet of prayer, varies in colour with the dress.

The officers whose duty it is to superintend the sacrificial rites prepare themselves by a course of abstinence from eating, Venere et vino, music, mourning for the dead, visiting the sick, and taking cognisance of capital offences; forfeiting a month's salary for failing in any one particular. The empress and imperial concubine of the several grades only officiate at the worship of the silk manufacture. (No. 10, Chinese Repository, Vol. iii.) But the most important perhaps of all is No. 8.

Confucius, the patriarch of Chinese literature. though an object of worship himself, was not intentionally the founder of a new creed. The aim of his studies was merely a system of moral philosophy, that might put an end to the troubles and rebellions that, during his lifetime, distracted his country, and enable man to attain a greater degree of happiness in this world, by learning, in short, " that useful science to be good." The leading feature of his doctrine is filial piety and submission to parental authority. " Under the five modes of punishment there are three thousand crimes, but the greatest of these is undutifulness to parents." He worshipped the visible azure heavens. " He that doeth good, heaven will reward him with good; but he that doeth evil, heaven will recompense him with evil." But it is not clear that he had any definite knowledge of the existence of a superior being beyond the heavens that he saw, and he always parried the questions put to him by his disciples concerning a future state. But as a moralist he was no ordinary man, and has influenced the habits of thought of more of his kind than any other uninspired authority. He stamped his character on his age and country; and at this day, after a lapse of more than two thousand years, a knowledge of such of his works as are extant may raise the son of a peasant to the highest civil rank under the sovereign, and has done so for many. Of doubtful legitimacy himself, the family of his father was amongst the most ancient and noble in China, tracing its origin and descent through a long series of kings and princes, from the Emperor Hoangte to Shuh-leangho, a magistrate of Shu-yih, who is said to have been of low stature, a bad figure, and severe temper; impatient of control, and, when pretty far advanced in years and a widower, with nine daughters by his first wife, and a deformed son by a concubine, to have proposed himself to the chief of Yeu as a suitor for one of his three daughters, and to have been accepted by the youngest Yeu-she, who in due time presented him with a son, named Kew, "Mountain," surnamed Chungne, who assumed the title of Kung-futse, Latinised into Confucius. Other accounts say that his mother was only a concubine of Shuhleang-ho. However that may be, his birth took place in the year 551 B.C., or the twenty-first year of the Emperor Ling-wang, on the 13th day of the eleventh moon of the forty-seventh year of the cycle, attended with extraordinary prodigies, all emblematic of his future greatness; among the rest various marks were found on his body, and for the first and last time the mysterious animal the Keling appeared alive on earth; the recollection of which is preserved by a representation of it on the wall of every house inhabited by a mandarin.

Having lost his father when only three years of age, he was left to the guardianship of an excellent mother, whose care he repaid with the utmost affection and reverence. His personal appearance was remarkable, his figure was gigantic, and his complexion of almost negro blackness; but the gravity and dignity of his deportment, and his calm and benevolent countenance commanded respect.

The task of his education was not very burdensome to his mother, learning seemed to come to him as if by inspiration; at school he soon left all rivalry behind, and at the age of seventeen had mastered whatever Chinese learning had then to oppose him. At nineteen he married, and in due time had a son, whom he named Pih-yu from a present of carp sent him by the King of Loo; at twenty he became inspector of pastures and flocks in his native province, an office that he held for two years, when, at the death of his mother, he set the example, since universally followed by his countrymen, of giving up all government employment for the next three years after the death of a parent.*

This seems to have been the crowning period of the life of Confucius, and perhaps of Chinese history; he retired to indulge his grief and respect for his mother, and to mature those plans of human improvement which he has left a time-honoured inheritance to his nation.

But it must have been about this time also that occurred the one circumstance that in a Chinaman's idea would leave a blot on his character. In a country where divorces are of rarer occurrence than even in our own, and, for any other reason than the single one of adultery, in the highest degree discreditable, he put away his wife, the mother of his only son, on the very insufficient plea that the married state interfered with his studies. One would almost be inclined to suppose, though I know of no positive authority for it, that the sage, as has been the case with some other great men, was not happy in his choice of a wife, and that his house

* In the report of the Foundling Hospital at Shanghae, the secretary says, " I, Tsinchin, have retired from office on account of my parent's death." And a better known illustration of the rule in the case of Wang, late secretary to the Imperial Commissioner Keying, Governor-general of the Leang-quang, or the provinces of Quang-tung and Quang-see, who was last year recalled to Pekin to account for having held his office after the death of his mother without officially reporting it.

was a very unphilosophical establishment; but, be that as it may, the three years of mourning were devoted to the study of music, ceremonies, arithmetic, writing, the use of arms, and the art of driving chariots and horses; which, in his time, before the population had increased to such an enormous multitude, were not uncommon.

At the age of thirty he resolved to devote the remainder of his life to philosophy, and to planning some oriental whole duty of man, a course which he pursued as steadily as the political commotions of the times would allow; and, having attained a good old age, was gathered to his fathers in his native province of Loo, now part of Shangtung, where his posterity still reside and flourish. Divorces, however discountenanced by his countrymen, would seem to have been hereditary amongst his immediate descendants. Pih-you, his only son, died in his father's lifetime, but not before he had put aside his wife, the mother of his son Tsye-Sye, who survived his father and grandfather to carry on the line, and in his turn followed their example in also divorcing his wife. The present direct hereditary representative, by name Kung-King-Yung, holding, with the title of Yen-King-Kung, " Most sacred Duke," an hereditary pension paid by government, is the representative of the longest known pedigree in existence, and head of a family numbering 40,000 members.

The office of Woo-king-po-sye, in the Hanlin-yuen, or College of the Han-lin at Pekin, is also held by the descendants of Confucius and Mencius, and their most distinguished disciples.

If we are to believe tradition, a few short records, carved in rude hieroglyphical characters on bamboo or metal, comprised the whole literature of his countrymen before his time; and Confucius gave them the four branches of philosophy, classics, politics, and history, in which the literary degrees are still conferred. The main root of his system is filial piety, of which he himself set so brilliant an example in the regard he always shewed for his mother. He taught that to cast away the remains of a parent, or consign them to the grave with little more ceremony than those of a mere animal, and to consider that as the last duty we owed them, was degrading to the dignity of man; but that by periodically repeating some act of homage to our ancestors at their tombs, or before some representation of them at home, their memories would be cherished, and a glow of filial piety and affection would be kept alive to transmit to posterity; and the same practice being continued among them would, as it were, perpetuate our existence. This may be the reason why dying without male issue is regarded as such a calamity; and should the wife fail to produce a son, the law allows the substitution of one or more concubines to prevent the name becoming extinct in the male line.

The transition from such homage to worship would be easy and natural, and the practice of it is now enforced by law; no excuse exempts any one; the priests of Taow and Fuh, who are strictly forbidden, on pain of punishment, to perform otherwise the rites of the state religion; the Mahometan and the proselyte to Christianity are all enjoined, and readily comply with the injunction, to visit the graves of their immediate parents, and worship the manes of their ancestors, and repair the tombs. In the third month, at the period called Tshing-Ming-tse, every one repairs to the tombs to Tse-saou, sacrifice and weep, and offer sacrifice; after which a piece of paper, Ya-chi, is fixed under a sod to bear witness that the ceremony has not been neglected. In autumn, during the eleventh month, the royal ceremony, Tung-tsee, takes place, when the officers of government assemble in the imperial hall, Wan-show-king, to make prostrations, I believe, to the winter solstice. These two festivals are held in honour of Confucius, and upwards of 1560 temples are erected to his memory. It is calculated that on the two occasions there are sacrificed, every year, 6 bullocks, 27,000 pigs, 5800 sheep, 2800 deer, and 27,000 rabbits; besides 27,000 pieces of silk that are burnt upon his altars. But the patriarch may have influenced the belief of his countrymen in one particular, the effects of which may be in the womb of time; in the sixth century, before our Saviour, he foretold that a prophet would arise in the west whom all would obey. Some have acknowledged him in Buddha, but others still look for his coming; and it need be no great stretch of imagination to suppose that as the country becomes more open to intercourse with foreigners, this prophecy may assist, as it may have done already, in gaining proselytes to one or other of the sects of Christianity.

The temples of Confucius usually cover an enormous area; one establishment at Ningpo occupies about ten acres of land, laid out in ornamental temples of all sizes, triumphal entrances, fountains and tanks, and courts planted with trees, mostly yew. But, except on occasion of a festival, these are rarely or never visited, and the grass grows in abundance through the interstices of the pavement. The only ornaments are carved beams and huge frames, containing maxims and sayings of the patriarch. I visited one in the city of Paou-shaw, " the Hill of white stags," in Kiang-tsu; having obtained permission from the chief magistrate, the Chi-Heen, who was a considerable time in finding the key, and when he found it, the lock was so rusty as almost to refuse us admittance. The interior court, although paved with flag-stones, was as green as a meadow. A large board over the entrance bears the name of the temple, before it stands a carved table bearing candlesticks, a bronze vase for incense, and some plates for fruit-offerings. The festivals are occasions for some of the most beautiful processions I ever saw. I witnessed one in Amoy, at which were collected all the *literati* from an environ of upwards of thirty miles, each man carried a lantern in form of some production of the earth, or that of a bird, quadruped, or fish. The larger of them are the size of life, and drawn on wheels, they were made of a thin silk, beautifully painted and ornamented, and lighted up with candles inside. None under the rank of Seu-tsai (the first degree) could join; all were in full dress; all walked, with the exception of mandarins in office, who were carried in sedan chairs, and every man, besides his lantern, carried some fruit, tree, fowl, or other offering; they walked two and two, and in rear of each of the larger animals, such as elephants, buffaloes, &c., was a band. The whole was said to extend three miles. At midnight a peal of cannon thundered from the walls, and the admiral (Shuy-tse-tetuh), the senior mandarin, stepping into his chair, gave the signal to advance, when, on the instant, a hundred of the most discordant bands of gongs and wind instruments struck up the most diabolical noise, and away went the procession. The city was illuminated with lanterns of every make and shape, the men were supposed to find places for themselves, while in front of each house were platforms for the ladies. It was as light as day, and every one, being well-dressed in silks and satins of the gayest colours, gave the whole scene an appearance of immense richness. The ladies of Amoy adorn their hair with innumerable flowers, which, with the variety of colour in their dress, added much to the general effect as the procession passed; each house vied with its opposite neighbour in the number and beauty of its various lanterns and fireworks; the thunder of which latter were quite a relief to the hideous bellowings of the band. But everything went off with the utmost regularity and good-humour, and all the streets of the town were paraded until daylight put an end to the festival of the spring.

Before I proceed to notice any other object of worship, it may not be out of place here to take a passing glance at another celebrated native of Shang-tung. Confucius had animadverted on the mal-administration of Mang-tsum, a native of Choo, and a magistrate of Chin, ancestor in the third or fourth generation to Meng-tse, or Mang-ko, Latinized into Mencius, who shed a lustre on

the period in which he flourished, second only, in
the estimation of his countrymen, to that of the
Patriarch. He was yet a child, when his father
died and left him to the guardianship of his mother,
Chang-she, who very soon discovered that the leading feature in her boy's character was a strong taste
for mimicry. The widow, it appears, was not rich,
but spared no pains in the care of her son's education, and is often cited as a model of parental
excellence. The house she occupied was near the
shambles of a butcher; at the first cry of the
animals the boy would rush to be present, and
watch the whole process of the slaughter, and then
return to his mother and give her a rehearsal of
what he had seen, that did more credit to his his-
trionic vein than was agreeable to her feelings.
Fearing that, from the repeated sight of blood, the
boy's heart might be hardened, the widow shifted
her residence, but the change was for the worse, as
he very soon tried to amuse her by representing
funerals, with the wailings and lamentation of the
mourners at the tombs, as he witnessed them in the
cemetery that adjoined her new abode. Lest he
should learn to make a jest of what of all things
is the most serious, the widow removed into the
city, and was more fortunate in securing the better
neighbourhood of a school, where he might harm-
lessly indulge the natural bent of his humour, to

his heart's content. Hence arose the proverb, "Mentze's mother chose her neighbours." Having received his education from Tsye-sye, the grandson of Confucius, after an unsuccessful application for employment, under the King of Tse, he entered the service of Hwang-wang, King of Leang, or Wei, now part of Honan, but did not long continue with him. The political troubles of the time interfering with his studies, he returned to his native province, to compose the works that have immortalized his name, and conferred on him the titles of Shing, or Second Saint, (Confucius being the first,) and Holy Prince of the country of Tsou. He died in the earlier part of the fourth century before our Saviour. Of his marriage and immediate family I have no account to give; but his descendants, at this day, share with that of Confucius the office of Woo-kin-po-sye, in the Hanlin College at Pekin.

CHAPTER VIII.

TAOUISM.

Its Founder a Contemporary of Confucius.—His Followers not
numerous.—Temples.—Gods.—Priests.—Temple at Ningpo.—
Temple of Ancestral Remains.—Invitation to a Religious Ceremony.—Description of it.

LEAON Keaun, or Leaow-tse, the founder of the
Taou, or sect of reason, was a contemporary of
Confucius, but his followers at the present day are
not numerous, and his doctrines nearly obsolete.
What few temples there are remaining are supported by a priesthood, dressed in flowing robes,
and differing from every other class in China, except
the Meaou-tse, in their mode of arranging the hair,
which is collected into a knot on the crown of the
head, and not plaited into a queue, or tail. Their
tenets are visionary and mysterious. The earlier
proselytes, like hermits, sought solitude in deserts
and caverns, and were little more or less than
maniacs, believing in all sorts of nonsense, good
and evil spirits, earthly immortality, and terrestrial

paradises, more especially Kwan-lin, the seat of everything that was delightful, situated somewhere in the west, with its groves, grottoes, delicious fruits, and warbling of birds, where was to be sought the great pillar, on which the world rests, measuring three hundred thousand miles in height, and the fountain sparkling with the waters of life, one drop of which conferred immortality. Of the few remaining temples, that at Ningpo, which I entered, contains, amongst its godhead, the deities of the cycle, sixty in number, one for each year. The chief ceremony performed, but which I had no opportunity of witnessing, is that of relieving the deity on the last day of the year. Besides these are the gods of fire, air, earth, and water, and the genii of the hills, rivers, thunder and lightning, &c. One struck me as very remarkable, it was a female figure, surrounded by small purses and pieces of silk, tied to every convenient part. She presided over conception and birth, and the tokens were not so much of regard to the goddess as to keep her in mind of the requests of the votaries. There is also a representation of the Kwan-lin, richly gilt, covering a whole wall with its different gods and genii. In another part are the household gods of hearing and sight, to whose care, in his absence, the prudent husband commends his wives and families. The one is painted of a furious red colour; his eyes, to which he points with his forefinger, are much dilated, and the expression of his countenance is most severe, conveying the intimation, that a fault, committed in the sight of so austere a divinity, would meet with no mercy. The other was painted green, of a very dark colour, almost black, with a most attentive look; the forefinger of·his right hand points to his ear, as much as to say, "whatever you say does not escape me."

The gods are very numerous, but the priests are few. Roaming about I entered an old room of very large dimensions, with a most unwholesome damp smell: it appeared never to have been inhabited, yet pictures and small models of joss-houses, such as are seen in most Chinese dwelling-houses, were scattered all over the floor, together with some huge boxes and heavy shelves filled with the same. I opened several of the chests, but for the life of me could not even form a conjecture of the use of these decayed articles, notwithstanding the vehement ejaculations of a stout old priest, whose manner made me laugh at, and abuse him, alternately, as he went through the most extraordinary antics, and then shewed by the shrug of the shoulders that he had very little idea of what I was talking about. Some days afterwards I again strolled into the temple, and found the old fellow as civil as the memory of a former, and the hope of a future *douceur* could make him. Immediately on seeing me he dragged me off, wondering where it all would end, to the same antique apartment, where to my great relief, I found an American missiouary, who soon satisfied my curiosity by informing me that this was a temple of ancestral remains; and these the household gods, images, and pictures of the deceased, whose families were extinct in that part of the country, and that here they would remain for ever or until perhaps the room became too full.

An old comprador belonging to one of the opium vessels became of great service to all Europeans, whom business took to Woosung, by establishing himself on shore and opening a regular trade in every kind of marketable article. In a short time he was seized with a devout fit, and took it into his head, that, unless the gods were propitiated, his business could not thrive; and accordingly in the dress of a maudarin, and wearing a gold button, a distinction he had about as much title to assume as I have, he called all round the shipping and gave a general invitation to his foreign friends to attend at the ceremony of a Chin-Chin joss.

Two rows of lanterns faced the water and formed a double line to his house, which was illuminated and fitted up with as much splendour as carving,

gilding, and silk hangings could give it, one portion was arranged as a joss-house, with as many
altars as it could conveniently hold: the trees were
illuminated. Opposite to one of the altars stood
a tent with a band of boys dressed in yellow, with
mandarins' caps, and seated round a table, each
carrying a musical instrument and a book. As we
entered, a book was handed to our host, who
made his selection of the performance. The leader
commenced a kind of oratorio; he would recite for
some time, now and then addressing one or more
of his band, and then suddenly seizing his instrument, strike off into a wild air, joined by the whole
company: at times after his oration, they would
all chant together, or some chant and others play.
This was renewed at intervals during the whole
evening. About nine, the chief priest led our host
and his principal wife into the house of prayer,
at the door of which stood as guardians, two
painted paper deities, at least fourteen feet in height.
The room was certainly well lighted, and had
a very rich, though very fantastic appearance. On
one side sat our hostess of the evening, to whom
we were all formally introduced, with some dam-
sels, her friends. On the other several Europeans most irreverently smoking cigars and drinking beer, brandy and water, &c., at the worthy
comprador's expense; while in the centre, sur-

rounded by priests, the pious man himself knelt and performed the Kotow, to each of about twenty altars: having gone through this ceremony, his lady wife did the same, and then the priests amongst the din of gongs and bells. The ceremony was repeated three several nights, with only one variety, viz., that on each succeeding night, our host's declared rib was not only much younger, but much better looking, a miracle which I have no doubt he would have attributed, if asked to account for it, to the mysteries of Taouism. I asked him whether he was a Taouist, as he employed priests of that persuasion; his answer was in the Canton figurative mode of expression, "Sing Song, all same pigeon," meaning, "Anything you please, all the same to me."

On the third night the large paper images were burnt with several sacrifices of meat-offerings; and a message sent by our host to the genii of the world of spirits, soliciting the favour of a speedy fortune and good success in his business. With that the ceremony closed; but it was evilly remarked that had it lasted a week, the old rascal had a fresh and younger wife for each night, and though they were debarred the honour of attending their lord and master at his devotions, yet they might console themselves that each day he shortened the performance, saved him a hundred dollars. These were as we speak of the wives of France, wives *du pays*, as the old gentleman had besides the subalterns of his matrimonial staff, a principal wife in his native province of Canton, another at the port of Amoy, another then with him at Woosung, and another in every port that he had ever touched at.

CHAPTER IX.

BUDDHISM.

Origin of Buddhist Religion.—Legend of " The Fragrant Hill."— Story of the Tiger.—Miracle performed by Buddha.—Introduction of Buddhism.—Beautiful situation of the Temples.—Description of Tien T'hung Joss-house.—Mode of Travelling.— Interior of a Monastery.—The Priests.—Their Ceremonies and Mode of Living.—Aqueducts.—Wild Hogs.—Civility of the Priests.—Origin of Tien T'hung.—Beautiful View from the Temple.—Plucking the Tea Leaf.—Grand Procession in Honour of Shinnung.

THE history of Buddha having been so often and so freely dilated upon by other authors, I shall merely give a few of the legends, illustrative of the introduction of the Buddhist religion, and proceed to describe some temples that I visited.

In the reign of the Emperor Tsung-Ning, A. D. 1125, it is related that an old priest appeared to a Buddhist recluse, as he sat wrapped in contemplation, in his hall, in Tëen Chuh, (either India or Ceylon) and accosted him, saying, "Why sittest thou and thinkest thus to practise thy religion? Soar for it above; every good principle is from on high; how else canst thou arrive at universal love? Study to serve Buddha and to imitate his glorious deeds, and thus have power over the wills of mankind."

"But how is this to be done?" said the Buddhist.

"Seest thou not that the dwellers of these parts worship the blessed Kwan yin? make known to them her history, and thus reap your own happiness." With these words, his mission was at an end, and he vanished. The Buddhist compiled the "History of the Fragrant Hill," and at its completion, the goddess appeared to him, borne on the clouds, of a pale gold colour, with a pitcher in one hand, and a willow in the other, and was seen by many.

THE FRAGRANT HILL.

The Emperor, Poo-kea, ruled over a most extensive empire, his wealth was prodigious, and his subjects adored him, his empress, a paragon of loveliness, was devotedly attached to him: one only cause of regret marred his otherwise complete happiness, though already the father of two lovely daughters, he had no son to succeed him. The empress felt for his distress, and addressed herself to heaven, and a miraculous conception was vouchsafed to her by Buddha, who appeared to her in a dream, but of a third daughter Meaou-shin.

The emperor was some time inconsolable, but at

last hit upon the plan of marrying his daughters to great nobles of the court, and adopting as his heir, such one of his grand-children whose superior merit should warrant his choice. The eldest became the wife of a civil, the second, of a military mandarin; both of high rank and distinction. But nothing could prevail on Meaon-shin, the offspring of the miraculous conception, to take to herself a husband: threats, persuasions, and ridicule alike failed, in spite of them all, she determined on retiring to a monastery, and devote her life to the service of Buddha. She had borne all the persecutions with the constancy of a martyr, but, being now free from them, in her new asylum, her humility was exemplary, and the sister nuns were edified by the imperial novice assuming the office of scullion, and being so far approved of by Buddha, that he sent her down animals to help her, and a dragon to open the well, when she stooped so low as to become the drawer of water to the establishment. But however grateful to Buddha and admirable to the nuns, the emperor did not approve of it. The old gentleman thought what persuasions would not accomplish, force might, so he sent a file of soldiers to destroy the temple by fire, but in vain, Buddha sent a shower of water and shewed to the abashed instrument of human will, with whom they had to contend. The nunnery stood entire, but Meaou-

shin was carried off. The lady was in earnest, so
was the father ;

> " So opposite to marriage that she shunned
> The wealthy curled darlings of the nation ;"

and, to repel future advances most effectually, dis-
figured her person. This expedient would seem to
have succeeded, or, at least, was the feather that
broke the back of the old gentleman's patience, he
gave orders for her execution, and the sentence was
carried into effect, to the great grief of all nature
and nations.

A tiger, specially provided by Buddha, saved the
trouble of a funeral, by carrying off the body to the
woods, while the soul passed into the regions of departed spirits, but did not long remain there. The
emperor, meanwhile, found himself troubled with
an illness that baffled the skill of all his physicians
even to relieve. In the midst of his agony, a Buddhist, and priest, gave him a gleam of hope, by re-
commending a pilgrimage to a venerated saint in
Heang Shang, in whom he found his daughter,
Meaon-shin, who had been restored to life, and
brought to that place, on the back of a tiger.
Their differences were soon settled. The father
was restored to health, and became a staunch sup-
porter of Buddhism ; and the daughter, after a long
and glorious life, took her place as a saint in the
azure heavens, to be worshipped as the Goddess,

Kwan-yin. The story of the tiger is consistent with the ideas of the Chinese of the present day, as the following extract from the Hong Kong newspaper, may shew.

In King-Yun, a village of Tsing-Yuen district, there is a man whose surname is Le, and name Hung-how, aged eighty years, who had always been diligent in business. In former days he supported his family by industry in farming. He has a son called Isae, who is not well educated, because his family is poor. This year, (1846,) on the twelfth day of the first month, his father went up into a rugged valley in the mountains, and having inadvertently slipped his foot, fell down upon his knees. He could not walk, and unexpectedly a tiger came to him. Seeing the old man was lamenting and weeping without ceasing, the tiger took and put him on his back and carried the aged man to his home: as his son was coming out to see his father, the tiger went away. On the next day the thing was made known to the chief-magistrate of the district, and his son was invited to tell the magistrate what had happened to his father; and the officers, knowing that the old man has a good heart and great virtue, and his son has a filial spirit and righteousness, rewarded them with twenty taels of silver, thereby to shew esteem for them, and to stimulate them to renewed exertion.

Shih-le-fang, with eighteen other Hoshang or priests of Fuh, *i. e.*, "bright appearance," or Buddha, came from Kea-chuh, (India or Ceylon,) the birthplace of that divinity, to the court of the Emperor, Che-wang-te, bringing with them representations of the San Fuh, or three Buddhas, and the principal deities of these persuasions, embroidered in gold thread, on fine cloth. Their reception was not a welcome one, for the Emperor ordered them to be imprisoned; but no sooner did Shih-le-fang and his fellow martyr find themselves in durance, than on their application to Buddha, a bright fire illuminated the skies, thunder and lightning shook the earth to its foundation, while Buddha himself, in form of an angel, appeared in the heavens; his colour was of gold, his stature fifteen cubits, and such was the awful brilliancy of his countenance that it blinded all beholders. The gates of the prison, of their own accord, unbound themselves, and liberated the captive priests. The jailors fled with the account of the whole affair to Che-wang-te, who fell down and worshipped Buddha, and ordered his priests to be escorted home to their own country, with great magnificence.

The date of these proceedings is somewhat obscure; the Emperor, Che-wang-te having taken into his head the eccentric idea of burning all books, and so passing himself off for the first monarch of China, and founder of his dynasty, but the time supposed, is about 220 B.C.

The original statue of Fuh, of enormous dimensions and pure gold, fell into the hands of the emperor Woo-te, as a trophy of war; by whom it was placed in the palace of sweet springs, and incense was ordered to be burned before it; but from the loss of the books, the worship fell into desuetude, until about the time of the Christian Era, in the reign of Ching-te, a scholar recovered some books, manuscripts, and pictures, by means of which it was revived. Another account dates the introduction of Buddhism in the reign of Ming-te, A.D. 63, who reigned at Loyang in Honan. This emperor originally professed Taouism, but his priests having promised and failed to procure him an interview with spirits, who, when called from the vasty deep, would not come, he began to doubt, when he had a vision of a colossal figure of a pale gold colour, with a ray of glory round his head, flying to him through the air. His wise men pronounced this to be the prophet of the west, foretold by Confucius, and readily induced the emperor to send an officer named Wang-Sung with two ministers, Tsae-Quan and Tsin-King, into the west to inquire into and report upon the doctrines of Fuh. The ambassadors proceeded as far as Thibet where they prevailed upon Shih-Mo-Tang, a Shaman or priest of Fuh, to return with them.

He brought with him representations of the deity embroidered in gold on fine Indian cloth, together with many of the sacred books of his creed, which were escorted into Loyang, the capital, with great magnificence. From this time Buddhism would seem to have been established in the country, though now and then severely persecuted.

There is scarcely a spot of real natural beauty that is not ornamented by a pagoda or other Buddhist temple. A natural grotto, let its access be ever so difficult, is enlarged and altered into a receptacle for idols. One at Amoy, called the White Stag, is singularly beautiful, from the peculiarity of its situation and novel contrivance. It stands near the summit of some lofty crags. In a bed of huge rocks is built the main temple, while its dependencies are, many of them, natural excavations; others, chambers formed by the vacant spaces between the rounded and detached pieces of granite. Many of the idols are carved out of the solid rock; in one instance nature has left one immense stone surmountingly balanced on another like the rocking stone. A solid stair-case winds round the lower, encompassing the top of which is a stone railing, while the space between the two is sufficient to admit of stone chairs and tables, which are placed here and there all round. Splendid overhanging terraces filled with exotics, are reached by spiral stairs hewn from the solid rock. A few melancholy looking priests are the sole tenants of this romantic spot.

Of all the joss-houses I have visited, that of Tien T'hung in the province of Che-Kiang is the most beautiful and extensive. In a recess formed by two mountains at the close of the fertile valley of Teaow-Pih, the road, which had hitherto been a flagged pathway, expands into a broad avenue extending about a mile, with lofty trees on each side, adorned at intervals each with a handsome ornamental summer-house. Passing over a well supplied water-course, the thrilling noise whereof is increased by a fall immediately under, from a height of about thirty feet into a large artificial basin below, at a sharp turning the astonished traveller comes suddenly on one of the most romantic scenes I ever witnessed. There is a majesty about the first appearance of the monastery seldom seen in China. Immediately in the rear are high topping hills, which appear to rise almost perpendicularly, covered with a magnificent forest. In front is a huge tank filled with the elegant lotus plant, reflecting in its calm waters the huge building. Facing the temple is a small seven-storied stone pagoda, on each side of which are three lofty urns.

The forest closes the area around an immense parallelogram, two thirds of which form the site of the joss-house; while the rest is occupied by the tank, round which is a broad flagged pavement; all traces of the road are lost, an extraordinary echo catches the veriest whisper, while the report of a gun would appear never to leave the ravine. Through the woods in all directions are foot-paths commanding every variety of scenery. A few steps conduct from very plain to highly ornamented parterres, then through a sudden opening between the trees may be seen a barren sterile plain farther on, the side of a hill teeming with the richest crop of corn, taking an almost perpendicular descent into some fairy-like *bosquet* of bamboos. Birds of beautiful plumage and the most silvery notes abound, and increase, and multiply, safe in the vicinity of the abodes of men, one of the tenets of whose religion is, "Thou shalt not kill." Tien T'hung is situated about twenty miles from the city of Ningpo; the trip from whence is one of great interest. A canal conveys the visitor about fif- teen miles; when, disembarking at the village of Sheaou-Pih, a well-paved road leads to the mo- nastery.

In leaving the Ta-hea river, the boat, which is

peculiarly built for canal service, is drawn by cap-
stans over an inclined plane when reaching a height
about four feet above high water mark, she is
launched into the canal: the crew consists of two
men, one skulls, while the other either poles or
tracks. The country through which the canal passes
is richly cultivated with rice and a variety of vegetables, with here and there a large village, joss,
or farm house, in the distance; the villages along
the banks are frequent and striking, but the most
elegant structures are the bridges, which are numerous, and no two of them alike either in shape
or make; of two, perhaps in sight of each other,
the one will rise by steps to a height of thirty
or forty feet over one arch, the other may consist of
three or four enormous beams of granite laid straight
across on supporters on either bank. About some
of them there are good carvings, and each is ornamented with a post, on which is a highly coloured
lantern in the centre.

Every here and there are monuments to commemorate the dead, and some to record the benevolent
and other good actions of magistrates, under whose
government agriculture or manufacture more than
usually flourished, or the building or repairs of a city
or temple in the neighbourhood; and sometimes in
honour of a more prudent mother, who, like the
mother of Mencius, had from her care and attention

to her offspring, acquired a sufficient notoriety to be deemed a good example to them, and worthy of public record. These monuments consist of two uprights of granite, or other stone, their higher ends joined by flags of elegantly-carved marble or stone, which bear the inscription. They may frequently cross a road. All boats in the canal, to prevent confusion, proceed on the left side going to, right returning from, Sheaou-Pih, a small village through which there is considerable traffic, being on the high road to Ningpo-Fu; all goods destined for which city are shipped there, and transported by canal. Here we quitted our boats, and for the remaining five miles, as the road was very steep, we engaged some of the mountain sedans—a very simple kind of vehicle, consisting merely of two long poles, from which are strung two bars, one to sit upon, the other to rest the feet.

Immediately on leaving this village a gradual rise for about two miles, through a country covered with dwarf oak, fern, and azalias of every variety, brought us to a small rest-house, through which the road runs, and immediately to the left of which stands a high seven-storied pagoda, apparently of great antiquity; this marks the boundary of the rich and extensive domain of the monastery. In the rear the city of Ningpo appears in the embrace of the distant hills. The fertile valley, intersected with

MOUNTAIN SEDANS, PROVINCE OF SHEAOU-PIH.

canals and the Ta-hea river, resembles a beautiful garden; while beyond, the vale of Teaou-pih, and its mountain stream, divides the attention and invites the traveller's descent. In the centre is a village of the same name, an emporium for teas which grow on the neighbouring hills, and are transported from hence to the city. During a stay of a fortnight at the monastery, we found a good market of fish, flesh, and fowl here.

Except being much larger in actual build, the joss-house is like most others, I shall, therefore, give the following cursory account of it. On entering are the colossal statues of the four kings of heaven, about forty feet in height, of dried clay beautifully painted; their appearance is very striking; the two

on each side are divided from each other by a stone
pillar, round which a dragon is carved in high relief; and what struck me as very remarkable, they
all bore on their breasts red crosses, such as one
might imagine to have been the badge of the old
knights in the time of the crusades; they are all in
a. sitting position on the right side; the first is
black in the face, with chain-armour and a drawn
sword in his right hand; opposite to him is one of
a light complexion, also with chain-armour but no
sword, a green dragon coils round his left arm;
both the above wear belts clasped with a lion's
head, and would appear to be gods of war. The
attributes of the remaining two seem of more
peaceable nature, both are of light complexion, and
instead of chain-armour their breasts are gilt, but
they wear the same red cross; their belts are
clasped by two fishes; the one on the right side is
playing on a musical instrument like a guitar, that
on the left bears an umbrella in his right hand; at
their feet are some figures the size of life, dressed
as peasants, to shew the contrast between the inhabitants of this and the other world. These occupy
the two sides of the entrance, while in the centre is
a small model temple, in which, facing the entrance, is a stout globular joss in a sedentary position, with a rosary of nine beads in his hand, whose
jolly countenance and laughing open mouth give

him a very Bacchanalian expression. Behind him, facing the other direction, is a warrior in gilt armour, supporting himself by a richly carved staff; his helmet is adorned with plumes, while so excellent is the carving that his different dresses, such as martial cloak, armour, under-suit, and coat, are all perceptible.

A huge drum and moderately large bell finish the paraphernalia of the religious furniture of this temple.

In this place lounged and slept our palankeen and luggage bearers, who seemed more bent on the excitement of cards and dominoes, than awed by solemnity of the place; a quadrangle ending in a flight of steps reaches the second temple, in which are the images of the San-paow-fuh, or three precious Buddhas, in colossal statues about fourteen feet high, each seated on a lotus flower, their names are (from right to left) Shah-kea-mow-ne-fuh, Joo-lae-fuh, and Me-to-fuh. These are highly gilt; at the back of each head is an enormous metal mirror to represent the halo of glory, while above a huge rich canopy, of magnificent carving and gilt, reaches the ceiling. These three figures are in the centre of the temple facing the door, paying homage to whom, and in attitude of prayer, in richly painted dresses, are, one on each side, two figures of men nine or ten feet high; they face a carved table, bearing a small model of a temple, an incense burner, two vases, and several candlesticks: above hangs a magnificent lantern; under the table are bronze vessels and small drums, used in the devotions by the priest; on the left is a drum nine feet in diameter, on the right a bell six feet high, both are slung six feet from the ground.

In front of the door outside stands an enormous metal vase for the ashes of burnt offerings; on it are several inscriptions, one of which certifies that the devout of the cities of Shaou-hing-fuh, Tac-chow-fuh, Ningpo-fŭh, Ting-hae-heen, and Chin-hae-heen presented it to the monastery; it stands seven feet high on a tripod, and bears the date of the Emperor Sun-che, A.D. 1644. At the back of the San-paow-fuh, and facing the other entrance, is a highly executed image of the goddess Kwan-yin; she is represented seated on a lotus flower on the back of a horse with clawed feet; she is surrounded with angels in attitude of worship, floating about the azure heavens; above is a crimson canopy, while below is a representation of the entrance of the infernal regions, guarded by a furious demon. The whole is highly coloured, and forms a tableau of about forty feet in height and twenty broad. In front is a table, on which stands a bronze figure, with innumerable arms, and on each side is a lantern. The three Buddhas and their attendant deities stand back to back to the goddess Kwan-yin and her satellites, flanking which are the big drum and bell; and these fill the centre shrine, on each side of which, at equal distances, are nine of the eighteen Lohan, or spirits, who guard the souls of the departed. In front of each deity throughout the temples, are invariably three small basins, one filled with water, one with rice, and the third with vegetables; these are shifted daily. On the ground in front of each is a cassock, exactly resembling those seen in a country church in England, while before the Triads are some forty or fifty of them. At the end of another quadrangle another flight of steps conducts to another temple, in the centre of which, on a raised platform, surrounded by a carved railing, is a high-backed chair, and before it a small table. The only articles of furniture hanging to the roof are several tablets with inscriptions in gold character. This is the prior's tribunal, and the seat only to be occupied by the Tae-ho-shang, or high priest, and now a days by him seldom more than on the single occasion of his inauguration. These three form the principal temples, and are each of the same size. The roofs are lofty and supported by huge pillars, some five feet in diameter; these are built, trenailed alternately at right angles and hooped. These rooms must be each about eighty feet in length, fifty in height, and sixty in breadth.

They are lighted by lofty windows, some of oiled ˙
paper, others of oyster shell; and under a roof, that
projected for some distance, is about six feet depth
of open work.

The roofs are highly ornamented with huge
dragons, fish, &c., in porcelain, while from each
angle hangs a small metal bell. The clapper consists of two cross sheets of metal, so thin as to
catch every breath of wind and keep up a constant
chime; the colours of the walls are universally
red without and white within, while the otherwise
ungilt and painted parts of idols, pillars, &c., is invariably of the former colour. Innumerable lanterns
and candles are used every night. Again at the
back of these is the dwelling-house of the Tae-
Hoshang, a large building moderately well furnished.

These three temples form the centre range, and
are divided by a paved way on each side from
another range of buildings. That to the right consists of innumerable smaller temples, cells for the
priests, library of monastic books and printing-press,
gardens, and a two-storied pagoda, in which is the
large bell, ten feet in diameter, covered with inscriptions; it has no clapper, but like all large bells
in China, is struck by swinging a heavy log of wood
slung for the purpose: while on the left are the
houses of the superiors of the monastery, the refec-

tory, kitchen, and houses for the reception of strangers. A deep gully, crossed by several bamboo
bridges, separates the offices and farm; among the
former are the bath-rooms, both hot and cold, well
supplied with water, store-houses of rice, paddy, or
rice in the husk, wood, seeds, &c.; in the latter a
good supply of water, buffaloes for the ploughing,
thrashing, grinding, and other agricultural machines
and implements.

The priesthood of Tien T'hung might be about
two hundred and fifty, one-fifth of whom are invariably travelling as mendicants into all parts of
the empire, and frequently beyond it. On their
travels it is said they do not always preserve the
purities of the Buddhist rule, as the following by
no means singular edict may shew.

"Ching-tsoo-lo and his colleagues have reported
respecting the seizure of a swindler, noted for several years past, and have offered the result of
their deliberations as to his punishment. This is
a case of a Buddhist priest, Shing-Lang of Shang-
hang, in the department of Ting-chow, in Fuh-
Këen, who has been guilty of illicit intercourse
with married and unmarried women: of sharing
in the profits of theft and plunder: of extort-
ing ransoms from persons under threats of de-
priving them of sight: of involving and trou-
bling many by falsehood and lies, with nume-

rous other transgressions of the laws. The magistrate of the said department, having of his own accord apprehended him, and brought him to trial: let all demerits marked against the said magistrate, on account of negligence, be remitted. Respect this."

There is a resident medical man in every monastery, the rest of the priests of the establishment are employed as agriculturists and domestic servants, leaving about sixty to officiate as priests. The duty of these latter, after making good the appearance of the josses, consists in three daily religious exercises, each prior to the morning, noon, and evening meal. There is a Tae-Hoshang, or high priest, and two sub-priors, the rest are in two grades. Their heads are shorn, and their dress consists of flowing robes of a French grey colour. The Tae-Hoshang wears a red sash from the right shoulder to the left waist, as also the sub-priors: the highest of the two grades is distinguished by a yellow sash clasped in the right hand. The three superiors wear very ecclesiastical-looking hats, the rest are uncovered. These priests are mostly the most illiterate men in China; few can either read or write, and from habit are almost idiots: they chant the ten thousand names of Buddha, and get by rote the Indian works in the Pali language, written in the Chinese character, but untranslated;

and they in reality know little or nothing about the mysteries of their religion.

To the sound of gong, bell, and drum, they assemble in the hall of the three precious Buddhas, and each assumes his place at a cassock, disposed at equal distances, on each side a larger one for the prior facing the triad; the sub-priors are on each side of the table, one with a bronze vase and stick, another has a small bell and hand-drum: as soon as the high priest has taken his place, the bell is beaten three times three times, and the whole being performed an equal number of times, chanting then commences; and now first those on the left of the high priest, Ko-tow, then those on the right, then all together: this continues for about half an hour to the varied tune of drum and bell, and beating on the bronze vase; when, still chanting, the high priest leads off those to the left, one of the priors those to the right, and they pass up and down, across, in and out, and back again to their respective cassocks. A short chant more ends the performance; a chance pilgrim, a foreigner, and a few, whom curiosity might have drawn, are the only congregation, if such a motley crew deserves that name. During this service candles and incense are burnt before each of the deities.

This ceremony is repeated three times a day, at cock-crow, noon, and sunset, and appears to be the whole duty of the mob of the priesthood; attending visitors round the joss-houses, arranging their offerings, &c. is imposed on a few.

The people can scarcely be said to attend at the regular service in the joss-houses at any time. Pilgrims, however, arrive from the most distant provinces, and perform their own devotions, which consist in burning candles and incense before the particular god, making offerings of all kinds, repeating a prayer and performing Ko-tow; after which there is a kind of lottery of fate between the devotee and the idol: the devotee generally wins. There are two modes of settling this affair; one is by the direction of the fall of two pieces of wood, round on one side and flat on the other, to which the initiated have a key, the other by placing some hundred of small slips of bamboo in a conical shaped wooden vessel, each of which is marked, and to each is a corresponding fortune. The inquirer, after making his oblations, shakes the vessel in so peculiar a manner, that one only of the slips fall to the ground; but in either case, if he be not satisfied, he tries again until better luck turns up.

Ladies assemble in the village joss-houses, to talk scandal and shew off their finery, as on such occasions they are arrayed in "furs, and silks, and jewels sheen."

It is the custom for these pilgrims, besides giving a pecuniary fee, to present some article of ornament or dress, either to the joss or house, which former are, as may be supposed, magnificently arrayed. In every temple of note are some valuable josses of gold, silver, jade or bronze; and these are generally in glass-cases in the private apartments of the Tae-Hoshang; the large figures are mostly of clay, and these of six feet and less of wood.

Immediately after prayers is the meal, and from the temple all proceed to the refectory, a large apartment seventy feet long by thirty broad, across which are long tables and stools for the priests. In the centre facing a niche, holding an idol, is the table and high chair of the prior: one side of each large table is occupied so that all face the superior: opposite to each priest on the other side of the tables, are arranged two basins and a pair of chopsticks. No sooner are they seated than a basin of rice is presented by a novice to the superior, who pronounces a blessing, and returns a few grains on a pair of chop-sticks, which are taken by the same novice to a small stone altar, and reverently deposited there. As soon as the ceremony is performed, servants enter laden with large tubs of either rice or vegetables, and continue filling the basins until they are replaced on the opposite side of the table empty, with the chop-sticks laid across them, the sign of having had enough. After the prior has said grace, all leave the apartment.

Rice is the chief commodity of food: salted vegetables of all kinds are used more as a relish; although the prior goes through the form of feeding with the priests—it must not be believed that he lives in that way. He invited a party, of whom I was one, to dine, and gave us as good a dinner as a Chinese could. There was no meat, but soups and meat imitations made of vegetables and gravies, &c.

To supply the enormous quantities of rice at times required, besides common sized pans for boiling, there is one with a furnace underneath, which across the rim is seven feet six in diameter, and holds fourteen piculs of grain. It bears the date and name of the Emperor of Tsung-Chung, 1640. The granaries were well stocked, and dried vegetables were in great profusion.

Not by any means the least curious part are the aqueducts, made of bamboo, running in all directions through every temple and passage, and conveying the most delicious and cool water; their length altogether would measure some miles.

One day we received a visit from the prior, who requested some powder and shot to destroy the wild hogs which he said eat his bamboo-shoots; on expressing a wish to be shewn the neighbourhood of these marauders, he himself walked about three miles at midnight with the party, who, though they heard several, failed in getting a shot at them.

Nothing could exceed the civility of the priests, from the superior downward. We hired a comfortable and well-furnished suite of apartments, sufficient to lodge our party, consisting of four, for a rupee a day, with convenience for cooking, &c.

Any thing we required from the village market, they would willingly procure for us, and, excepting a little very natural curiosity, we could find fault with nothing. The priests are certainly dirty in their persons. Washing I believe to be a matter of duty in summer, but wholly neglected in winter, and consequently, they are almost all sufferers from cutaneous diseases.

The origin of the establishment of Tien-tung, like most places, and of men of note in China, is lost in the depth of antiquity. According to the Abbot, about two thousand years ago, a member of the Taouist persuasion built himself a hermitage on the present site. He was a devout, religious man, and in great favour with the gods, who, in return for his zeal, granted him, at his request, an unprecedented power in the art of healing. Such was the fame of

M

the Doctor of Reason, that people flocked to his
hermitage from all parts of the empire. The gift
descended, by heavenly grant, into the hands of his
disciples, who, in the course of years, becoming more
enlightened, worshipped the azure heavens, under
the doctrine of the sublime Fŭh, when a medicinal
power was given to the waters of the valley. The
hermitage gradually increased, from time to time,
from the munificent grants of land, and donations
of money, by emperors, princes, and the people,
until in the reign of Tsung Ching, the last Emperor of the Chinese dynasty, it had assumed its
present size, A.D. 1640. Each emperor of the Ta
Tsing, or Tartar dynasty, has enriched the godhead,
and has either a tablet or vase erected in the
temple, to commemorate his liberality.

The situation chosen for the temple can scarcely
be equalled in point of beauty of surrounding scenery:
from the summit of the hill, at the back, you look
down, with a bird's-eye view, into the spacious
courts below; to the east are innumerable beautiful islands, whose very summits are covered with
the verdure of agriculture. Among these, are the
famed island of Chusan, and the Silver Island, the
supposed retreat of the defeated mandarins, during
the late war; Nimrod's Sound, studded with its
thousands of islets, abounding in pheasant, wood-
cocks, hares, deer, ducks, geese, swan, curlew, and

other water-fowl, lies immediately below, to the
southward; so called from her majesty's ship, Nimrod, in an early part of the war, having surveyed it.
Looking north, can just be seen the mouth of the
great bay of Hang Chow, whose tide is so extremely strong as to have altered the determination of
the heads of the late expedition, and saved the city
of Hang Chow Fŭ, after the fall of Chapoo, the
sea-port. In this direction heaven and earth appear to meet in the Blue Mountains, whose distance
otherwise ends the scene. Winding in serpentine
form the Ta Hea appears, studded with towns, cities,
and villages; that of Chin Hae, crowned with its citadel, the most conspicuous; while the means of communication through the splendid plain of Ningpo
are supplied by the numerous canals, ornamented
in all directions with boats. On the west, the view
is closed by the high hills, which stand beyond the
elegant lakes of Tong-u, studded with its small islands, about seven miles from the monastery. In
every picturesque nook is seen, in all directions, a
Buddhist temple, or pagoda. The hills abound in tea-
plants. The teas grown here are hyson, hyson-skin,
and twankey. The tea-tree stands from three to four
feet high, generally on the southern side of the hill.
In May the females throw a white handkerchief
over their heads, and, surmounting that with a
straw hat, ornamented with flowers and glass beads,

with bamboo baskets in their hands, sally out in parties to pluck the leaf. When it is all culled, the moisture is extracted by pressing it heavily, backwards and forwards, on a table, made of strips of the bamboo; from this it is laid on mats, and dried for several days in the sun. Prior to bringing to market, it is fired, *i. e.* placed, in a large pan, over a wood fire, and thus rendered perfectly dry; it is then assorted, and, according to its quality, sold from twenty to seventy dollars a picul, (120 lbs.) I bought some fifty catty, at 140 cash a catty, which I had assisted some well disposed and proper Chinese girls to pick and dry.

This tea would have cost me double the money had I bought it in the town of Ningpo, and that too after it had been rendered unwholesome, by the ridiculous process of firing it on a copper plate, covered with verdigris, to give it a higher green colour.

One afternoon, sauntering from the monastery, I, all of a sudden, came upon a splendid procession, that was making a tour of the valley, in honour of Shinnung, the divine husbandman and presiding deity of the mysteries of agriculture and medicine. Crossing the road, almost at the end of the avenue, was a temporary erection over a table, groaning under a weight of pigs, goats, ducks, fowls, &c., roasted whole, and other offerings to the deity.

Every person between this and the procession was in chains and handcuffs, undergoing a voluntary penance, and, never turning their backs, knelt and ko-towed, again and again, until they reached the offerings, when, to the amount of hundreds, they all placed themselves on the opposite side to the procession, and ko-towed nine times nine. These were the sick, and those who had been so lately, and had vowed, if they recovered, to worship the divine doctor, at his next appearance. The order of the procession was as follows : first, the cards or boards, bearing the honorary titles of the god, hung with lanterns, as also was every article in the procession. Bands of trumpets, gongs, drums, in sedans, highly ornamented, were here and there interspersed, and in the commencement, and near the end, was a huge lantern dragon, not less than forty feet long, supported by eight bearers, who, when the procession halted, so frisked it about as to give it the resemblance of life. In a painted red car, filled with exotics, and carried by eight men, was seated a handsomely dressed youth; on his left hand, supported by a splint beneath the dress, stood a magnificently dressed young girl, balancing herself by two wands. In the youth's right hand was a wand, with which he attracted the eye of his female friend, and, by keeping his hand steady, assisted her in her balance. Great must have been the pain suffered

by these two young people, for, immediately on
halting, a man from the bystanders rushed in with
long crutches and relieved the girl therewith,
while another sprinkled their faces with water, to
keep them from fainting. A well-dressed person,
in the garb of a mandarin, walked on each side the
car, and in its rear a servant carried the crimson
umbrella of state. These youths were of the village, and it was considered a great honour to be
chosen, beauty giving the preference. Youths carrying banners, followed by servants bearing crimson
umbrellas, while others, dressed as horsemen, on
imitation lantern horses, were followed by labourers,
carrying as offerings, imitations (as lanterns) of
the fruits of the soil. Shopmen bearing teas and
other dried herbs and fruits, as offerings; youths
bearing banners, literati with tabards, inscribed with
the wisdom of Kung-foo-tse; executioners of the
deity, with instruments of torture, used in the infernal regions; youths bearing banners; while at
the last came a large image of the god himself,
dressed in the imperial (yellow) dress of satin, on
its head a golden crown, the face of a high vermilion colour; it was borne in a sedan-chair, by
twelve bearers, and attended by all the paraphernalia of a mandarin of the first rank. This procession was thoroughly of the Confucius school, and
only gazed upon by the priests of Fu, in the pre-

cincts of whose domains it was enacted. At twelve at night, amid the firing of cannon, and with the noise of gongs and hideous music, it again made the tour of the valley, this time illuminated by thousands of lanterns.

CHAPTER X.

THE ISLE OF POO-TO.

Number of Priests and Temples.—Visit of the Dutch.—Extent of
the Island.—Famine from Dearth of Water in the Chusan
Group of Islands.—Two Wooden Deities bring Rain.—Origin of
the name Poo-to.—Scenery of the Island.—Large Temple.—
Mausoleum.—The Tae Hoshang.—Smaller Temples.—Suicide's
Leap.—Productions.—Water Buffaloes.—Description of Kung
Shang.—Its Library.—Nunneries.

THE island of Poo-to, near Chusan, is said to
contain six or seven hundred Buddhist priests,
under whose charge are three hundred temples
of all sizes; of these, three are of the largest size,
about six of a second, some fifty of a third, while the
remainder dwindle into mere natural grottoes, or
artificial excavations of the solid rock. The whole
establishment was founded in the Leang dynasty,
A.D. 550, to record the mercies of the gracious
Kwang-Yin, who is said to have honoured this
island with a visit. Among the stories of old times
of the island, one relates that in 1666, the fifth
year of Kang-He, some red-haired men (Dutch)
profaned the island, and carried away some of the

idols of Buddha; with these they proceeded to Japan, and, by means of trade, gained two hundred thousand pieces of gold. But on their return home the ship spontaneously caught fire, and all were consumed or drowned in the ocean,—an instance of the avenging power of Fŭh.

This island, one of the Chusan group, is of a sterile craggy nature, about twelve miles in circumference, being about five long and about one and a half broad.

All the temples have a southerly aspect, and are sheltered by high perpendicular hills from the northeast monsoon. It has one decided advantage. over the neighbouring islands in being replete with mountain springs, whose waters are drawn by means of bamboo aqueducts into large reservoirs or tanks.

In the summer of 1846, when, from the dearth of rain, a famine spread over the Chusan group, the crops in Poo-to alone flourished.

In the city of Ting-Hae, the capital of Chusan, the people, the soldiers, the mandarins, all joined in processions, prostrations, and oblations to all the gods in the calendar, praying incessantly for rain. Their prayers, hitherto unheeded, were only accepted (or seemed to be) on the appearance of two wooden deities, supposed to preside over the springs of heaven and earth; which, at the solicitation of the high general and imperial commissioner, Heen-

Leang, (whose presence was required to receive back for his sovereign the till then occupied island,) were allowed by the good priests of Poo-to to be carried with great pomp, firing of guns, beating of gongs, cymbals, and other martial instruments, from their long occupied and exalted position, and were received, on landing at Ting-Hae, by nine mandarins, kneeling and bowing their heads, to the admiration of the countless soldiery and peasantry.

Scarcely had these idols left their sanctified niches, when, from the sea, gradually rolled one of those thick mists so peculiar to an insular position. The sacred images themselves, dressed in gaudy satin robes, were soon drenched with rain, and before they left the island not one of the retinue had a dry rag on.

Their voyage was prosperous, rounding the point of Sin-cu-Moon, a south-east wind took them into Chusan with the first of the rain. Great was the joy, and strong the belief of the islanders, who did not consider that, from the lowering state of the atmosphere for some days past, rain was inevitable, but only remembered that the blessing had been sought for at the shrine of these idols, and by them granted. A shock of an earthquake was felt on the same night.

The name of Poo-to is a corruption of Fuh-too, one of the names of Buddha. Besides the temples, there are a few dwellings belonging to the laity of the place; some keep small shops and sell to the pilgrims the incense candles, and other articles of oblation, together with *bijoux* and pictures of the island.

Landing in a small bay, to the north-west, the scene is very picturesque; on the left, on an over-hanging cliff, is a blue-coloured temple, some of the apartments of which, like the nest of the sea-bird, appear to be merely hanging from the rocks; a winding step-road approaches it. The bay is generally well filled with large trading-boats, which transport hence a considerable part of the pro-ductions of the island, and with the pilgrims and priests produce a very lively appearance. Round this bay is a well-built stone wharf, at the right extremity of which is a very fine triumphal gate-way of carved and painted wood. Peeping through the dense foliage, on the side of the hill, are fronts or gables of several joss-houses. Passing the ar-tificial gateway, the road is beautiful, high hedges on either side, replete with sweet-scented and gaudy flowers, such as the jessamine, sweetbriar, rose, orange-flower, azalias of every colour, magnolias, and pomegranates, blossom-flowers in high per-fection; on either hand are open arches through which may be seen inviting lanes leading to tem-ples in the various ravines. Passing through some of these lanes, a winding stair, cut through the heart of the granite, leads to caverns ornamented with deities hewn from the solid stone, and through which purling streams meander into the vales below; a pavilion, with seats for the wayfarer, crowns the highest point of this road. Looking back, countless islands seem almost to cover the vast expanse of water, and nothing can exceed the novelty of the view; all around, wherever possible, every inch of ground is cultivated, and amid crags, in almost inaccessible parts of the varions hills, seem to hang grotesquely shaped edifices. Passing down into a charming valley, on the right-hand side is a monument inscribed with the Pali characters, and a translation of them in Chinese, in the Seal character; under it is an altar like a tomb hewn out of the solid rock, and hollowed for the burning of incense. At the foot of the hill you pass under a magnificent pile of perpendicular and longitudinal granite beams of stupendous size, and view the principal temple which, with its attendant pavilions, occupies about ten acres of ground, leading through an open pavilion containing a marble tablet on the back of a huge tortoise; a flat stone causeway, or bridge, on the middle of which is another open pavilion, reaches the central porch of the joss-house, this causeway stands in contrast to a handsome single-arched bridge on the right, (the arch of which is about three-quarters of a circle,) and the two divide an extensive tank into three parts, that to the right is filled with the sacred lotus plants, whose flowers of crimson and white, add much to the general beauty of the scene. This temple. like that of Tien-Tung, is dedicated to the Triad Fŭh and the goddess Kwan-Yin, and, with slight exceptions, is generally similar. The tiling is of a bright yellow colour, shewing that it is imperially endowed, and the high priest said that the Emperors Sun-Che and Kea-King, of the present dynasty, had sent presents of money and silks to the temples of this holy isle, and that most of the princes of the Ming dynasty, and especially the last of that race, Tsung-Ching, had done the same. Pilgrims from all parts of China visit it in the spring; and its refectories, together with the plump appearance of its priests, bear ample testimony of their liberality.

Looking from the arched bridge on the right stands an immense monumental pile, of three stories in height, the old mausoleum of the establishment. Back from this, in a hidden ravine, is the new mausoleum, a huge structure of stone, built square with three surmounting towers one over the other, in use for the same purpose.

In front is a marble table, and at the back an arched bridge joins a thick wall, which, at the height

ANCIENT MONUMENT, CONTAINING THE ASHES OF A DECEASED PRIEST.

of ten feet, runs round three sides. On this is a rampart gained on each side by a staircase. On the right and left side of the mausoleum are stone doors, through the walls of six feet in thickness they cast the burnt ashes of the dead priests into the abyss within. The object of the bridge in the rear, is, that when the interior be filled to the doors at the side, this may be available to reach a higher one at the back. The whole is about a hundred feet square, and reached by a flight of stone steps from the path : the mausoleum is about forty feet high.

Near this spot was one of the most valuable but small joss-houses, now in ruins. The whole of its deities were of bronze metal, but from the pilferings of some Englishmen, I am ashamed to say, the priests found it necessary to remove these valuables to a safer position.

Leaving the large temple the road passes through a small village, unblest by woman, whose appearance on this island, except for the devout purpose of offering to the gods, is prohibited, and the prohibition strictly enforced. "Thou shalt not marry," is one of the principal doctrines observed by the Buddhist priesthood. Passing this village the most cultivated part of the island is entered. The hedges again commence, and on either side are fine gateways, opening to view long vistas of green lanes. Flowers and trees, by their engaging position, invited the wayfarer to visit the hidden treasures within, consisting, in some far back position gained by ascending terraces, of the gardens of a joss-house, half-temple, half-farm: inhabited by a mixed crew of priests and laymen. From this point the road, stretching to the south-east, winds round a splendid sandy bay into which the surf rolls with much force and loud sound. At the eastern extremity stands the second grand temple, partly hidden by a magnificent park of lofty trees. It is entered through a green tiled pavilion, in the upper story of which lives a bonze, a man about forty years of age, whose office is to incessantly strike a small hand-drum, repeating at the same time the names of every saint in the Buddhist calendar. His dress was filthy and in rags, and his long matted hair was bound round the temples by a brass band. From generally sitting with his legs crossed they had become so contracted as to cause him to waddle with difficulty when he wanted to shift his position. At the back of seven temples, divided each by a paved court, and dedicated to some presiding deity, in an elevated position stood the dwelling of the Tae Hoshang.

He was a young man of very respectable appearance, with his house very neatly furnished: in one room he had the most valuable josses, of gold and jade stone, in glass cases, the door of their recess was locked with five iron locks. He had many books, and among them a translation of the Bible, and a history of the world in Chinese, printed at New York, one map of the world shewed the track outward and homeward of a ship which had circumnavigated the globe, rounding the Cape of Good Hope, touching at Chusan, and returning *via* Cape Horn; another was illustrated by the animal productions of each kingdom; another represented the heavenly bodies, these appeared as much thumbed and filled with written comments, &c., as the Bible appeared free from them. In his complacency he even offered me the sacred volume, which I declined, stating that I already possessed one, and hoped that he might at some future day profit by the doctrines therein taught. He smiled, as much as to say, I'll take time to think about it. This temple was undergoing repairs, having fallen into much decay.

ANCIENT TEMPLE AT POO-TO.

Behind the temple the road ascends a ladder-hill, about fifteen hundred feet high; half way up is the residence of a hermit, whose nest of filth almost forbids the hope of a slight rest to the weary traveller. He and the bonze are somewhat similar in dress and appearance, and both natives of Nankin. More of them I know not, except that he continually called on "Omiedo Fuh!" a name of Buddha.

Arrived at the summit, the fine road again, through

N

beautiful lanes branching to smaller temples, leads
to the third of the large joss-houses.   It is similar
in many respects to most of the others, except that
in one room I counted seventy-nine different deities
all in good order, and gilt, besides which the joss-
house contained the usual number, together with a
tablet hall, in which are written, for a small sum, the
virtues of a deceased relative.   In this joss-house
I lived for ten days in the month of August, and
notwithstanding its being the hottest month in the
north, found it delightfully cool ; each day the morning shone out fine and clear, while just as the day
would be getting unpleasantly hot in rolled from the
sea a heavy mist.

Above this on the highest point of the island is
a small hermitage, with a single joss-house.   Descend where you will from this, caverns, carved
rocks, and farm-temples, everywhere meet the eye ;
should a heavy crag otherwise baulk the scene, it
is rendered picturesque by cutting there on either
deities themselves, or inscriptions in honour of
them.

On a high jutting rock forming a beautiful but
unsafe little harbour, on the south side of the island,
stands one of the second-rate temples.   Here, after
some days' search for a perforated rock, (described
as being in so enticing a position as to invite the
discontented with this world of woe, who believe

in transmigration, to launch themselves into the foaming tide beneath—it had attained the name of the Suicide's Leap,) I was dawdling along one evening, when of a sudden a tremendous roar drew my attention at a moment, and a bamboo bar caught me by the middle and nearly tumbled me over. It was the bar of the Suicide's Leap: and immediately underneath, at a depth of a hundred feet, foamed the advancing surge. The rock being perforated, it forced its way for several hundred yards into a sub-marine channel that is dry at low water.

The productions of this island are sweet potatoes, rice, and vegetables of all kinds, also arrowroot and water melons. Water buffaloes are used for the plough: of these I may relate the following anecdote, which occurred to me on this island. Walking one day with a lieutenant, R.N., and a major of the company's service, where we thought it not unlikely that we might come across some of these creatures, I warned my companions, that, if we did meet any, I should vote discretion the better part of valour, pocket my dignity, and trust to my heels, a plan which my naval friend most cordially approved of, — not so the gallant *militaire*. "Nonsense, turn tail to a buffalo, catch me at it! faced hundreds in India, and not going to "run now"—and he kept his word, whether he would

or not. We had both double-barrelled guns; but
the major had an umbrella and some tracts, translated into Chinese, which a pious lady of Ningpo
had requested him to distribute among the priests
of Poo-to. A sharp turn into a farm-yard brought
the lieutenant and me most unexpectedly into
very disagreeably close quarters with a huge brute
and two calves. The major was a little behind;
scarcely had we got into a place of safety, my
friend on the wall, and myself on a bean-stack,
shouting all the time to give him warning, when
he reached the door, just at the moment that
the frightened buffalo, eyes shut, head down, at
full speed, was making his exit: up went the
major, umbrella, hat, spectacles, tracts, and all, and
descended into the soft embraces of the moist run-
nings from a dung-heap, while the animal pro-
fited by the opportunity to run off more frightened than the vanquished major. This animal has
a most unaccountable antipathy to foreigners: under
command of a native urchin, whose directions it
follows, it was quiet as need be, but in sight of a
foreigner it becomes furious, and will, if escape be
difficult, attack most resolutely.

But the finest sanctuary of Buddhism is the King-
Shang, or "golden isle," not inaptly named, and
lying in the Yang-tse-Kiang river, about forty
miles below Nankin, which I had not time, I re-

gret to say, thoroughly to examine. It consists of a single rock rising out of the water, of about half a mile in circumference, much resembling the prints of, for I never saw the original, St. Michael's Mount. Here was formerly the summer residence of the emperors, when Nankin was the capital; it is splendidly adorned with a pagoda, like the celebrated tower of Nankin, except that it is of seven instead of nine stories in height; the picturesque and beautiful buildings that once formed the palace are much decayed; but there are still magnificent tombs raised to the memory of the members of royalty who have died here. It swarms with joss-houses and Buddhist priests, but has not a single female inhabitant; in fact, it is an establishment something like that of Mafra near Lisbon, at once a palace, temple, and monastery combined, but deserted by its royalty.

The most remarkable and valuable part of it I did not see, which was the library—we were treading on unknown ground, and the contents of it, which we alone of all nations might have made lawful prize, were by us left behind : it was the largest and most valuable library of books in the empire, and contained amongst other things, a most unique collection of European engravings, presented by the earlier missionaries, long out of print, which would have been invaluable. I still think, but do not know that I dare say more, the whole will some day or other turn up in Europe, though unfortunately not in London.

Nunneries are not uncommon—there is one at Shanghae; the ladies are from their birth dedicated to the service of Buddha, and brought up as priestesses. One advantage they gain by it is, avoiding the tortures of having their feet cramped; their hair is shaved, and the dress much resembles that of a male priest: and celibacy, ostensibly at least, is required. The interior of this establishment is much the same as a monastery, but the exterior is distinguished by being painted yellow —the royal colour.

CHAPTER XI.

CHRISTIANITY.

Few Converts to Christianity.—Plan adopted by Roman Catholics.
— The success of Protestant Missions. — Advantages of the
Jesuits over the Protestants. — Anecdotes of Missionaries. —
Andrè, a Corean Roman Catholic Priest.—His Account of his
Travels.—Domestic Tragedy at Pekin.—Sect of the Devils.

OF Christianity in China I am afraid I cannot
give a very satisfactory account; as for a real native
Christian, I do not suppose one exists in the empire, the converts all adhere to the worship of their
ancestors, and partial success has attended the
preaching of the Roman Catholics alone, who cannot overcome this rooted obedience to the leading
precept of the Confucian system. The plan adopted
by these worthy fathers is to enter the country
thoroughly prepared ; they acquire the language at
some outpost, together with a knowledge of medicine, or other art that may be turned to good account; and having let their hair grow into a tail,
à la Chinoise, and left European habits behind them,
they take ship and enter the country as common
sailors or fishermen, and devote themselves to gain-

ing the confidence of the natives. The extent of their success I am ignorant of, but the following extract from the Chinese Repository, June, 1846, will shew that they are not idle.

"Apostolic Vicariate, Fu-kien. This province is assigned to the Spanish dominicans. Bishop Carpena is vicar-apostolic, and there are, in connection with the mission, one coadjutor, five European priests, and nine native, and more than forty thousand members."

I wish I could say as much for the success of the Church of England mission, but at Koo-lung-su (Kin-lang-Shuy, meaning "gold cold water," or the island of the golden springs), where I was for upwards of a year, the only two Protestant converts that I could hear of, were suspected of running off with the communion plate. And yet we read and are expected to believe such precious romances as the following: —"We have had rather a long season of rain ; when it intermits, as it has to-day, many come over from Amoy. It is at such times especially that our situation appears favourable for a mission. It combines the advantages enjoyed by Paul at Ephesus and Rome. We need not go to the school of one Tyrannus, but can dispute daily with multitudes who come to our own hired house."

But the Jesuit possesses great advantages over the Protestant. Amongst bells, candles, incense, chanting, flowing robes, and celibacy of the priesthood, the Buddhist and Catholic are equally at home. And the Church of England does not tolerate the worship of ancestors; but blame must attach somewhere for the paucity of churches, one at Macao and a mat-shed at Hong Kong comprised all that I could hear of. The Dissenters are better provided with buildings, but are equally unsuccessful at conversion. And yet there are many hard-working and zealous men, both English and American, in the Protestant missions; and perfect toleration is granted to all other sects of Christianity in the five ports equally, as the edict somewhat naïvely remarks, with the worshipers of images. But the subjects of the following anecdotes are lamentable exceptions to the general rule. On the occasion of the death of an officer of her majesty's service at Chusan, in reply to a military surgeon who had asked an English missionary why he did not attend the hospitals to administer the consolations of religion to the sick, the amateur apostle who, no doubt, flattered himself he was not like the publicans, said,—" Soldiers and sailors are so very bad, it is of no use, I never like to go near them." Not so at Koo-lung-su thought Monsieur Barrentin, a Jesuit, I believe, and I mention his name without apology to him, and will contrast his conduct with that of an American missionary who, as there was no clergyman of the Church of England on the spot, undertook the cure of souls of an English regiment, at a salary of 250*l.* per annum, paid weekly by our government; his duty was church service once a week, and attendance on the sick, and, in short, the usual duties of a chaplain.

An unfortunate young soldier was in hospital in a state of madness from delirium tremens caused by drinking. A few hours before his death he came to his senses, and hearing that the surgeon had given him over, begged that a clergyman might be sent for. The clergyman was sent for, and came— as far as the foot of the staircase—when, hearing what the case was, the holy man merely gasped "Delirium tremens!" in a tone of pious horror, turned upon his heel and went his way. Father Barrentin was in hospital at the time visiting some Catholic patients belonging to the regiment (the officers told me he attends most assiduously to his duty, and gratuitously, inasmuch as it forms no part of his regular mission; and though his stipend, under the Bishop of Macao, is only ninety dollars per annum, yet upon that he lives, and declines all offers of further payment). He had seen the dying man, when told that there was no hope of his obtaining the consolations of religion as prescribed by his own church. At the soldier's own request, communicated to him through the hospital attendant, the good father administered to him the last offices of the Roman Catholic Church, in communion with which I need hardly say the poor man died.

Some of the natives, although only partial converts, have sealed their faith with their blood. When at Shanghae I met with a Corean of noble birth, and by profession a Roman Catholic priest, who gave me the following particulars of himself. He said that when very young he had been taken away from his country to be educated at Macao, where he received the baptismal name of Andrè, and was brought up as a Catholic. His father, grandfather, and great grandfather, had all died for that religion. After completing his education he was landed from a junk at Ningpo to find his way from thence to his own country on foot, a distance of at least fourteen hundred miles. He passed through Pekin at a time when popular feeling was much excited by the death of a daughter of the emperor by his lawful wife. His majesty had two daughters of the same age, one by the empress, the other by a Manchou concubine, of whom he was very fond. As they grew up the latter was pressed more into his notice than the legitimate child, of whom the jealous concubine never failed to speak ill when an opportunity presented itself. The daughter of the empress was said to have been clever, amiable, and beautiful; and at a family inspection of their respective performances, the artful concubine substituted as her own daughter's the productions of her niece, in writing, composing, needlework, &c.,

and by the most ingenious malice had so worked upon the emperor's humour, who was enraged at the meanness of what had been presented to him as the work of his lawful daughter, that when the latter knelt to him to crave his blessing, he kicked her so violently that she died. The bereaved empress soon discovered the cheat, and the concubine and her daughter were banished. Such was the domestic tragedy that Andrè said he heard at Pekin. It is but proper to add that this was only hearsay of the good priest, but that the Chinese universally speak of their emperor with affection, as a benevolent and most fatherly man.

From thence he travelled northwards towards Tartary, and arrived on foot at the frontier, cold, hungry, and disheartened, in the depth of winter; he roamed about for several days to escape the vigilance of the guards, by whom he was frequently chased, until one night, although he knew it to be certain death, he lay down in the snow and was soon asleep, but he was awakened by a mysterious voice, saying, "Andrè, arise and follow!" He arose and followed, he knew not how, but when he came to his senses he found himself beyond the frontier, and safe in Corea. His religion has met with many persecutions there, all the French missionaries had been either driven out of the country or murdered, and more than once he had witnessed a partial massacre of his flock, and had himself been hunted down by dogs. He described his country as being tributary to China, which it resembles on a poorer scale, the emperor pretty well dictating to the king of it as he pleases. In writing on foreign intercourse during the last war, the Son of Heaven directed that barbarian ships might be driven from the coast, and on no account should a foreigner be permitted to land. " Let one land, and, like rats in a granary, they will increase and multiply, and devour your very substance. In voracity they are dogs, and in habits, pigs." The government is obnoxious to the people, and the strongest anxiety prevails for foreign trade. The productions are metals, coal, grain, silk, cotton, and most of the productions of China, though in less profusion, and the silk by no means so good. Their paper is of very fine manufacture in large sheets, much larger and superior to Chinese. The dress much the same except that sandals of leather are worn as shoes, and the hair is collected into a knot at the top of the head, and ornamented with wooden knobs, on which a hat is fitted with an enormous brim, and a crown about eight inches in height.

The religion, in general, is the same as Chinese, but he mentioned, with great respect, and as if he really believed what he was talking about, one sect, called—The Devils,—initiation into which, is by going at midnight into a certain wood, and invoking and defying his Satanic Majesty, which of course much provokes him, and he is only kept from attacking you by your keeping your presence of mind, and reading for an hour out of a certain book, with which it is necessary to be provided, when Beelzebub is beat, and voting you as good a devil as himself, gives you a ticket to that effect, as a certificate to shew to your friends.

The reason of his again quitting his country, was to meet a French Bishop, lately appointed, and to save him the trouble of a land journey. For this purpose, he had brought a junk not unlike a Chinese vessel in shape, but entirely destitute of paint and made of wood, joined together with wooden fastenings, without a particle of iron or metal of any kind, in its composition. A good chart, a compass, an English quadrant, and French tables, formed the sum of his astronomical utensils, and a few old matchlocks and pistols his protection. Being aware of the prohibition of trade between Corea and Shanghae, he managed to lose his masts off the Yang-tse-kiang and was brought into port in tow of a Chinese junk, when he entered himself both at the Hae-kwan's and the British Consul's office, as a Portuguese, on pretence that he was a subject of Portugal, from living so many years at Macao.

He always wore his Corean dress, a hat of fine

bamboo framework, covered with black gauze, and a long flowing white robe: his crew consisted of nine men in all, and he performed divine service every morning and evening for them on board. What with the singularity of his dress and appearance, and the construction of his vessel, he excited a greater degree of curiosity among the Chinese, than I had even witnessed on the arrival of an English vessel, and never stirred on land without an immense crowd following him. He dined with us once or twice on board, and we found him a clever, agreeable, well-informed man, with a fund of anecdotes, and very good manner. He spoke French, Italian, Spanish, Portuguese, Chinese, and Corean, with a small smattering of Japanese, and had travelled all over China, Manchou, and Mongul. On his leaving for Corea, he presented me with his hat, which might have passed the Corean, safer than the English custom-house, where it must have met with an admirer, and in consequence, I have not seen it since.

The Bishop arriving, the junk started, but meeting adverse winds, put back into Woosung, whence she again sailed, and I am sure, with the good wishes of all who had known poor Andrè. The last I heard of him was a report, though afterwards contradicted, of his junk having been cast ashore on the Shang-tung province, and only one man saved.

A MILITARY MANDARIN.

CHAPTER XII.

MILITARY.

British and Chinese Troops compared.—Chinese Military Maxims disregarded. — Want of Discipline. — Expresses and Posts.— Protection of the Frontier.—Emigration.—Barracks.—Soldiers'. Arms bad. — Ordnance. — Soldiers' Dress. — Fight ill in a body. — Military Mandarins. — Intercepted Government Despatch. — Division of Troops into Tartar and Chinese. — Attempted Intercourse with the Mandarins during the War.— Mr. Thom's Narrative of its ill Success.

In looking at a Chinese army it seems astonishing that the small handful of emaciated British troops, with the few Indian regiments under Lord Gough, could have escaped utter annihilation. The Chinese coolie can lift and carry a heavier weight than a British soldier, and is often larger than our life-guards-men, and the Tartar, from his northern birth and education, is stronger still, though not of such large build. But the discipline is wanting. Their military maxims are often beautiful in theory; take for instance, "The army may be one hundred years unemployed, but not a single day unprepared," and their articles of war and some of their military laws, which I have taken the liberty of transcribing from Sir George Staunton, in order to comment upon them, are such as, if judiciously enforced, ought to insure a formidable army.

Art. I. "In the day of battle press forward bravely; whoever, through fear, saves his life shall be decapitated, and his head exposed as a warning. To kill an enemy shall be rewarded as a meritorious act. If a soldier is killed, his family are compassionated. The coward, *i. e.*, the conquered, cannot live: if he rushes forward it is not certain that he dies, but if he draws back, it is impossible that he can live. Let the officers inculcate this principle on the men, that they may doubtless be brave, and killing the thieves, their enemies, meritoriously distinguish themselves."

The policy of this article is, to say the least, questionable; and lamentable effects of it were seen at Chang-keang-foo, which was defended solely by Tartars, whose ancestors had, two hundred years before, put the finishing stroke to the conquest

of China, by a most brilliant exploit in that very
place.   It was then one of the largest cities in the
country, and, in its own province of Kiang-tsu,
second only in importance to Nankin, the capital.
The Tartars crossed the Yang-tse-kiang, on the ice,
and took the city by a *coup de main*. The first
Emperor of the Manchou dynasty, gave it them as
a prize, and in their hands it had since remained,
subject entirely to Tartar laws and customs. The
original natives inhabited the suburbs which grew
up round it, and became their servants. In the
first watch a curfew tolled for the close of the
gates, when all Chinese had to leave the walled
city, which was essentially Tartar, and of all places,
threatened the greatest resistance to a foreign foe.
But the city walls were deserted, or nearly so, and
the greater part of the garrison as they retreated
from street to street, made but a slight defence,
while not a few preferred suicide, some, perhaps,
from a high but mistaken sense of honour, which
forbade them flying or falling alive into the enemies' hands, others from a dread of the hard fate
which awaited them at the hands of their own
countrymen, if they survived the capture of their
posts.

It is strange that men should shrink from meeting
their enemies and dying honourably in defence of
their country, and should prefer ignominiously em-

ploying in their own destruction the very hands
that providence has given them to defend, and not
take their own lives. Yet the Tartar general can
scarcely be called a coward, who, surrounded by a
weeping family, refused to fly, and having caused a
pile of his furniture and ancestral pictures to be
raised under him, coolly awaited the decisive report
of his city being in the hands of the enemy, when
he gave orders to his secretary to fire the pile, and,
surrounded by his wives and family, met his death
with the utmost composure. The secretary was
taken prisoner, and, when on board H. M. S. Cornwallis, several times attempted to commit suicide,
but was prevented: he was released on his promise
to carry a letter from Lord Palmerston to the Emperor's ministers, at Pekin, but after his landing we
heard no more of him.

How much better would it be for the generals,
when all is lost but honour, to succour their defeated
troops, and by a judicious retreat, preserve the gallant remnant of a disciplined army, than by a
wanton act forced upon them deprive their men
of a leader, and set a most injudicious example?
Had Sir John Moore been a Chinese general, and
survived Corunna, his glorious retreat might have
forfeited his life and reputation.

Art. 2. "On entering into battle, powder and
arrows are not to be expended at a distance, but

reserved for the exact moment of efficacy. To waste them before the time arrives, is like tying one's hands and waiting to be killed."

In passing the Yang-tse-kiang, at a place afterwards named Cape Disappointment, from our having expected a glorious action, which ended in smoke, a tremendous cannonade from a fort situated at the foot of a high hill, was observed and heard on board the headmost vessels of the fleet, at a distance of from a mile and a half to two miles a-head, the recochets of the balls were observable in a direct line across the river, at right angles to us who were ascending the river, the head of the squadron was disposed as follows:—Modeste and Phlegethon a-head, sounding, Cornwallis, towed by the Vixen, followed. As soon as the probable strength of the Barker was ascertained Sir W. Parker made signal to the Modeste to proceed and engage the battery; as she advanced she continually crowded sail until nearly abreast of the battery, which was still firing, when one pipe reduced the canvass to topsails, and a whole broadside, well directed, was poured in, and that was sufficient. The sides of the hill were immediately covered with the enemy, retreating, and the boats' crews of the Modeste spiked and destroyed the guns. In less than half an hour we had anchored and went ashore for a stroll without let or hindrance.

Art. 3. "The utmost pains must be taken to preserve their arms in good order and keep their ammunition dry."

Let a man be as careful as he may, the cartouche-boxes are of so inferior an order, that a shower of rain would render a Chinese army, who depended on their fire-arms only, totally inefficient. It is strange that so ingenious a people should not long ago have remedied this; but, from the length of peace they have enjoyed, the implements and art of war may not have been much studied. The Chinese soldier has no bayonet nor manœuvres with the matchlock on parade, as the European, nor in time of peace does he mount guard with arms, hence, except at reviews, the fire-arms are un-touched.

Art. 4. "When an officer is wounded or taken, the men shall make the utmost efforts to carry him off or rescue him, if they neglect to do so, and defeat ensues, the guilty men shall be decapitated."

As far as my experience goes, this article is a dead letter, the officers being generally those whose lives were forfeited by a retreat. They, by their personal valour have done something to uphold the dignity of the nation. Mate (now Lieutenant) Hodgson, of the Cornwallis, had two hand-to-hand engagements with mandarins, at Sye-ke, he kill-ed his antagonists, but no attempt was made to

rescue either them or Quan, the Admiral, who fell
at the Bogues.   At Woosang, nearly all the rank
and file fled, leaving their guns to be worked by
the superior mandarins, the chief of whom fell at
his post, and I have often seen his effigy as a dei-
fied hero in the temple of the tea-gardens at Shanghae, in the dress and boots which were the insignia
of his office during life, his widow was allowed to
write, or have written, the biography of her lord,
and his children were ennobled and rewarded, and
every possible honour paid to his memory.

Art. 5. "Soldiers must not quit the pursuit of a
flying foe for plunder."

I cannot authenticate an instance of their quitting
a flying foe for plunder, but in the late war the
authorities often acknowledged that their own
soldiers plundered more than their enemies, and
the protection of the barbarians against natives
was often, especially at Shang-Kiang-Fu, sought
for and accorded.

Art. 6. "The utmost vigilance and silence is required of men on duty at any pass or post. On
obtaining any information they must depute able
men to communicate it speedily and secretly."

On the night before the taking of Woosung, such
was the din of gongs and howling, and the light
established by each Chinese soldier carrying a
lighted lantern, that, guided by them, the captains

of our surveying vessels not only sounded the entrance and the line of battering positions, but also marked by anchored buoys, the positions for the several ships as they were taken up on the following morning.

Art. 7. "All plundering to be severely punished." Note, article 5.

Art. 8. "The soldier who bravely kills one enemy shall be rewarded; but he who is detected in lying pretexts about his own merits, or who by false tales usurps the merits of others as his own, shall be decapitated."

In an attempt to force a letter on the authorities of Amoy from Lord Palmerston to the Emperor's ministers, a Chinese soldier fired an arrow, which so nearly hit Mr. Thom, who was doing duty as interpreter in a boat of H.M.S. Blonde, that I have heard him say he bowed just in time to allow it to graze him and pass on; as he did not resume his original position, the soldier who shot it was recommended to the Emperor for having killed the barbarian eye, for which he was gazetted a mandarin at considerable length in the King Chow, *i. e.,* "Pekin Gazette." In the course of events, the conference in the Meaon Sin, at Nankin, called the heroes of both countries to an amicable dinner, at which the guests were waited on by mandarins. This very mandarin, the slayer of the barbarian eye, was admitted into the inner chamber, and as fortune would have it, stood behind the very man's chair for whose death he had been raised from the ranks, and retained his title after the mistake was discovered.

Art. 9. "The horses and camels belonging to the army must be treated with affection and kindness, and good water and provender provided for them. Should they stray at night, let them be forthwith sought for and brought to the wells in regular succession, so that the water may not be fouled by their being permitted to strive against one another in crowds. Neglect of this duty must be severely punished."

With the exception of a few saddle-horses of the mandarins, I never saw either cavalry or camels, though both, I believe, are to be found in the north.

Art. 10. "While encamped, the patrols must be vigilant, and particularly so at night. None must be permitted to walk about without cause. In the tents, especially, care must be taken against fire. On any alarm none must act hurriedly or with levity. Secret orders must be carefully obeyed, and not allowed to transpire from one another."

At the night attack on Ningpo, thousands of Chinese fell from every soldier carrying a lantern. As soon as the gate-guards had been reinforced, the

Chinese were repulsed, and directed by the light of their own lanterns, each musket and field-piece ball took effect on them. It is the custom of every man, woman, and child, be he who he may, to carry a lantern after dark.

The other military regulations are as much disregarded as the above articles of war. In short, in a Chinese camp of the present day, there is little or no discipline. This should not be the case where merit alone (at least so say the edicts) can make a military mandarin, all alike rising from the ranks. I have given these few examples from the events of the late war, but am not of opinion that such a state of things will always exist, or that the Chinese in future will prove a contemptible enemy. Two hundred years of almost uninterrupted peace may have relaxed their discipline, but from the care that, at the time of my departure, was being bestowed on the repairs of fortifications, embodying regiments, drilling recruits, the size and strength of the men, and the enormous population to draft from, I am inclined to think that a few years of active hostilities would teach them the art of war, and enable them on land to defy invasion by any power in Europe. Under the head of military laws may be mentioned the following:— Protection of the palace, the person of the Emperor, and his apartments, together with those of his em-

press, the empress-mother, and grandmother. Tres-
passing on the imperial privacy is punished with
death. Military forces, except in great emergency,
cannot be called out without the sanction of the
Emperor, and every movement must be reported
to the commander-in-chief, by him to the military
board, and by them to the Emperor. (I shall presently show that the Emperor may be very ill
informed of what is going on.) Betrayal of trust,
including defeat, severely punished according to
rank. The regulations of the nocturnal police are
to be observed in all cities and fortifications of the
empire, and no person, except on public business, or
on urgent private affairs, shall move about in them
from twelve minutes past nine P.M. to twelve
minutes past 5 A.M., during which time the gates
are shut. This does not apply to foreigners at
Shanghae, where the word Fan-kwei was to open
sesame. Expresses and posts are solely for the
conveyance of public despatches. Three hundred
Le (three to a mile) is the journey of a day and
night, and if exceeded by an hour and half, twenty
blows are the penalty, and ten more for every
additional hour, until they amount to fifty. The
distance between Canton and Pekin (twelve hundred
English miles) is accomplished in twelve days; but
Pekin gazettes take thirty, and officers are allowed
ninety days for the journey.

Protection of the frontier is under military surveillance. No person is allowed to pass without a licence, under a penalty of blows. Passports must not be granted to exiles or natives. Nor must those who are properly furnished with a licence be unnecessarily detained. Persons seeking to carry inventions out of, or introducing themselves into, or plotting the means of removing themselves out of the country, shall be beheaded; and more effectually to prohibit intercourse with foreigners by sea, the law forbids the building on or inhabiting the small islands along the coast.

This latter enactment is not much observed. Emigration goes on to a great extent; the straits islands, with Luconia and Borneo, are filled with Chinese labourers; some find their way as far as St. Helena and Rio Janeiro. In Canton a few are to be met with whose education has been partly gone through in England or America. No difficulty seems to be in the way of their return. Many having amassed money return home to marry, as the women are very infrequent companions of their travels. The islands on the coast, instead of being barren and deserted, are highly cultivated and thickly peopled. Their inhabitants would be invaluable for the cultivation of our West Indian Islands; inasmuch as they are indefatigable labourers, inured to a hot climate, willing to emigrate, and work at a very low rate of wages. At the same time this emigration ought to be under very strict surveillance. I knew a case of a man on his death-bed confessing that he had come over to Hong Kong for the purpose of decoying the natives away, and embarking them for the Brazils, and there selling them as slaves.

A Chinese barracks is always a conspicuous object. In front of a low white-walled house, surmounted with dragon-roofs, stand two poles bearing the banners of the mandarin in command; a red ball, surmounting a half moon, is painted between every two windows, of which there are generally three on each side of the door. To the left of the building, in front, is a look-out station, like a sentry-box on stilts, and to the left of that again are three small chimneys for watch-fires. Besides marking a military station, these chimneys are in line at visible distances from each other along the whole length of the coast, for the purpose of conveying intelligence of an attack.

Matchlocks were introduced into the Chinese army in the reign of Kea-Tsing, of the Ming dynasty, A.D. 1520. The Chinese soldier labours under every disadvantage, his arms are bad, the matchlock is of the rudest kind, and not brought up in a line with the eye as an English musket; the powder is of the coarsest brand, and loose. Each soldier, besides his cartouch-box, is provided with a measure with which he loads his piece. The lances are of the roughest order, being simply a pike placed on the head of a piece of bamboo.

The bow might have been considered a superior weapon of its kind in the early part of the Ta-tsing dynasty, but decidedly not fitted for modern warfare. It is very difficult to string the processes by placing one end between the ankles, bringing the other over the back, and slipping the string on in front; the value depends on the number of catties (one pound and a quarter) required to draw it to a bend sufficient for stringing, which varies from one to two hundred catties.

A Tartar general, at Chusan, before the war, petitioned the emperor to abolish the use of bows and arrows, and substitute the matchlock, as a more efficient weapon. An edict appeared in the Pekin Gazette, to the following effect. "Ignorant fool that you are, know you not, that, for the last 200 years, our army has been placed on the firmest basis of military power, and would you now that I should alter it? Had a Chinese petitioned me, I should have treated his ignorance with the contempt it would have deserved. But for you, a Tartar, I order you to be degraded from your rank, and rendered incapable of ever after redeeming it." In six months after, Chusan fell, and the inutility of the bow and arrow was fully shewn. The artillery of a regiment consists of a few large matchlocks, each supported on the shoulder of one man, while another takes aim; these carry balls of from one to two pounds' weight.

The ordnance department is much on a par. The brass pieces are generally from four and five to twenty pounders, while the iron guns range as high as sixty-eight pounds; they are nearly all of the same shape. In the battery of Woosung, about three hundred guns were mounted, the oldest of which bore the date of 8th moon, 4th year of Tsung-ching, (or A.D. 1632,) the last Chinese emperor. They are rudely cast, somewhat in the shape of an European gun; but some have the breach separate, hence, in the cannonade at Woosung, many of these were blown off and destroyed the men at them. On the upper part of the right side is the date, as 7th moon, 21st year of Taon-Quang; (the present emperor;) on the left the name of the piece, as "Tamer of the barbarians that come from afar." Such names especially were on the guns cast for the war. On the centre is the name of the foundry, city, province, and governor-general. They were all fixtures in their huge carriages. The guns were painted black, with red stripes, and the carriages red. The powder is provided in a large box.

As at all other places taken in China, the brass

guns at Woosung were shipped, and the iron spiked, their arms knocked off and thrown over the rampart into a marsh. But here we learnt a lesson that was new to us, for we afterwards saw the same guns re-bored, and shouldered, by casting a large piece of iron round the part to support the newly introduced arms, or trunnions; and for Chinese guns they were as good as ever. Not the least curious part of the business was the mode of raising them out of a swamp, entirely by hand labour; a rope was introduced round each end of the gun, and bamboo poles were attached to it, crossways to each other, their number increasing until the men, by simultaneously applying their shoulders underneath the poles, could lift the weight off the ground. In this way fifty men might be employed in removing the same gun, with the labour so beautifully distributed, that one would have no more burden to carry than another.

The dress in no way varies from that of a peasant, except in the jacket and cap; the former is blue, with facings varying in colour according to the regiment. A round white patch in front and rear receives the name of the soldier and his corps, which takes some high-flown title, as "The Invincibles," "The Never Conquered," &c. The cap is surmounted by a red tassel, and, in the case of an officer, with a ball besides.

The sword is rather a novel contrivance, it consists of two blades and handles, in one scabbard, so beautifully fitted together, that, when drawn out, it is one or two weapons, to be used in one or both hands, according to the will of the wearer, who is usually very expert with it in either way. In one of the edicts the soldiers were ordered to strike the blades together, and so make a noise that the barbarians would be terrified. The target, or shield, of the Tartar troops, is no insignificant weapon for offence as well as defence, in their opinion; it is painted with some hideous device. The "Tiger Guards" had a furious head of a tiger, which, with the awful grimace and antics, "the bearing of the truly brave in action," cannot fail, say the mandarins, to awe and terrify barbarians. "You are about," said the present Emperor to his Tigers, "to face an enemy, who wear so tight garments, that, if once they are down, it is impossible for them to rise; waste not your powder, but frighten them so that they fall down, and then they shall be at your mercy." It may be as well here to mention, that tiger's flesh, dried and eaten in powder, supplies what we call (without offence to the Hollanders, I hope) Dutch courage.

Individual bravery was often exhibited in the late war, but in no one instance did the Chinese fight well in a body. The obstinate defence of the joss-house, at Sye Kee, was not an act of bravery, but desperation. They had deserved to die for mutilating the bodies of the fallen British soldiers, and feared the resentment of the Royal Irish, whose colonel had fallen in the attack. But, if few of the military mandarins came off with anything like honour to themselves or country, I think it right to give them what credit I can, though it be but a single instance. Poor fellows, their cases were hard; they had to face a powerful foe on the one hand, and their ignorant, prejudiced, and more merciless compatriots on the other.

After taking possession of the city of Shanghae on the 19th June, 1842, the admiral directed Her Majesty's steamer Nemesis to ascend a small river or creek, and reconnoitre. Towards sundown she came in sight of a fort and military station, with a strong detachment of troops drawn out in battle array, who exchanged a few shots with her, and retired in good order. The steamer returned, it being deemed advisable to do so before dark. When Chin-Kiang-Fu was taken, Her Majesty's ship Childers was lying above the grand canal to intercept communication. A small boat, sculled by one oar, was observed from her quietly advancing close in shore. A boat was despatched to bring her alongside, when a government despatch was found secreted aboard. It proved to be a report from his Excel-

lency Jan-Wei-wan, of Ting-Hae, in Che-Kiang,
chief magistrate of Shaughae, narrating that although the city had suffered an occupation for a few
hours he had removed the treasure, and from the
commanding position taken up by the troops he had
called out to guard it, the barbarian eye had been
so awed and terrified that he immediately vomited
huge clouds of smoke and fire, and retired amid the
din of cheering from his Invincibles. The potent
argument of having saved the money was convincing,
as we afterwards understood. Not only he and his
officers, but their children also were honoured and
rewarded. Thus far I have used the term Chinese
generally; but more properly speaking there are two
separate armies; the Tartar Pa-ke and the native,
which, in truth, are little more or less than an embo-
died militia, called Luh-ying, or "troops of the
green standard." The Tartars muster under eight
banners. Yellow with border; yellow without;
white with; red with; white without; red with;
blue with, and blue without borders. The Tartar
and Chinese generals in the different provinces are
entirely independent of each other, and have fixed
official residences. A Tartar cannot command Chinese, nor a Chinese Tartar troops. Their numbers
it would be impossible to arrive at, but as every
tenth male capable of bearing arms is drawn by lot
to serve, the force must be prodigious. The Chinese

work at their several trades, and some of them hold land; but the Tartars are soldiers by profession. The pay of a common soldier is a mace, fourpence a-day. The military mandarins wear chain armour and helmets, presented to them by the Emperor on their arriving at that rank, and in common with all other mandarins are entitled to use the Joe, an emblem of rank and office; its use is to rest the arms upon when sitting. It is supposed, though I cannot vouch for the accuracy of the circumstance, that a moustache betokens a father, and a beard a grandfather.

I have once or twice mentioned Lord Palmerston's letters. I am indebted to the late Mr. Thom for the following narrative of his attempt to deliver one. A notice had been previously read, and explained to some of the servants of the mandarins in hopes of their forwarding it to their masters. One head servant took a copy of it, but returned the original, saying that the mandarins could not come aboard, but would receive a visit on shore. The notice was as follows:—

" The Commander-in-chief of the great English nation addresses this to the honourable officers presiding over this district (at Amoy) in order that peace and harmony may be kept, and war and calamity avoided.

" Behold! it hath been said by the ancient sages,

the ten thousand kingdoms of this earth form but one house, and all mankind are but one great family of brothers. Thus, although they may at times have their differences, yet in the end all hope to drop their enmity and love each other as before. This is a principle of human nature applicable alike to all countries. The object of this, then, is to say, that a misunderstanding having unfortunately arisen between the two great nations England and China, in order to restore their brotherly harmony as of old it will be necessary for quiet and peaceably disposed people to be continually coming and going between both parties, for the purpose of speaking kind words, delivering letters, or such like. These people go utterly unarmed, and carry a white flag which, with the exception of savages, is looked upon by all nations as a sacred sign. No violence is ever offered to their persons: on the contrary, all mankind look upon them accordingly. It answers very much to the same purpose, as Mëen-chin-pae, ' avoid fighting,' in your honourable country. We, therefore, beg that you may communicate the same to all your fellow-officers that they may know accordingly. At the same time distinct warning is hereby given that if any of your people fire off guns or matchlocks at such white flags, it will be impossible for me, the great English chief, to prevent my people exacting the most fearful vengeance!

" Beware, therefore, beware !"

MR. THOM'S NARRATIVE.

"At three, p. m., accompanied by the second Lieutenant, Sir Frederick Nicholson, Bart., we went in the cutter and pulled right for the beach close beside the fort. We had a white flag at the cutter's bow, and were unarmed. To our amazement, instead of the kind reception we expected, several officers, and two or three hundred soldiers were drawn up on the beach, and manifesting the most hostile disposition; we ran the cutter's bow on the beach, when myself and the lieutenant went forward, and pointing to the flag, said, we had a letter for the admiral, and wished to land in order to deliver it. In reply, it was stated that the admiral was at Chin-Chew, and that if we dared set foot on shore, they would kill us or bind us hand and foot, and send us to Foo-Chow-Fu. They shewed themselves prepared to support what they said by deeds, for their spear-men and matchlock-men approached till their weapons were within a yard of our persons, and we could not jump on shore without rushing on them. The conversation on our part was confined to begging them to receive and forward the letter, all of which was done with perfect politeness; and their only answer was 'Off! off! gone, get you gone!' with abuses and imprecations. Finding it impossible, we returned; Captain Boucher, (H.M.S. Blonde,) in the meantime, seized a junk, and by the captain of her sent a letter on shore, stating he would seize their vessels and stop their trade. No answer was returned, and the junk escaped in the morning. On Friday the Blonde shifted her berth to three hundred yards from the battery. I now went on shore in the jolly-boat, unarmed, rowed, and steered with five men and boys to ensure the intention being understood: the following notice was printed in Chinese on a piece of calico, and with the flag of truce placed in a conspicuous position.

"'A clear distinct notice, Behold! I the foreign *employé* have received orders from my superior officers to land here and deliver an important despatch to the honourable officers of this district, who, in their turn, are to hand the same up to His Excellency the Admiral of the station; which being done, we depart hence immediately, having in fact no other business here. Now, this is to say, that, having received a commission from my commander, I dare not do otherwise than execute it, and am determined, therefore, to deliver the said despatch into the hands of the honourable officers of this district; and as for your threats of killing me or binding me, I regard them not! If you consent to receive this despatch you will thereby avoid giving birth to a very serious affair. If you decline to receive it, you will thereby bring on yourselves a greater calamity. Lo! happiness and misery are in your hands : say, not that we failed to give you due warning beforehand. These words are true.'

"At this time the landing-place had become an encampment — guns were mounting in all directions, and armed junks were preparing for the offensive.

"When I reached the landing-place, the troops were drawn up as the day before, and a considerable crowd of spectators had assembled. Fearing treachery, I had directed the boat to be backed in the beach (the bow being thus brought ready to pull from the landing); and in the event of my being seized, the boat was to make the best of her way back to the frigate.

"When about five or six yards off shore, I sat over the boat's stern, and holding out my notice to the mandarins, requested them to peruse it. Their fury was beyond all bounds, and seemed to be aggravated by the crowd's perusal of it. I told them that, being most friendly disposed towards the Chinese, I came at peril and hazard to speak to them words of peace and kindness, as I could not bear the idea of injuring them. They replied with threats and curses, making signs of decapitation. At this time we were scarce two yards from the beach, and the boatmen called my attention to some soldiers wading in the water to seize the boat; upon this we pulled to eight or ten yards, when, standing up in the boat, I said in a loud voice, 'I now ask for the last time, will you receive it, or not?' 'No!' they all roared simultaneously, 'we fear you not;' and other expressions of defiance. Seeing all hopes of delivering it gone, I desired the men to pull back to the ship, the force of the oars pulling jerked the boat. I lost my balance and fell, and a lucky fall it proved; as, just at that very moment, a well-directed arrow flew over the spot I had quitted, and struck on the bottom of the boat with such force as to shiver its head to pieces: one moment sooner it had passed through my body. A bullet hit the stern a few inches from the coxswain's seat, several more passed over our heads; a couple of field-pieces were discharged either at us or the ship, and the troops were getting ready for a general discharge at us, when a circumstance took place which completely turned the tables in our favour, and most justly punished the offenders for their cold-blooded cruelty. Two thirty-two pound shot from the guns of the frigate, sent officers, soldiers, and spectators wildly scampering for their lives, leaving the lifeless bodies of some ten or a dozen behind."

DINNER AT THE PUBLIC COLLEGE, NINGPO.

CHAPTER XIII.

REVIEW.

Public Dinner at Ningpo.—An Insurrection.—The Mandarin Shoo.
—Attempt to obtain an Interview with the Governor-General
at Ningpo.—Obtained with difficulty.—Review of three
Regiments.—Their Manœuvres.—Orders given by waving of
Flags.—Colours.—Civility to the Author on the Parade.

WHILE at Ningpo I was fortunate enough to dine
with H. E. Leang-paow-Chang, of Tien-tsin-hëen in
the province of Chele, the governor-general of the
Che-kiang province, commander of the several naval
and military brigades, and head commissioner of the
commissariat department of the province, (I like to

give the whole name said the Vicar of Wakefield,) and to see him preside at a grand review of the forces of the district. The circumstances were as follow: he was making a survey of all the fortifications and cities of Che-kiang, his presence having been requisite to quell an insurrection that had broken out in the district of Fungu-a, in consequence of Chin-Chekei, governor of Ningpo-fu, and Taow-tai or intendant of the circuit of Ningpo, Shaou-hing-fu, and Tai-chow-fu, insisting on the payment of the usual tribute without abatement, notwithstanding the

ARRIVAL OF H. E. LEANG-PAOW-CHANG AT THE MILITARY TEMPLE.

pressure at the time of a partial famine. The insurgents had repulsed the military with great loss, and taken the Taow-tai and several mandarins prisoners, but released them on an old degraded mandarin named Shoo, who was much and deservedly respected, interceding with them, and offering himself to be responsible for the tribute not being insisted on; at the same time promising that a true account of the whole transaction should be sent to the emperor, the former official communication having been rather wide of the truth. The Taow-tai was in a scrape, having bambooed some of the literati of Fung-wa, whose position ought to have exempted them from such a degradation. The poor fellow and the second magistrate were summoned to Pekin, where I am afraid their punishment was a severe one, but I never heard what. The Emperor ordered a distribution of rice, from the public granaries, among the distressed, and proclaimed a general amnesty to the insurgents, and Shoo was shortly to be reinstated in his rank. The cause of his disgrace had been rather a misfortune than a crime, viz. the loss of Ningpo to the British, when he would have lost his head, but having shewn great kindness to Captain Anstruther, Mrs. Noble, and other English prisoners, Sir Henry Pottinger interceded for his life, which was spared on condition of his serving the emperor, without pay or button, for seven years when called upon.

On the 18th of November 1845, Mr. Thom, Her Majesty's Consul, Captain Gordon, R. N., Lieute-

nant Rogers, R. N., the Vice-Consul, and myself,
were carried in sedan-chairs through the Salt
Gate (so called because by that alone salt is allowed to enter) into the city, to visit the intendant
and discover whether the governor-general would
allow us to pay our respects to him, and how he
would in that case receive us. On our arrival
at his house we found old Shoo waiting to receive us, who said that the intendant was engaged
with the governor-general, and had desired him not
to wait dinner, but do the honours of the table
himself. Down we sat to a very good Chinese dinner of sea-slugs, birds' nests, and all the delicacies in
season, washed down with some very tolerable samshoo. In the middle of it our host arrived, and
though he tried to put a good face on the matter, it
was painfully evident that his interview with the
great man had not been satisfactory to himself, and
we afterwards found that some late news from Pekin
connected with the insurrection, was the cause of
his discomfiture; however he made the entertainment as agreeable as he could, and we did our best
to second him until, when the centre dish had been
replaced nearly thirty times, each with some new
delicacy in it, we prevailed on him, with some little
difficulty, to bring the affair to an end, and enter
with Mr. Thom on the diplomacy about the visit to
the great man.

"But," said the intendant, "you are not of equal rank, and cannot expect him to receive you as if you were."

"No," said Mr. Thom, "but with about the same honour as yourself."

"Good; but I am not allowed to sit in his presence."

"Then I must make my own terms, or not go at all. These gentlemen and myself shall be received and allowed to sit down in the presence of the governor-general, and he shall not on the day fixed deny himself to us on any pretext whatsoever. 'Not at home,' on the day fixed for an interview, is a mode of shewing superiority more frequent than agreeable."

The answer was promised that night, and we took our leave. On the next morning the Taow-tai sent his card with a message that the governor-general would have much pleasure in meeting Mr. Thom and his friends, on the terms stated, at three o'clock on the 21st instant, which was followed by the arrival on board of the Taow-tai in person, to return our visit. Captain Gordon gave him an English dinner, which he seemed to relish, and shewed him over the ship.

Punctually at three o'clock on the 21st we again passed through the Salt Gate in sedan-chairs, full uniforms, and as much state as we could command,

and were set down in the outer hall of the Taow-tai's house amid a glorious salute of guns firing, gongs sounding, and a most diabolical band executing in a most execrable manner the Chinese national airs;

ENTERING NINGPO BY THE SALT-GATE.

here we remained drinking tea until we had given him time to announce us at the governor-general's apartments in the public college, where he was residing (in every town there is a college containing apartments always ready for the use of great men who may happen to be on a visit there). We again mounted our chairs and, passing through a dense crowd, arrived at the hall of the college, where we were met by our friend the Taow-tai with whom we proceeded to an inner chamber and were introduced to the governor-general, a fine tall stout healthy-looking old man, with a very good-humoured expression of countenance, wearing spectacles, dressed in the plainest manner, his long robe surmounted by a jacket made of skins of young lambs; to have dressed well would, according to their etiquette, have placed himself on a footing with the consul; he rose to receive us, and shook hands, but did not condescend further.

A dinner was prepared, round which we all sat and conversed, through the medium of Mr. Thom, the best linguist of all the Europeans in China. During the dinner, the governor stated that on the following day he would return Mr. Thom's visit, and at the same time would look at Her Majesty's ship Wolf, but begged to be excused coming on board.

The dinner was much the same as all Chinese dinners, differing only in one particular, viz. that all the attendants wore the dress and buttons of mandarins of the low class.

In consideration of our being allowed to sit, the great man condescended to allow his countryman the Taow-tai to sit down also. The conversation was mostly on the railroads and steamers; our host was a gentleman, but could not conceal a look of incredulity at some of the accounts of the powers of steam. Dinner over, we took our leave, our host rising from his seat, and shaking hands with us, but nothing more.

On the 22nd, at three, a large boat, handsomely painted, and decorated with flags, was seen slowly gliding down the river from the Salt Gate of the town. The walls of the city and the banks of the river were crowded with well-dressed Chinese. Down she came with the governor-general on board and, when nearly abreast of Her Majesty's ship, the crew of which, already aloft, lay out on the yards as the first gun fired, of which three were fired (three constitute a mandarin's salute in China).

We now went on shore to meet him at Mr. Thom's house, where a capital *déjeuner* was prepared; a guard of marines from the ship were drawn up in the court-yard to receive him.

Champagne, sweet wines, and cordials are much preferred to port or sherry by the Chinese; of the former they are very fond. Dinner over, he departed with the same manning yards and salute as on arriving.

Amid the excitement, the report got wind that a review of three thousand men would take place on the grand parade ground, and a party of officers of Her Majesty's ship Wolf, including myself, started off, anxious to be present at so novel a sight. On landing at daylight the Invincibles were in bed, and we were told that his excellency had changed his mind and did not intend holding the review that day, but had postponed it *sine die*. The fact was it

was put off till next day, and the report was circu-
lated to get rid of the English. The device succeeded with all but myself. The next morning at
sunrise found me the only European on the parade.

Three regiments highly distinguished, at least
with mottoes on their respective backs, were advancing in close column towards a temple filled with
mandarins and their attendants. Shortly afterwards,
amid a considerable sensation, appeared his excellency the governor-general, riding on a very sorry
nag. Notwithstanding his age, and awkwardness of
dress, for he wore petticoats, he displayed some
agility in dismounting, which was a signal to all the
mandarins to perform the Ko-tow, or throw themselves flat on their faces, the Taow-tai alone excepted, who falling on his knees at the head of the steps
leading to the temple of the god of war, there
remained until graciously raised by his excellency,
all the other mandarins rising at the same time.
The ceremony of introduction to the superior officers
having been gone through, the review commenced
by each regiment being marched up in front of the
temple, and put through a few manœuvres, the principal of which were changing front by counter-
marching of files, forming squares every now and
then, with a good deal of firing, but very few evolu-
tions. Each regiment is divided into three parts,
the first the artillery, or ginjall men, carrying huge

Q

matchlocks requiring two men to manage; secondly, the musketeers, carrying small matchlocks about the size of a carbine; then the pike men. Every man has also a sword. At the head of each regiment, in advance, were five flagbearers to act as

THREE REGIMENTS IN SQUARE.

fuglemen, bearing each a red flag to repeat the orders of the adjutant-general, who was stationed in a square tower on the left of the temple; over him the national standard (Tai-tsing-kwo), or flag of the great Tsing nation was waving (Tsing, or " pure," is the name of the present dynasty). His orders were given by waving, one at a time, of three flags in different directions, perpendicularly, horizontally, or obliquely, which being repeated by the fuglemen were immediately executed. Thus great regularity prevailed during the whole business, and not a word was spoken; but adjutants' towers are not always conveniently at hand when wanted in actual warfare. The order to fire was waving the black flag horizontally, which being repeated, the fuglemen fell flat on their faces, and rose after the fire. When a regiment had performed any evolution its colonel was called by his excellency and praised or censured according to his merits, the praise apparently much predominating; but if I had been allowed to give an opinion on one point, the less he said on the bands of music the better.

FIRING A VOLLEY.

New colours were presented to each regiment, of which each has three, the principal one carried by a mandarin of superior rank.   The colours of the centre regiment bore the constellation of the great bear on a white field, the other two golden dragons on a green field, one with crimson, the other with yellow borders.   Oranges, apples, nuts, cakes, &c. were hawked about the parade-ground.

The people were exceedingly civil during the whole business, which was more than I expected from so dense a crowd, which might have caught a little excitement from such a display of military glory.

A police force was in attendance to keep the ground clear for the army.   On one occasion I found myself a little ahead of the mob, accompanied by only one Chinaman, which was no sooner seen than a policeman ordered him back, not taking any notice of me; my friend appeared a little indignant, and made some remark, at the same time pointing at me, which was no sooner done than three or four policemen set upon him and threshed the poor devil most unmercifully; I presume he had dared them to turn me off.

CHAPTER XIV.

NAVY.

The Emperor's Opinion of a Sailor's Duty.—Navy on same footing
as Army.—Policy of the Admiral at Amoy during the War.—
Murder of the Inhabitants of Tapeba-Shan.—Coast Surveying.—
Arms of the Navy.—Immense numbers living in Boats.—De-
scription of Junks.—Pleasure Boats.—Canal Travelling.—Grain
Junks.—Itinerant Trades afloat.

In illustrating the Chinese navy, I cannot do
better than give the august opinion of the Son
of Heaven, the Emperor of the World, Reason's
Glory, promulgated on the

17th day, 9th moon,
13th year of Taow-Kwang (the present Emperor).

"On shore a man's ability is measured by his
archery and horsemanship : but a sailor's talent by his
ability to fight both with and on the water ; a sailor
must know the winds, the clouds, the lands, and
the lines of passages among the sands. He must
be thoroughly versed in breaking a spear with, *i. e.*
beating against the winds.

"He must know, like a god, how to break through the billows, handle his ships, and be always in regular order for action; then, when his spears are thrown they will pierce, and his guns will follow to give them effect. The spitting tornado of your powder will all reach truly their mark: and whenever pirates are met with they will be vanquished wondrously. No aim will miss its mark. The pirate banditti will be impoverished and crippled, and even on the higher seas, when they take to flight, they will be caught and slaughtered. Thus the monsters of the deep, and the waves will be still, and the sea becoming a perfect calm, not a ripple will be raised.

"But far different from this has it been of late, the navy is a nullity, there is the name of going to sea, but there is no going to sea in reality. Cases of piracy are perpetually occurring, and even barbarian barks anchor in our inner seas."

The navy is on the same footing as the army, officers have the same title, with the addition of Shuy-tsze, "sons of water;" the actual captain and crew of the vessel are unconnected with the military service, in short, it may be compared to the time of Blake and others, who, at the head of a party of soldiers, embarked as war men, while the navigation was in the hands of the master mariner, boatswain, and crew.

The admiral at Amoy (officially the Te - Tuh Shuy-tsze) although exceedingly fond of visiting H.M.S. always evaded the offer of a return visit to his junk, at the same time he was very anxious that we should come and see him at his residence in the town, of which he was the Foo-Yuen, or, lient.-governor.　He, on one occasion, called to state that a number of pirates had been reported, and that he was going to sea on the following day. Curiosity led us to promise or threaten him with an early visit on his embarkation; this he could not at the moment refuse, but daylight proved his anxiety to have anticipated our intention, admiral, fleet, and all had sailed.

In 1841 the same admiral governed Amoy. Hearing that the barbarian eye was on his way to take the city with a fleet of ships, he solemnly took leave of his countrymen, commended himself and his expedition to the care and favour of the gods, wrote a valiant epistle to the Emperor, stating his intention of annihilating the barbarians in their San pans, i. e. "three planks," and returning victoriously to reap the gracious favours as the fruits of his valour.　Amoy fell, and the admiral's official residence was burnt (by which means a valuable library was lost).　Soon after he returned, he wrote an account to the Emperor of his missing the enemy, and the unfortunate consequence.　The *on dit* was, that he was anchored safely in the Straits of Que moy, within hearing of the cannonade. For his real or supposed valiant intentions his life was spared, but he was condemned to rebuild the house and office at his own expense, and to serve his Imperial Majesty for the space of ten years, without pay or emolument. This man was no coward, or, at least, did not appear so, but he was more enlightened than the generality of his countrymen, and has often expressed his opinions in disgust of his service, and vessels afloat.

Being at anchor off the Tapeba-Shan (the great musical instrument) island in H.M. surveying vessel Plover, in 1843, we were astonished at the arrival, in so remote a situation, of a large fleet of war junks; they entered in two lines, with streamers flying, and gongs beating, the high colours of junks and flags heightened the effect of the splendid scenery. Scarcely had they anchored than a mandarin came on board, stating himself to be the aid-de-camp of his Excellency Liŭ-Yunko, of Wanshing Heen, in the province of Shan-tung, Te-tŭh of the green banner, governor-general, commander-in-chief, and director-general of the commissariat departments of the province of Fuh-kien, to take, burn, and destroy certain nests of furious pirates, of whose depredations complaint had been made by the most influential merchants of the city of Fu-chau. He

congratulated us on hearing no communication had
as yet taken place with the people, as most likely,
he stated, being but few in number, had we landed,
we should have been surrounded and cut to
pieces. After paying his respects to the captain,
whose relative rank was Foo-tseang, or colonel,
and whose name (as the following will explain)
was well known to him, his mission was to beg
that we should on no account interfere between the
pirates and justice, nor even intercede for mercy
on the vagabonds whose lives were forfeited. I
was sent to return the call and compliments, and
found the men under arms, preparing for a landing,
under a canopy in the centre of the deck of the
principal junk: I was introduced to the admiral,
who immediately offered tea and a pipe. He knew
our mission, and asked several questions regarding
it, he said he was about to land in person, and that
before sun-set not a soul now on the island would
be left alive. There was nothing sanguinary in the
appearance of the admiral, yet he kept his word,
and man, woman, and child, to the number of near
five hundred were mercilessly put to the sword.
There was nothing remarkable in the furniture of
his apartment, if a tent on the deck of a vessel
deserves such a name, several lanterns and scrolls
ornamented the sides, a high chair, over which
stood a huge red silk umbrella of state, with three

or four smaller chairs and tables, made up the sum total. He was very civil, and as I quitted from one side, his men being in the boats, he left on the other. We watched from the ship with glasses; the town or village was on the opposite side, and nothing was visible on shore but a few·cultivated fields, to prove that the island was inhabited. Having landed, they marched to the top of a hill without noise, when they beat their gongs, and were soon out of sight. We weighed our anchor, and standing out of the harbour, could distinctly hear the firing, presently a deep volume of smoke arose, which left no doubt in our minds that the mission had been too severely executed.

In regard to the Chinese admiral being acquainted with the captain's name, the supplementary treaty has a clause admitting surveying foreign ships into the inner waters of the coast, provided the Emperor has a faithful copy of the result. The high commissioner, Ke-ying, while on his first visit to Hong-Kong, promised to send the name of the captain of the Plover to the various high officers on the coast, in order that he might be received as of the rank of Foo-tseang, or colonel, and by honour Pa-to-loo, titled brave, or knight (Captain Collinson was a C.B.) which insured him great respect from the mandarins. On one occasion the Foo-yuen of a large city in the Hae-tan straits sent his aid-de-camp to offer his compliments, and to say that, should it be deemed requisite, he would pay the first visit. This aid-de-camp could not be persuaded but that we sold opium, ours being an English vessel, and nothing would convince him but we had it, and were afraid to sell it to him as a government officer: he entreated, grew angry, offered high sums, promised inviolable secrecy to no purpose, and at last left the ship, quite angry at the supposed injury.

As an improvement the Chinese have two or three English-shaped ships that never go outside the Canton river, but they are miserably handled, and filthily dirty. The arms of the navy are the same as the army; their guns are miserably made, mounted on immovable carriages, the powder is brought on deck in a huge red painted case, and, as happened to Admiral Quan's fleet at the Bogue, are not unfrequently blown up in consequence.

An enormous portion of the population of China may be termed amphibious, inasmuch as, except for the purpose of shopping, they are seldom out of their boats; thus, grandsires and a host of children and grandchildren, are the joint inhabitants of the same family-junk; a part of the children's dress is a large gourd tied to the waist, to prevent them from sinking if they fall overboard. Boys and girls, as the first plaything, have small oars with which they imitate the rowing and sculling of their elders, and thus become sailors from their earliest infancy.

In the coasting trade, and in vessels making short voyages, the wives and families form a part of the crew, but on longer expeditions, as to the Malaccas or Luconias, they are left behind.

The word junk is not a Chinese expression, their general name for a vessel, of whatever size, is San-pan, *i. e.* " three planks," which are the three first laid on a foundation for the building, and answers to the keel of our vessels; larger craft are often called Chwan, and Ping Chwan, or " soldier-ship," is the term for a British ship-of-war.

Under the term junk, as used by foreigners in China, are comprised almost every native vessel, from the beautiful pleasure boat of the high man-darin, to the filthy tenement of the water beggar. Anchors are mostly of hard wood, with only one fluke or arm, and the stock lashed on the crown or head of the anchor. The rigging and cables are of bamboo thongs twisted into rope, and the sails of matting. Iron anchors and chain cables are at times, though very rarely, met with, as for instance, in the government grain tribute junks, and in many traders to foreign lands. The large junk is an enormous unwieldy structure, sometimes upwards of a thousand tons; the high poop and forecastle, together with the general build, strongly resemble the pictures of the ancient craft of this country, and representations on old tapestry. Except a small space allotted for the crew in the fore part of the vessel, the whole hull, which is built in compartments, is given up for cargo. Of the sailors who inhabit the fore part there are two distinct kinds, the one Tow-muh, which may be translated "able seamen," have all the seaman's duty to perform, while the other, the Ho-ke, are learning their trade of the former; each has his separate bed-place, like the berth of a steamer, which he is allowed to let if he pleases to a passenger, but the latter shift for themselves as best they can about the decks. Besides the above, and ranking below, are the priest, cook, and barber. Every man has a small share in the vessel, or cargo, and sometimes both.

Over the stern is built the house for the captain and pilot; the captain's duty is more that of a supercargo, and to assist in its execution he has one or more clerks, while the pilot is more properly the captain of the ship, directing her course, &c. Under him are one or more sub-pilots, who may answer to the mates of our merchant vessels. The galley or cooking apparatus is on deck. In times of danger from wind or shore, the confusion can be easier imagined than described, each person having a small share in the vessel conceives he has a right to give his opinion; thus anything occurring out of

the ordinary way is attended with difficulty, and
frequently with accident.

These large junks have from three to four masts
and on each a single sail, so extremely large and
difficult to manage that to hoist it requires the
whole strength of the crew, and is seldom lowered
altogether until the port is gained ; when the wind
freshens it is lowered a reef into slings from the
mast-head, where, from being battened at equal
lengths it lies like a Venetian blind, in convenient
shape.   If the vessel be merely leaving the harbour
for another anchorage, she is towed out by innumerable small boats, and the large sails are not
hoisted.   The rudder is of stupendous size, and in
harbour is raised from the water and covered in
with matting, as also all the sails and cordage.   The
compass is the most direct assistant, the Chinese
pilot having no idea of astronomy beyond the compass bearing of the heavenly bodies, he is otherwise
at a loss for his position, except in sight of land,
which he seldom loses.   Nautical instruments are
unknown to him, though their charts are by no
means so incorrect as their rude appearance might
lead one to suppose, being outlines more of pa-
noramic scenery than tracings of coast surveys.
On a surveying voyage along the coast of China,
in H.M.S. Plover, we had Chinese charts, and
found them useful in many instances, in deter-

mining local pronunciations for the various names, by asking the fishermen to repeat them.

They sound by lead and line marked off to fathoms, and in shoal water by a long bamboo pole.

In the captain's cabin is a small temple to the goddess Kwan-yin, the great patroness of sailors, by whom she is supposed to have been a native of Fuh-keen, (the school of maritime adventure in China,) and to have had a brother, a sailor, whose life she saved from drowning by a miracle. Before the vessel leaves port the deity is taken on shore to the temple, and there oblations and prostrations are made by the captain and pilot, and a play performed in her honour, after which she is taken in great pomp to the junk amid the din of gongs, &c. where theatre, feasting, and illuminations finish the ceremony of the day. During the calms or adverse winds she is constantly applied to, and sacrifices are offered. She is generally accompanied by a few other deities. The bow is sacred, and ornamented by a painting of an eye on each side. Rice is the only food laid in for the crew and passengers, but each is allowed to take with him a certain quantity of live pigs, ducks, fowls, or goats, or dried and salted meats, or vegetables, &c.

Pleasure boats of all sizes abound in the rivers and are elegantly fitted with carving and painting, the crew are in a separate part of the vessel from

the passengers; one of a large size has all the convenience, and somewhat the appearance of a house,
with sitting rooms, bed-rooms, and kitchen, and, on
the top is often a well-laid out parterre of exotics;
the furniture is good, and for pic-nic or other excur-
sions they are very comfortable.

Except by boats, almost all other transport is by
manual labour. The frequency of rivers and canals
gives great occasion for variety in make, shape, and
size of the various boats. The rates of travelling
are cheap; the fare from Ningpo to Chusan, a
distance of twenty-five miles, by passage-boat is
sixty cash or twopence-farthing. All travel on an
equal footing, no fore and after part with its tariff of
prices; the beggar and the merchant may sit together
cheek by jowl, both watching the same property,
but with different views. Robbery must be frequent, but the captain of the vessel is not answer-
able for the loss of property, he merely sticks up a
warning, such as "Look to your purses!" and it is
no business of his if you do not profit by it. Excepting in the hilly countries, there are universally
navigable canals, with good accommodation barges;
for keeping a sufficient depth of water a sloping
dam is made, over which the barge, of perhaps from
one to two thousand tons burthen, is drawn by
means of a rough wooden capstan. The quantity of
fish in these canals is prodigious; one is at a loss to

know how they have not long ago become extinct from the ingenuity that is exercised in taking them, nets, traps, hooks, in every variety, with the fishing cormorant; but the neatest thing that I saw was the mode of catching crabs; the fisherman ties a piece of meat to the end of a stick and puts it into a hole in a bank, when a crab bites he drags it with his right, and, under the hole, extends his left hand, into which the crab falls, and the bait serves again.

Families increasing have often large junks with a tender, *i.e.* a smaller boat, that some members of the family work in, while the other stands in the capacity of a house.

The most ornamental and highly-finished vessels are the government grain junks of from one to two hundred tons burthen. They traverse, by canal, from Pekin to the various cities of the empire, collecting the tribute or grain tax. At Shanghae they arrived to the number of eighty, each ten being under the command of a mandarin of the office of Leang-chow-taow, "superintendant of the grain department." The centre of the deck is raised, in which are suites of apartments for passengers, elegantly furnished; a considerable quantity of carving is lavished on each. The great peculiarity in them is the cut and texture of their sails, which are of cloth; from being divided by laths of bamboo, when set as well as lowered, they resemble in shape the common fan. Each carries a certain quantity of grain for government, according to her tonnage, and the rest of the room belongs to the captain and crew, who, it is said, take at least their full share. When all are full they start together; they are fitted with three sets of masts and sails, the longest for canals, to catch every breeze over the land, and the shorter for the passage of the Poyang and other lakes; in their passage along the canals they are also dragged by men, every district supplying its quota of relays.

Each mandarin has his official boat, and generally a private excursion yacht; these are always known by the flags and the insignia of office in the fore part, as hats and bamboos of the executioners, and heraldic boards.

Notwithstanding their unwieldy appearance many of the junks are good sailers, and the smaller craft turn to windward exceedingly well.

Afloat are many of the cries of itinerant trades, and particularly the barber and the *restaurateur*, while the beggar's tenement is by no means an uncommon one, and their mode of exaction is raising a basket on the end of a pole to the stern, and howling until satisfied.

CHAPTER XV.

NAUTICAL SURVEYS.

Useful information to Captains of Vessels navigating the Chinese waters.—Chusan.—Its approach.—Situation of the Quesans Islands.—Best Entrance to Chusan Harbour.—The South-east Passage.—South Passage.—Passages to Ningpo.—Tahiah River and its three Passages.—Approach to Yang-tse-Keang.—The Ruggeds of Gutzlaff.—The Navigation of the Yang-tse-Keang. —Entrance of the Shanghae River.

THE subject of the present chapter being entirely nautical, I think it right to the non-professional reader to apprise him so; but with the advantage of the able assistance of Lieut. Harry Hewitt, of the Indian navy, who commanded a war steamer during hostilities, and did the state much service in surveying the coast and approaches, and of Mr. Benjamin Hooper, acting master of H.M.S. Wolf, I have thought that the following particulars might be useful to captains of vessels navigating these waters in future.

As a general rule in ascending the Yang-tse-kiang, the southern bank should be kept about two miles distant, and the northern avoided. Should a vessel get on shore, to the southward the ground is firm, but to the northward shifting; and in the case of such mishap, the ship should be instantly shored up and hatchways battened down, the rise and fall being so great as to allow but little time to look about. With a contrary wind put the helm down as soon as the water shoals, particularly on the north side, as the bank is steep.

CHUSAN.

On approaching Chusan from the sea, vessels make the Quesans Islands—eleven in number, besides rocks. The south-easternmost, which is Patahecock, is in lat. 29° 22′ N., and long. 122° 13′ 40″ E. It is four hundred and fifty feet high, and may be known by its being in the shape of a sugar-loaf with the point cut off. The highest part of the large Quesan forms a sharp peak near the western extreme, and is four hundred and ninety feet high. The north-eastern inlet is a narrow cliff; after rounding this the channel lies about N.W. ½ W. ten miles to Starboard Jack, which is a low flat rock with two rocks to the eastward, having the Mouse, a small rock nearly level with the sea at high water, on the starboard hand, and a group of four islands, called the Whelps, on the port. On nearing Starboard Jack you get the Corkers, which are a group of rocks, the eastern ones occasionally covered, but the sea generally breaks on them. Starboard Jack may be passed close to the westward, but off its east end are two rocks. The distance between Starboard Jack and Corkers is about three miles and a half, in five and six fathoms water. From thence to Tree or Top Island (which is one hundred and eighty feet high, and has a pile of stones on the top instead of a tree), the entrance to Gough Passage, a course N. W. $\frac{1}{2}$ N. 10′ will carry you in about six fathoms water, leaving the Tinker and Yanjelt Islands, with large islands of Lowang, on the starboard hand, and Buffaloes Nose on the port. The Tinker is N. 39° E. $1\frac{1}{4}$ from Starboard Jack, a cliff steep rock eighty feet above water. There is a passage between them in $6\frac{1}{2}$, and might be taken, being more to windward. A sunken rock lies S. 56° E. from the Tinker, distant two cables. Lanyits lie three quarters of a mile N. E. of Tinker. There are four large and several smaller ones, the largest about four hundred feet high. Its barren summit forms one of the most remarkable features in the Buffaloes Nose Passage. Sunken rocks extend from both shores. The southern face of Lowang has two deep sandy bays; a reef extends from the point opposite to Lanyit, three cables; a reef also extends from the north extremity of Lanyit, five cables; narrowing the pas-

sage between them to less than a mile. Off the
first bay is a group of rocks south; one mile from
this is a bank with 3¼ on it, to avoid it, in steering
from the Lanyit, keep the island close on board.
Buffaloes Nose is one mile and a quarter from
north to south, and three quarters from east to
west. Off the west extreme lies a small islet. Its
eastern shore rocky; has three peaks on it, the centre one, the highest, being five hundred feet; it is
also perforated near the north extreme. There is
good anchorage in the north-east monsoon close
under Lowang; and between Buffaloes Nose and
the Ploughman, about one mile wide, in from five to
eighteen fathoms. The Ploughman is an even, flat-
topped island, having a reef off its north-east extreme. The best passage from Tree or Top is
Gough's to the westward; it being only one-fourth
of a mile through, and five cables wide, formed by
Fatoo-shan on the east, and the central islands, four
in number on the west. In the passage the shores
are steep, too, and very deep water, but the tide sets
fair through. South of the southern islet of the
central group is a small shoal, of which the lead gives
warning. The course after you are through Gough's
Passage for Keto Point (which is the extreme
north-east point of the main land, very high), will
be N. 41° E., nine miles and a half. Anchorage
will be found anywhere along the Keto shore,

until one mile north of Singlosan, a small islet near the shore, where the water deepens suddenly, and as there is no anchorage beyond this until you get to Elephant Island, or to anchorage north-east from Keto Point, close over on the Chusan shore, in about eight or nine fathoms.   The channel from Gough's to Keto is about four miles wide, and bounded on the south-east by the islands Lowang, Vernon, and Grouss, and Taou-hwa-shan, with channels between them, none of which I should recommend but the south-east, which is south-east from Keto Point and Former.   Between Taon-hwa-shan and Vernon—a description of which will be given hereafter—entering from seaward, about one mile N. N. E. of Keto Point, is Roundabout Island, with a deep, channel between them.

The first of flood-tide between Gough Passage and Keto Point sets from the northward, three hours before it takes its proper direction with the ocean tide.   The best entrance to Chusan harbour is that round Tower Hill, which may be known by its round appearance and high peak of one thousand three hundred and sixty-six feet; the course to its south extreme from Keto Point, or Roundabout Island, will be W. by N. eight miles, passing Deer Island, which may be known by its red appearance, having some small island off its southern face, one, the largest and rather a black islet, called the Deer-

watcher, which, with Elephant Island (known by
its having a long point running from the south extreme due east, resembling the trunk), forms the
south channel, about N. W. by W. from Round-
about; also on the main land on the port hand, the
depth of water varies from thirty-five to one hundred and ten fathoms, and no anchoring ground to
be found. After rounding Tower Hill you may
steer to the eastward for Tea Island, between
Tower Hill and Bell Island, which is the next
island north of Tower Hill, the depth being from
thirty to forty fathoms.   On the north-west side of
Tower Hill is a bank with three to four fathoms
about a cable's length off.   The course from off the
south point of Tower Hill will be northerly, alter-
ing gradually as you get round for three or four
miles. You steer then about east; a ship should
endeavour, on leaving Keto, to start so that on
reaching this place, to have the first of the ebb tide
to go into Chusan; and care should be taken, steering easterly with light winds, that the tides, which
run about four knots at springs, do not set you into
the Archipelago, between Tea Island and Elephant,
where the channel is narrow with foul ground.
The course through the Tea Island channel is about
north, leaving Tea Island on the starboard hand,
and Bell on the port.   There is good anchorage in
this channel, from ten to twelve fathoms.   Ships

remaining here should anchor, before they open the channel, between Bell Island and the south point of Chusan, as the tides are strong and the ground loose. Proceeding from thence to the inner harbour of Tinghai, another anchorage will be found on the Chusan shore, between a canal entrance and Guard-house Island, in from three to eight and twelve fathoms. A sunken rock to the westward of this, with two and a half fathoms, lies south of a small hillock in the valley, and two and a quarter cables from shore. In light winds vessels should avoid the strength of the ebb tide, otherwise they are liable to be set through and out of the south passage, the water being very deep here, from thirty to forty fathoms, but the shores are steep, too. A ledge of rocks extends off the north-east extreme of Tea Island one cable. The entrance to Chusan harbour is between a middle ground, with only two feet on its shoalest part, and Macclesfield Island. The best guide is to steer for Macclesfield Island, till a white post on trumball, touches the north end of Macclesfield, which must be kept on until Tower Hill peak comes on, with the slope upon the south rise of Tea Island, which will carry you in four fathoms; you then steer in, and anchor where convenient. On the western edge of this middle ground the water shoals suddenly.

Latitude of observation at the point abreast of

Guard-House Island, 30° 0' 25" N., long. 122° 5' 18" E. H. W. F. C. 11h. 0. Springs rise twelve feet; neaps, six fathoms. The streams run nearly two hours after high water.

For the south-east passage. If after making Patahecock, and it is desirous to take the south-east passage, a course from Patahecock, N. by E. twenty-three miles, allowing for the set of tide, will take a vessel to its entrance. Along this course will be seen the Lanyits, already described; and the south-east extreme of Lowang, which rises to the height of eight hundred and sixty-five feet, being a conical bare hill with several islands in front. Off the south-east extreme is an island called Tung-luh-san, on which is Beak Head; the island is five miles long; and Beak Head very bluff of black rock. The next is Vernon Island, about two miles and four fifths across; to the eastern extremes these two islands form a channel, which is rather intricate, from a number of islands and rocks near the centre.

The south-east passage lies five miles further northward; it is formed by Vernon Island on the south, and Taou-hwa-shan on the north; the east extreme of the former Island is rugged with large shoulders of granite; there is a cove at this end of the island, which runs in three-quarters of a mile, and would afford good shelter for boats; the passage, till six miles through, is about one mile and a half wide, when six miles in, it narrows to three and a half cables; two small islands, and some rocks on the Taon-hwa-shan shore, and an island with a sharp peak, (half a cable off the northern extreme of which is a rock,) form the boundaries. The shore of Taon-hwa-shan is bold and precipitous; the peak rises one thousand six hundred and eighty feet; near the western end the island is low, rising again at the extreme, where it is surmounted by a peculiar crag. The depth in the channel is sixty fathoms in some parts, and tides very strong; it is eight miles through, and should not be attempted unless the wind is fair through either south-east or north-west; leaving Chusan it would be very advantageous, during the north-west monsoon, for soon getting to sea. It is not safe to attempt it in light winds, or the winds scant, as you are subject to flaws and baffling wind off the high land of Taou-hwa-shan; when through this narrow part, you see Victoria Point and Round-about, and will act as before directed.

Vessels intending to take the south passage, (or Melville as it is mostly termed,) which is situated between Deer Watcher Island, already described, and Elephant, wind and tide not suiting to go into harbour, anchorage will be found abreast of Elephant in sixteen to eighteen fathoms water: the bottom is gravel, and not good holding ground ; but better may be found on a bank between Deer-watcher, and the south-west point of Deer Island, in from seven to fourteen fathoms, about a cable and a half north-west from the Deer-watcher, sandy bottom. From thence the Melville channel lies N. by W. ½ W., the leading mark being Maccles-field Island kept open eastward of the high peak on Chusan. This channel is joined by the Ledge Cap and Black Rocks, and part of Tea Island, on the west hand, and the Deer Islands and Sarah Galley on the east, with deep and uneven sounding, and two sunken rocks, one the Melville with ten feet, and Dundas with nine. There are also very strong eddies in this channel, which adds to the danger, and should not be attempted without a fine commanding fair wind. The marks for Mel-ville Rock are the Cap, a small island which joins the western boundary on the north, the Saddle of Kingtang W. by N., and the Joss-house Hill, at Chusan, showing between Sarah Galley and Trum-ball Island, N. ½ E., Dundas Rock, a tree on the eastern slope of Ta-ken-shan, better known as the eastern of the Sarah Galleys, on with the middle beacon on Tsing-lug-tow, N. E. ¼ E., and north end of Black Rocks, in one with south side of the Cap W. S. W. Another good mark is the Deer-watcher, shut in on the south-west extreme of Deer Island ;

should neither of these marks be seen, you steer in and pass the Ledge and Cap, about half a cable, steer for Macclesfield, and round close, and proceed into the harbour, as before directed. There is another very good channel you come in from the Deer-watcher, and keep Deer Island on board, leaving Sarah Galley and Ta-ken-shan on the port hand, in about a north-east direction the channel is deep, and south-east from the Sarah Galley the mud-bank extends about a cable and a half, gradually decreasing to nothing towards the west end of Ta-ken-shan. The mud-bank runs some distance off the north end of Deer Island, and both steep, to a third of a mile from Ta-ken-Shan is a stone beacon on a rock, which may be passed within half or one-third of a cable; you may then proceed to the westward and round Macclesfield as before into the harbour, or, if the wind is favourable, proceed for the east end of the harbour, which, from the beacon, lies about N. N. W., a good guide would be to keep the Joss-house Hill open of Grave Island. When well up to Grave Island, open the beacon rock in the harbour of Grave Island, and pass eastward of both, and anchor as convenient. From the Deer Island Channel to Grave Island, the soundings decrease to five fathoms, and after passing Grave Island deepen again to irregular soundings with strong eddies. There is good an-

chorage at the back of Trumball and Macclesfield,
in from eleven and a half, to ten, seven, and five
fathoms; the best is Joss-house Hill, well open of
Trumball, and the passage between Trumball and
Macclesfield well open in ten fathoms.

NINGPO.

The Tahiah river is entered by three passages,
formed by the islets called the Triangles, all of
which are difficult.

The first danger in the southern channel, is a
rock which is covered at half-tide, lying N. 70° E.,
two and a half cables from the summit of the
eastern Triangle (Tayew-shan). If the inner Triangle, or Passage Island, is kept open of the south
point of the outer one, this danger will be avoided
(on this rock is a white beacon, and it is called
Nemesis Rock).

Having passed the east point of the outer Triangle, keep it and the middle Triangle close on
board, to avoid a sunken rock with eight feet water
on it, which lies in mid-channel, and to the southward of the latter. When on the reef, a small
island eight miles to the west of Chinhae, is in a
line with the extreme high bluff land beyond it,
then steer to pass half a cable east of the inner
Triangle. Then steer for the foot of the Joss-
house Hill at Chinhae, taking care that the tide

does not set you over to the eastern shore, the water shoaling to two fathoms five cables from that side.

The second passage, or that between the middle and inner Triangle, is perhaps the best of the three. A mud spit extends westerly from the middle Triangle a cable and a half, which will be avoided by keeping the joss-house on the hill open of the west point of the inner Triangle; pass, as before, a cable to the eastward of the latter, which must not be approached nearer than half, or receded from more than a cable's length.

The channel between the inner triangle and the joss-house point, has only two fathoms water: it is, however, the broadest and best for vessels of light draught. The only danger in it is the Tiger's-tail Reef, which lies more than one cable N. 40° W. from the highest part of the inner Triangle. The marks for the Tiger's-tail are Hoowu-Tsiao, or the little peaked islet at the south end of the stakes, in line with River Hill, and also the south-east foot of Joss-house Hill, in line with the first cone. The Joss-house point is steep, and vessels will find good shelter under the fort.

The river is staked across at the entrance under the Joss-house Hill, and there are sunken junks on each side of the opening through them.

Ningpo is eleven and a half miles from Chinhae

by the river, which is nearly straight; the reaches all lying to the southward of west, except one, which is short. There are no dangers; the depth in mid-channel varies from five to two and a quarter fathoms. Vessels, therefore, drawing more than thirteen feet should wait for half flood. The average width of the river is two cables.

At the city the river separates into two branches on the north-west, the other south-west direction, the latter is barely a cable wide, and is crossed by a bridge of boats, a quarter of a mile above the junction. A spit extends from each point at the entrance to the former, and has a depth from two and a half to six fathoms.

YANG-TSE-KEANG.

On leaving Chusan for the northward the small passage formed by Guard-house Island and Tea Island should be passed with a commanding breeze, the object being to round the north-west point of Tea Island as close as possible, and to keep as much on the Tea Island shore as you can, otherwise the tide running here very strong, indeed, is likely to set a vessel into the Bell Island passage which you are recommended not to try, as being dangerous and deep. Keeping the Tea Island still on board anchorage can be found off the Red House, three or four cables by shutting in the Bell Rock passage

from her.   The passage between Tower Hill and
Bell Rock is quite clear, then steer W. by N. to
Just-in-the-way, making allowances for tide.   Anchorage can be procured any where between the
rock and Kingtang south shore, but varies much in
depth.   The bearing N.W.W. one and a half or
two miles from Just-in-the-way will give the best
anchorage in ten to twelve fathoms.   Off the south-
west point of Kingtang are two rocks about a cable's
length : these are the only dangers to be avoided.
Having cleared the island of Kintang the only difficulty in working to the Ruggeds is in the attention
required to the tides, making as much northern as
you can to enable you to make use of the E. S. E.
tide if possible, which sets to the E. S. E. ; flood running W. N. W. about two and a-half knots at neap-
tides, and four at spring tides.   Square Island should
never be brought to the eastward of south, as there
is a middle bank with nine feet water on it, which
lies about three and a-half miles to the north
of it.

After rounding the Volcanoes, and coming up to
the Ruggeds on the western side, a vessel can work
to the N. E. in seven or eight fathoms.   Vessels
should not near the low land of the Yang-tse-Keang
S.E. point, on which are two trees and a hut, nearer
than one mile, as the bank runs off half that distance, but which is very deep.   This point bears

N.W. about ten miles from the Ruggeds (but vesse
are recommended not to go far to the westward,
the tides are likely to set them on to the Han
chow river) and W. by N. of Gutzlaff (where tl
Levant packet was lost, June, 1843).   From tl
point the bank runs off about ten miles east, wor:
ing from the Ruggeds to Gutzlaff. Vessels not dra'
ing more than fifteen or sixteen feet can pass insi(
the Hen and Chickens, and work to the N. E. t
she brings them to bear S. W., and Gutzlaff E. S.I
or S. E. E., when by paying attention to the le;
they can borrow to get a cast on the southe:
shoal, from which she will be about two miles
five fathoms.

On leaving Gutzlaff you are recommended n
to bring it farther to the east than S. E. ; wh(
Gutzlaff bears south twelve miles shape your cour
N. W. for fifteen miles, when you will make tl
low land to the westward covered with grass a:
small bushes here and there.

After passing Gutzlaff in entering the Yang-t;
Kiang you ought to make certain of being able
make the low land before night; or being obliged
anchor, it is therefore better, should there be a prol
bility of not doing so, to anchor Gutzlaff south
near as possible, just in sight, and wait for a favou
able opportunity for starting, with the departu:

The same caution is requisite on leaving the river not to lose sight of the low land without a certainty of making Gutzlaff.

Six miles above the first point is another, on which are several huts and trees, with quantities of cattle constantly grazing. From this the bank runs off a mile and a half; a course of N. W. W., two miles from the south shore, will take you clear, and allowing for the tides you can continue at that distance until within sight of Woosung. Ships in beating either up or down should, as soon as they lessen their water, put the helm down, making each tack about a mile, or a mile and a quarter, as the bank steeps to an angle of forty-five degrees. Well in on the north bank is a low sand island, on which are several huts and small trees. A bearing of this will assist in placing the position of the ship, the principal but being ten miles from Woosung. When about six miles from the entrance of Woosung there are four trees on the bank here : this you can approach to three quarters of a mile. When abreast the soundings deepen to seven or eight fathoms and a half. A mile from the shore are several detached rocks on the edge of the mud flat; by keeping Paou-shan point to the north of W. N. ½ N. you will clear them.

On opening the entrance of the Shanghae river,

on the south point of which is a single tree, you must stand the W. N. W., until the remains of a large fort of grey appearance bears W. S. W., for which you must steer.   On each side are mud banks, with only two fathoms on them : on measuring this channel you will find from seven or eight to four and five fathoms.

On a white patch on the bund, with a black diamond in the centre, or with a pinnacle of the pagoda at Paow-shan, clears you of the south bank, until a square mark, with a red ball in the centre, at the water's edge, by Cornwallis or the Grey Fort, comes in with the centre of three trees (or marks) to the northward of the fort: the marks for clearing the banks in working in or out are the mark on the beach, or with either of the outer trees (or marks).

The three joss-poles of Woosung pagoda S. S. W. will enter the Shanghai river.

Keep on the north side of the river until you pass the second creek, then cross over to the southern and keep the shore boldly on board, passing batteries until you pass the second landing place, when you steer for the centre of the river.   On opening the Soo-chow creek you must be cautious lest the tide set you on to the north bank.

When anchored sixteen miles N. W. $\frac{1}{2}$ W. of Gutzlaff, Amherst Rocks bear E. N. $\frac{1}{2}$ N. 16°. The Ariadne Rock bears N. E. nearly from Gutzlaff about twenty-one miles, and W. S. from Amherst. On approaching from the sea make Saddle Island, and steer for Gutzlaff, the northern bank being too dangerous to be attempted.

CELEBRATION OF THE NEW YEAR AT SHANGHAE.

CHAPTER XVI.

MISCELLANEOUS.

Observance of Festival of the New Year at Shanghae.—Exchange of Compliments.—Visiting Cards.—Address for a Letter.—Business of the Host at a Feast.—Ceremony of making Calls and saluting Friends on the second Day.—Settlement of Disputes deferred to the New Year.—The Button the distinction of the Mandarin.—Badges of distinction.—Small Feet of Chinese Ladies.—Other curious Fancies.—Marriage and its Ceremonies.—Funeral Rites.

> " Each age has deemed the new-born year,
> The fittest time for festal cheer—
> In China, as well as elsewhere."

On the 26th of February, 1845, while walking through the streets of Shaughae, I was startled

by the sound of a serenade, that brought immediately to my mind our Christmas waits, coming
from a band that consisted of five or six performers
on bamboo castanets, wooden drums, &c. Everybody was busily preparing for the approaching festival of the new year that was to commence on
the morrow, The shops were gaily decorated, especially the butchers, who, as with us, displayed
their fattest meat, but it was mostly of pig decked
out with green boughs. We all assembled on the
twenty-seventh at the consulate, and, according to
etiquette, started off in full uniform to pay our respects and congratulations to our numerous native
friends. Everybody visits everybody in gayest attire
and as the ceremony differs a little from our own, a
few particulars may not be out of place : we had, the
day before, sent round our cards printed in Chinese
characters, and a verbal message to name the hour,
when we would do ourselves the honour of paying
our respects to the mandarins punctually. At the
time appointed, we were carried in sedan-chairs,
and most hospitably received with bands and sa-
lutes of guns and gongs, and obliged to make some
show of eating at each visit.

The houses invariably were hung with a diamond-
shaped board, bearing the characters of Fuh, "happiness." After a lapse of two or three days, our
visits were returned, first of all, a messenger brought

the cards, on each of which was simply the names of the mandarin. The following were three that we received from a civil, military, and naval mandarin, respectively, Lan-wei-wan, How-pang-fung, and Shing-ping-yuen. On the morrow, each sent two cards, bearing besides the name, the following sentence, " Bows, congratulates, and wishes happiness this new year," with another which differed according to the rank or office of the visitor. That of the civilian, as follows : " Lan-wei-wan, magistrate of the district of Shanghae, in Sung-Kiang-Fu, in the province of Kiang-tse, graciously raised to the rank of sub-prefect of the great pure dynasty, bows his head, and pays his respects." The colonel's, " How-pang-fung, sub-colonel in command at Shanghae, graciously raised to the rank of coionel," &c., &c., that of the naval, " Shing-ping-Yuen, sub-prefect of the coast-guard of Sung-Kiang-Fu, of the great pure dynasty, &c. &c."

If the former be sent to a native, a compliment is added according to the profession of the party: thus to a merchant, " May your property this year produce ten thousand pieces of gold." To a scholar, " May you this year rise to a golden button."

The ordinary visiting-card from one gentleman to another has the following, " Your younger brother, (here the name,) who stands to receive instruction, bows." An invitation is thus worded, "To-morrow, I shall prepare a little wine, and wait to be illumined by your presence, your friend and pupil, (here the name,) bows and appoints the day."

An address for a letter thus: " I will trouble you to take this to Shanghae, and deliver it to (here the name) open : sent from (here the name.)" On the reverse, " A happy and private letter." It is customary at the end or commencement of the year, for each governor-general, or high-commissioner, to address himself to his imperial majesty, and inquire after his health. When Canton was taken, a card was found in Commissioner Lin's office; the following is, as near as I can recollect, a translation of this laconic epistle: " Lin, (here followed his titles,) on his knees, and performing the Ko-tow, hopes the Son of Heaven is well." To which the Son of Heaven had replied on the same card, and returned it, " I am well. Taou Quan."

I have used the term card ; but the conveyance of all these delicate compliments is a red paper of about four feet in length, by nine inches in breadth, folded up with the inscription on one of the folds. On the day after receiving them, a messenger calls, and they are sent back. If the visitor is to be received with great ceremony, the host meets him at the threshold of the house; if on an equality, at the door of the apartment; if as an inferior, sitting in the room. The same rule is observable on taking leave; but, in the two former cases, the guest at each passage makes a show of trying to prevail upon the host not to come further, each, meanwhile, closing the two fists together and bowing: this in Canton phrase is called the Chin-chin.

At a feast the host always opens the business by presenting to the guests separately a small portion of any particular dish, when they all set to work with exemplary diligence. But to return to the new year, the first day, (27th February,) being unfortunately wet, the people contented themselves with paying their adorations at home to the household gods, instead of going to the temples, and the streets were nearly deserted.

On the 28th, everybody appeared abroad in holiday attire, making calls; the higher orders in sedan chairs, the rest on foot; and whenever a man met a friend he performed the Chin-chin, and bowed his head as low as he could, as is usual, amid festivity. In China, the bands were decidedly a nuisance, and excitement was constantly kept up by a running fire of crackers; shops were closed, and everybody appeared happy, and in the evening all the junks on the rivers and canals were beautifully illuminated. On the 29th I entered the public gardens, with some difficulty, owing to the density of the crowd; the principal object seemed to be to amuse the children, taking them to see sights, purchasing little presents, shewing them peepshows, punch, jugglers, tight-rope dancing, and mountebanks of all sorts. Every child carried some little gift, and I saw the parents of many returning home loaded with gaudy toys that they had purchased, or received as presents. These festivities lasted till the 15th day of the moon, and ended with a grand illumination and procession of lanterns, as in the spring festival of Confucius. I wish I could say that the whole went off as good-humouredly, but on the second day, having returned home early, I witnessed, from on board, a faction fight, that was attended with fatal consequences.

The inhabitants of two villages, situated at the entrance of the Soo-chow creek, had, in the course of the last year, disputed about the right to some land that had been recovered from the river, and, on the affair looking serious, they mutually agreed to postpone their differences to the end of the year, and then settle them by the achievement of a comfortable fight. The heads of the villages accordingly entered into an agreement, in writing, to abide by the result of the battle, which was arranged to come off on the second day of the year, and that neither party should in any way allow a report of the thing to transpire. All arms were to be fair, and accordingly they met, and, after a short struggle with pikes, muskets, agricultural implements, and whatever they could lay their hands on, two, belonging to one of the parties, were wounded and taken prisoners, which was the signal for their comrades to take to their heels and decamp. But the most barbarous part was, that the unfortunate men who had been taken were dragged to the doors of their own houses, and, in sight of their wives and families, most mercilessly butchered, and their houses pulled down, when the soldiers came in and made prisoners of some of the victors. I hope that they met their due.

The new year comes unwelcome to some; it is the season of settling accounts; there is no bankruptcy and insolvent court to whitewash the unfortunate, and woe be to the defaulter. All property must be sold off, and the last farthing exacted, and, if that be not sufficient, the poor debtor, besides bearing the opprobium consequent on his misfortunes, is obliged to apprentice himself, wives, and family, to raise money at the exorbitant rate of three per cent. per month, and sometimes higher, until the whole is paid.

It has been commonly supposed that the colour of the button worn on the lass distinguishes the different grades of the mandarins. This I am inclined to think an error, and that, though the button be the distinction of the mandarin in general, it is not peculiar to any grade. I have seen the lowest military officer wearing a brass button, and the Governor of Chung-chow-fu, the city of which Amoy is the seaport, received in a brass button, also a party of officers, of which I was one, while an officer of a very inferior degree, who came with a message to inquire the object of our visit, wore a white button, hitherto supposed to rank as the third in the empire. Old age, that is to say, a cycle, or sixty years, will entitle a beggar to a brass button. I should rather imagine that the distinction of rank lay in the heraldic badge, in front and behind the body of the dress, consisting of a bird on a civil, and a tiger or other animal on a military officer. Peacocks' feathers are only worn by superior officers, but the boots are the most general badge. Once, at Chusan, calling on Shoo, (who, after four years' degradation, had been restored and made governor of the island, when given up by the British,) to ask his permission to bury a man, who had died of a fever, in a spot formerly used as a burial-ground, but since walled in by order of the mandarins, I entered his audience room, unannounced, and just caught a glimpse of him retreating, boots in hand. Having transferred them to his legs, he re-appeared and told me that, without them, he was not in uniform. They are

universally of black satin, with thick white soles.
When a popular mandarin sends in his resignation
of office, and it is accepted by his imperial majesty,
it not unfrequently happens that he is met, on
the frontiers of his late government, by the heads
of departments, and his boots are formally requested of him, to be deposited in the temple, and, in
return, each makes him a handsome present in
money; this is a great compliment, equivalent to
a presentation of plate with us. The wife of the
mandarin takes rank and title with her lord; her
dress is as magnificent as satin, silk, and embroidery
can make it. The hair is beautifully adorned, and,
as an appendage, is not unfrequently the peacock's
feather, as a badge of rank.

The feet are perhaps the point on which ladies
pique themselves most, and to render them the
most useless to themselves would appear to be the
desideratum of Chinese female happiness, but Chinese only. The Tartars have never adopted the
fashion, and the empress herself wears rationally
large feet; but all the Chinese who can afford it,
and that is nearly the whole female population, except in the environs of Canton, and some other
sea-ports to the southward, cause the unformed bone
of the infant's feet, at a very early age, to be
broken, and the toes bent beneath the palm of
the foot. In this way the foot is bandaged, and

not allowed to grow; the consequences are a very small foot, but a huge unwieldy ankle, and no calf. The pain of the alteration in the direction of the bone, as it forms, frequently kills the sufferer; yet mothers pride themselves on their own feet, and subject their offspring to the same treatment, knowing the pain they must endure. In order to walk, some of these beauties are constrained to totter with the help of a stick, which, with a white powder, used to blanch their countenances, called forth the following verse, from an inspired oriental poet :—

" Pale as rice, and graceful as the bamboo."

Another curious fancy of these ladies, is letting the nails of the fingers grow so long as to render the hands totally useless. I have in my possession a cover, made of white copper, to fit on the finger like a thimble, to protect one nail, of an inch and a half long, which, together with a shoe and its clog, three inches and a half long, was taken out of a respectable house at the storming of Chang-kung-fu. The eyebrows are pencilled with Indian ink, and the eyelashes put into correct shape by the barbers. The ladies of quality are seldom or never seen, but are shut up like Turks; their lives pass in music, tea-drinking, embroidery, smoking, and playing chess. About one in ten of them are educated.

The marriage ceremony is an imperative duty to every Chinese; not to have a son to worship at

his tomb is the dread of all, and the sooner this
difficulty is overcome the better. The terms honourable and illustrious are used to the father, while the
bachelor is looked upon with certain horror. To
the poor man the acquirement of a son is what
he looks forward to, and the hope nerves his arm
to new toils, whereby to acquire a sufficiency to
marry with, *i. e.*, to buy his wife. Sons are looked

A BRIDE.

upon as profitable and honourable, while daughters
as almost the contrary, and the rearing of them
is a matter of question with the parents, literally,
whether it will pay or not ; according to the accom-
plishments of the lady, so is her price or remunera-
tion to the parents. Bearing the same surname is
about the only one bar to marriage in general, and

although this may appear but a trifling one, still, from the few surnames in China, it is a grave impediment.

Marriageable age is from fifteen on either side. A go-between, or public match-maker, frequently arranges the affair, but more commonly it is settled by one of the parents. Mothers not uncommonly in conversation, when in the happy state that those who love their lords wish to be, mutually promise that if of opposite sexes, their offspring shall in due time be man and wife. Love has not often a hand in the matter. The anxious parents of the youth having, by one means or other, procured a bride for him, presents of geese, cakes, samshoo, &c., pass between the families. I was present at the wedding of a worthy grocer, at Chusan, who from time to time, during our stay, had supplied our mess in the general line.

As soon as it was given out that he was going to marry, all friends of various grades sent congratulating cards, enclosing, each according to his means, from a hundred to a thousand or more Le cash; this he told me was purchasing a seat at the bridal feast for the donor and his wife.

Early in the morning the young female friends attend to dress the bride and weep; why the latter, I know not. When all is ready, the bride enters a

BRIDE'S FEAST.

carved red and gilt sedan (to be hired in all villages, and used for marriages only). First walk the band, not very emblematic of harmony perhaps, but that does not matter, followed by the household goods and wearing apparel of the bride, carried in red painted boxes, attended by her relations and friends. When arrived at the house of the bridegroom, he opens the door of the sedan, and, receiving his bride, steps with her over a pan of charcoal, conveniently placed on the threshold, then, entering the house, they eat rice and drink tea together; which, with some verbal promises, completes the nuptials. On calling on the bridegroom at his residence, and expressing a wish to see the bride, I was ushered into a well-furnished apartment, about which were strewed the newly

BRIDE AND BRIDAL CHAMBER.

arrived effects, and on one side a new grand bed-stead, ornamented with red and gold; in front of it, arrayed in a dress of red silk, and head-dress of gilt and silk, stood the bride, attended by her female friends; this is the ceremonial costume, and often hired, beneath which she is attired in silks and satins. Having been presented, and taken the liberty of presenting to the lady a small English purse, which was thankfully received, I made my bow and took leave of her. I next joined the bride-groom at an entertainment given to his friends (*i. e.*, all who had sent cards and money). Much samshoo was drank, and after the feasting was over a kind of game was played, one party threw out a number of fingers, and called them; while at the same time the other anticipated, and threw out

BRIDEGROOM'S FEAST.

a similar number, the failure in doing so incurred the obligation of drinking off a cup of samshoo. In another apartment, at the same time, the bride entertained her friends.

In the evening a temporary theatre is erected in front of the house; and performances, fireworks, and the din of gongs and music lasts till daylight, when all disperse. On the following day servants, sedan-bearers, performers, and all who have waited the day before are feasted, and thus ends the ceremony. The bride becomes the slave of her lord, whom perhaps she has never seen before. If her mother-in-law be alive, she becomes only second in the household, being entirely under the guidance of her mother-in-law for her life. And

THEATRICAL PERFORMANCE AT A MARRIAGE.

should she not in due season present her lord with an offspring, or should repeated presentations prove females he is by law at liberty to take a concubine, whose position in household affairs is secondary to the wife's; and again, should that lady prove barren, or not produce a male, a second or more follow. But it is not lawful for a man to put aside his wife and marry one of these concubines. But matrimony is not always the realization of hope, as I trust it was with my friend the grocer. A merchant in Ningpo having seen and admired the fair daughter of a fellow townsman, got his parents to arrange a marriage; when all was ready, he opened the bridal chair, and led into the house his intended's sister, who was not only ugly, but

terribly pitted with small pox: it was too late
to retreat, he had got her for better and worse, and
there was no redress obtainable. I heard the story
from the poor fellow's own lips.

There is a little story, I believe, hitherto untranslated, in a collection of tales of filial piety,
which may illustrate the feelings of parents towards their male offspring. The following is an
outline: — A mother and son, with his wife and
their son, living together in the last stage of poverty, the son and daughter-in-law consult together
upon the state of affairs, and agree that the small
store by them cannot support them all; but that,
unless something be done, there is danger of their
all dying of starvation. The first thought is to
kill their young offspring; but the wife urges that
the old mother cannot, in the common course
of nature, last long, and that it would be better
to sacrifice her first, and try whether the diminished number cannot survive until better times.
This is agreed upon between them, and that the
old lady may not want for the proper rites of
burial, the son goes forward previously to dig her
grave, when the first stroke of his spade uncovers
a large amount of sycee silver and a scroll, informing him that such is the reward that Buddha
sends to such piety as would not spare a mother
to save a son.

There is an old saying, that to render life perfectly happy, it is necessary to be born at Soo-Choo to be handsome; to live at Canton to be luxurious; and to die in the province of Keang-tsu, whose forests produce beautiful wood for making coffins. The coffin is mostly provided before death, and retained in the house sometimes for years, generally richly carved, painted, and decorated, of huge dimensions, and, when occupied, cemented down.

No sooner is the breath out of a man's body, than a message is sent to announce it to all relations; and women are hired to wail and lament; seated on each side of the coffin, clothed in sack-cloth and white garments, they howl and cry without cessation, assisted by the female relations of the deceased on their arrival. If a father dies, the eldest son, supported by his friends, carries a basin with some small money to the nearest well—throwing in the coin, he draws some water with which the body and face of the deceased are washed. This ceremony is performed by the nearest of kin. On the second day priests attend, and erecting an altar in the hall of ancestors, present offerings, and perform prostrations to the household gods for the welfare of the soul of the deceased, in which ceremony the females, clothed entirely in white, also attend, while the nearest male relations perform the Ko-tow, and repeat prayers to the most dismal tune.

No sooner is this ceremony over than three guns are fired to conclude the ceremony for the day, in honour of the deceased, which is followed by a wake.

On the outside of the door of the house is pasted a yellow paper, setting forth the virtues, rank, &c. of the deceased; and all friends call to condole with the bereaved, who not unfrequently answer these attentions by a placard some days after, also pasted on the front of the house, " thanking all parties for kind inquiries."

After the washing, the body is placed in the coffin, and a tablet bearing the inscription intended for the tombstone placed thereon: these tablets are of wood, painted red and gold, with a black field for the inscription, which is in gold cha-racters. The inscription for a male runs thus, "(after the name,) the deceased, who shone illus-trious in his days, finished his state of probation in the seventh day, second moon, twenty-third year of Taow-Kwang, in the dynasty of Ts'hing.".

The oblations and prostrations of priests and relatives, together with the lamentations of hire-lings, music and feasting, last for seven days with-out cessation, and off and on till the twenty-first, when the coffin is taken out to the burial-place.

In front march a band, then some small banners borne by boys, priests, and a sedan-chair, bearing the tablet and dress, boots, shoes, and stockings especially, together with all the insignia of office of the deceased, preceding the coffin, with which as mourners are the deceased's male friends and relations dressed in white and sackcloth; following are the female relations, who waddling along Ko-tow and howl incessantly. The coffin is placed above or below ground, and built over, or otherwise, according to the wealth of the deceased's kindred. In Kwangtung each family has its mausoleum, the ground plan of which is in shape of a capital omega, Ω, built of stone or brick, with a courtyard in front, the whole enclosed by a low wall. In the middle provinces the tombs are built round the coffins, generally of one generation of a family, and surmounted by a mound of earth, from the top of which grow clusters of strong grass, and surrounded by trees, much similar in appearance to an ice-house in a gentleman's park in England; while in the northern provinces three mounds of earth, in a large enclosure of trees, form the burial place of a clan. In all cases a stone tablet is raised to each individual, and placed in front of the tomb.

In the vicinity of large towns are public burial places, in which the poor are placed under ground, somewhat similarly to the mode in this country, marked with a headstone. Soldiers are so buried, and over the grave is an oval stone, on which is painted, in front, the name of the deceased, and in rear that of his regiment. The scattered bones of the ancestors of poor people are collected and placed in large chatties, each bearing inscriptions, and, in some instances, if the relations are very poor, the coffin is placed on a bench in the field, with only a little straw or grass to protect it from rain and weather. At Shanghae, when the English merchants bought land on which to erect their factories, whenever it interfered with a burial place, (and there are scarcely a thousand yards together, all over China, that does not,) they had to pay extra to the relatives for the expense and trouble they were at in removing the coffin, and providing them with new ground.

Where there is a large water population, there are houses of reception for the coffins of those who were not land-holders. These coffins, which are handsomely decorated, are on stools in line on both sides of long rooms, as close as they can be ranged together. Here they are visited by the friends of the deceased, and candles and other offerings burnt in honour of them.

After the coffin is placed, the wooden tablet is brought back to the house and formally placed with the others of the family in the hall of ancestors, and incense burnt before it; a feast closes the day, and until the forty-ninth day after the death, offerings and prostrations are made to it morning and evening, when the ceremony ends, only revived in the feast of the dead, when houses, clothes, money, and every imaginable want, in paper imitation, is burnt, being supposed by the relatives to be carried in reality by invisible spirits for the use of their friends in the next world.

CHAPTER XVII.

THE TREATY AND TAKING POSSESSION OF LABUAN.

Conquest of Labuan.—Situation of the Town.—Murders committed by order of the Sultan.—Cession of Labuan to the British Government. — Taking possession in the name of Queen Victoria.—Speech of Captain Mundy on the occasion.—Character of the Sultan.—His overreaching Conduct.—Pedigree of his Family.

THE large island of Borneo is said to have been conquered some 380 years ago by the Malays: how far they may have extended their conquests inland is not known, but the whole line of coast is in their possession. These Malays are at present in many separate governments, but at the head of all, not so much in a political as a religious sense is the Sultan of Borneo Proper, Omar Ali. A high Mussulman is looked upon as the religious chief of chiefs. His capital is situated about twenty miles up the Brunè river, which name it takes.

The town stands out on the river, and is built on piles: the branches of the river form the four principal streets. Each house, which is built of wood and mats, has a ladder to the water, and all exit must be made in boats. The mosque, surmounted by flags, and the home of Pangeran Moormëen, the prime minister or grand vizier, are in the principal street, but cut a very sorry figure: the dwellings appeared but miserable, as also the inhabitants, who paddle about in their canoes almost naked.

The Sultan caused to be murdered his uncle, the Pangeran Muda Hussim, and several others, who were known to be friends of the British. Partly to avenge their deaths, and partly to punish some acts of piracy, and an attempt to murder Captain Egerton, the forts in the River Brunè were destroyed, with the loss of thirty or forty guns taken, and the town of Brunè deserted by the Sultan and his subjects. A promise was then held out of putting an end to hostilities, provided the Sultan would give up his piracies, and cede the island of Labuan, situated at the mouth of the Brunè, to the British for ever.

The admiral, having communicated with government, despatched H. M. S. Iris and Wolf, on the 1st of December, 1846, to Brunè, there to conclude a treaty, and thus take formal possession of the island. On the 10th of December, the ships being anchored off the island of Mora, at the entrance, the boats of the Iris, in command of Lieut. (now Commander) Little, those of the Wolf, under

my command, started at nine in the morning for
Brunè. The scenery on the banks is remarkably
beautiful in many parts; numbers of small canoes
skimmed the river, while every here and there
smoke rising among the trees, or a canoe or two
moored to the bushes, told of the vicinity of a
small concealed village.

About eleven we anchored in line off the Sultan's
house, and as Captain Mundy landed, the men in
the boat stood up and took their hats off, and a guard
of marines saluted him, when the Sultan, Pangeran, and several of the higher classes, received him
on the wharf.

In the centre of his hall of audience, a plain barn-
like room, with a matted floor, sat his majesty Omar
Ali, Sultan of Borneo, dressed in a jacket of yellow
crape, slashed with satin, a turban of black and gold,
and black inexpressibles. Behind him stood his
sword and betel bearers, and other attendants, with
horsetails, much the same as those worn in state by
Pachas in Turkey. The only other Malay seated
on a chair was the Pangeran (or prince) Moormëen.
The treaty was explained by Lieut. Heath as interpreter (it being written in Arabic, the Malay
written character). After much discussion between
the Sultan and the gentry seated around, orders
were given to the chancellor, another Pangeran,
to prepare the seal (which was made of metal and

inserted in Arabic characters) : this he did by holding it over a huge candle, made of pure beeswax; when well blacked he rubbed it smooth, then, having wet the parchment, he pressed it thereon. This leaves the characters white on a black field.

Conversation now turned upon the relative advantages and disadvantages to be derived by both parties. Trade, it was agreed, would materially benefit both sides, as, on the one hand, the Malay would be clothed, while, on the other, gold, antimony, diamonds, coal, sago, pepper, and beeswax would be plentifully supplied to the British. Under the head disadvantage to the chiefs was mentioned the loss of their slaves, who would no doubt flee to British ground; on our side the climate, as it rains six months in the year.

TAKING POSSESSION OF LABUAN.

On the 24th of Dec., 1846, at 8 A. M., H. M. S. Iris and Wolf, being at anchor in the harbour of Labuan, crossed top-gallant-yards and dressed. At 1 the small arms-men and marines landed, the flagstaff having been previously erected, the marines lined the path leading to it, while the seamen were drawn up in a line facing the water. At the foot of the flag-staff was placed a stone, setting forth that, "On the 24th Dec., 1846, this island was taken possession of, in the name of Victoria, Queen, &c., by order of Sir Thomas Cochrane, &c., and Captain R. Mundy, of H. M. S. Iris." At 1, 30, Captains Mundy and Gordon, with Pangeran Moormëen and suite landed, and passing through the line, ascended a raised platform, where, under the shade of two huge umbrellas, Captain Mundy delivered the following speech, which was translated into Malay, by Lieutenant (now Commander) Heath. "Let it be known to all here present that on this day I take possession of this Island of Labuan, and the islands adjacent, in the name of her Majesty Queen Victoria, by order of Sir Thomas Cochrane. You are therefore now standing on British ground. People of all nations will be protected by the English nation. The English Admiral will order his steamers and ships to destroy all pirates by land or by sea, killing them and burning their villages. The Sultan of Borneo and the Queen of England are now friends. Pirates making war against him will be destroyed by the great English nation."

At the end of this speech the flag was gradually hoisted together with several others about the beach. Immediately on its reaching the head of the staff, the ships commenced firing, which was soon answered by a four-gun battery on shore, and volleys from the small-arm men and marines, as the last gun fired, all "right about face," and gave three hearty cheers.   This ended the ceremony of taking possession, but not the day.

A cold collation having been prepared by Captain Mundy, we all assembled under a marquee, eight Pangerans honoured us with their company, and drank her Majesty's health; they left at about four o'clock.

One of the Malays had stolen a bottle, and being licked for it was fool enough not to be satisfied, but complained to Pangeran Moormëen, who seized a stick from the beach and broke it over his back, and then told Captain Mundy that if he were not satisfied with that, he would order him to be decapitated on the spot,—a very kind offer, but it was declined.   Having reached their boats, they set sail for Brunè, and we returned to the marquee, to finish dinner, and spend the evening.

The island of Labuan is low and much wooded, about thirty miles in circumference.   Fresh water abounds.

On the 21st, Captain Mundy sent me to Borneo, to purchase bullocks.   My interview with his majesty shewed me royalty under a new aspect. We arrived on the morning of the 22nd, off the Palace, and immediately landed, and were met by a Pangeran, who invited us to go and be presented to the Sultan—the Omar Ali of private life *—an

* An ugly little man with two thumbs on his right hand, about forty-five years of age.

U

imbecile, but with all the sly cunning that is now and then seen supplying the want of common sense ; a smart man at a bargain, who might let any Jewish pedlar in for a wrinkle or two, at the same time an overgrown baby, who asked for everything he saw.   No sooner was I seated in his august presence than he ordered six fowls and rice of two kinds to be sent to the boat for our breakfasts, and then inquired the reason of our visit, and promised to let us have seven bullocks, at two pieces of calico per head.   After which, I returned to the boat to breakfast; I had scarcely got there, when his majesty sent to beg bread, cigars, copper caps, and sugar, and I sent a small quantity of each.   Then he sent for me, and having finished my breakfast, I went, when he asked me for everything he could see, and obtained the buttons off my coat, a pair of flannel trowsers, a pen-knife, a looking glass, and a small spy-glass, for which he promised me a kris, in fourteen days.   Determined to have something at once to shew, I asked him for his autograph, but he told me that Sultans never signed but sealed, I asked for and obtained the impression of his seal, made as above.   He then asked me to fire at a mark with my musket, which I did, and he in return shewed me his weapons, consisting of a kris, about two feet long; a spear, eight feet ; an Illanun sword, a kind of scymetar, four feet long ; a supitan, six feet, this is a spear with a hollow staff, like the cherry-stick of a Turk's pipe, made of iron wood, with a bundle attached to it containing the poisoned arrows, which are small pieces of cane very sharp, and about ten inches long; they are put into the mouth and blown through the staff with considerable force, and I have a Malay's authority for saying that if not within the sound of a gong, they carry certain death; a gun, four feet long; a shield, made of wood and fish skin, six feet; and the state sword, three feet,—mere tinsel.

Having done this, he asked for everything he could think of, but I had nothing more to give him. He begged soap from the men, one of whom, finding himself on such easy terms, thought he might sit down without taking any very great liberty with a man who would ask him how he was off for soap? and did so accordingly in a chair I had just vacated; but he reckoned without his host, whose royal blood immediately was up, and who became the monarch again. He rushed forward, and seized him with his own royal hands, and dragged him out. All his subjects entering his presence squat on their hams, then lifting their hands, clasped together, to the forehead, bend until the hands nearly reach the ground. Having now been with him nearly all day, I went to the boat and brought out a bottle of sherry, intending, as

I thought, to share it with him, but his majesty thought differently, and I confess he *did* me, for he seized the bottle immediately, and ordered one of his servants to take it into the harem, telling me that he was a good Mussulman, and so could not drink in company, but would drink my health that night. During the whole day he either chewed betel-nut and tobacco, or smoked cigars; he offered me cakes and tea, which, of course, I accepted. He wrote my name on the back of an old book, as he assured me, I rather thought it more likely to be " Omar Ali, his mark." I doubt whether he can write, as, wishing while I was with him to send off a letter on business, he ordered one of his ministers to write it, and he himself merely sealed without reading it. As it was beginning to get dark, I jogged his memory about the bullocks, when he told me that unfortunately he could only get two, and asked for the cloth for them beforehand. It was rash, I own, but I let him have it to expedite business, and two bullocks made their appearance, one good and one very bad. I took them to the boat, and then sent the interpreter to tell his majesty I was very angry with him for cheating me in the way he had done, after promising large bullocks, and that unless reparation were made, I should relate the whole of the circumstances to the captain. A change came o'er the spirit of his dream, and he immediately sent a very fine one in place of the lean kine, and I went up to take leave of him. We parted the best of friends, he did not shew any angry feeling at my having accused him of cheating me—not in the least, he knew it before, and volunteered a promise that the kris should be forthcoming in fourteen days, and deceived me again, for he kept his word this time.

There is no money as yet in circulation in Borneo, trade is carried on by barter, a fathom's length of cloth is the price of a fowl or duck, six of a goat, ten of a calf, two pieces a bullock. An empty bottle five eggs, or a heap of vegetables.

The following is the pedigree of Omar Ali.

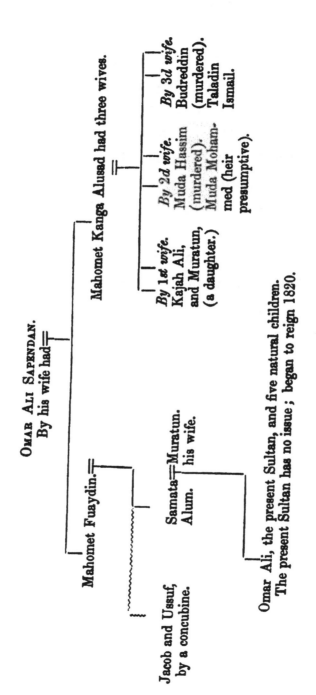

OMAR ALI SAPENDAN.
By his wife had

Mahomet Kanga Alusad had three wives.

By 1st wife.
Kajah Ali,
and Muratun,
(a daughter.)

By 2d wife.
Muda Hassim
(murdered).
Muda Moham-
med (heir
presumptive).

By 3d wife.
Budreddin
(murdered).
Taladin
Ismail.

Mahomet Fuaydin.

Jacob and Ussuf,
by a concubine.

Samata═Muratun.
Alum.   his wife.

Omar Ali, the present Sultan, and five natural children.
The present Sultan has no issue ; began to reign 1820.

CHAPTER XVIII.

MASSACRE OF BRUNÉ.

Despatch received from the Sultan by the British Authorities.—Translation.—The Pangeran Suliman's Tale.—Arrival of Captain Heath.—Settlement of the Disputes.

ON the 11th of February Pangeran Illeman delivered a despatch from his master, the Sultan, stating at the same time that his highness had been much disturbed by the threats of an anti-foreign party, who had been formerly expelled, but had lately returned to the city of Brunè, and were in the habit of prowling about at night, firing off muskets, and creating other disturbances, until they had become so bold as to threaten the royal person; and they were nightly expected to fire the palace. He said that the Sultan bade him explain that these desperadoes were to him as a sort of nightmare.

The despatch was written in Arabic, and translated as follows :—

" Whereas this friendly epistle, which springs

from a white heart, and from a heart filled with purity; that is to say, from the Sultan Omar-Ali-sep-Aldin, son of the deceased royal Sultan, Mahomed, the elegance of the world.

" May it please the Lord of all the hosts in the world, to cause this to arrive before the beautiful countenance of our dear friend, Captain Heath, the high officer who is appointed by the Queen Rajah of Europe, and who is all-powerful in the island of Labuan.

" We now send word to you, our dear friend, that Hadji Samun is in our royal city of Brunè, for we have heard it from Nakhoda Ruhsid. This we have but lately known of with certainty; now we wish to perform our duty (appointed to us), but we are not strong enough,* and we are afraid shall get blamed by our dear friend.† Thus, then, enough is known to our dear friend.

" What may be the wish of our dear friend that we should do?

" That we shall deliver him unto our dear friend.

---

* When Captain Heath had read thus far, the Pangeran said he had to explain that the powder-magazine of Brunè was but poorly stocked; and that since the war the muskets had become rusty and old.

† After all had been settled, the Sultan confessed that he had no fear of Hadji Samun and his party; but he was much afraid, unless he discountenanced his return, of the anger of Mr. Brooke and the admiral.

"We have nothing to add, but many many compliments.

"The Hope which protected us is gone."

This was sealed with the royal seal; and in consequence acting Commander Heath proceeded to Brunè in H. M. S. Wolf, and left me in charge of the Island of Labuan.

The following account was given me by Pangeran Suliman, of the causes of the bad odour in which Hadji Samun now stood at the court of Brunè.

"Before Mr. Brooke * obtained the patent of Rajah of the Sarawak, an uncle of the Sultan's had reigned over it, named Muda Hassim, who, with his brother Budreddin, returned to Brunè with a strong prejudice in favour of Mr. Brooke. The Sultan being in reality an imbecile, the duties of the government were in a great measure in the hands of the uncle Pangerans, and the consequence was, that for some time a strong party grew

* The Rajah of Sarawak needs no eulogium from me. I have the honour of his acquaintance, and know that his modesty would shrink from anything of the kind. I shall merely say here, that though what he has already achieved be almost super-human; yet the effects of his policy are still to be seen, and if his own generation do not reap the full benefit of it, another will acknowledge him as perhaps the greatest, wisest, and ablest in the long catalogue of heroes that illumine the history of the British empire in the east.

up in Brunè in favour of the foreigner; that Budreddin presuming on British protection, became
proud and overbearing in the extreme, and this
made innumerable enemies among the most bold,
of whom was Hadji Samun, whose self-gained rank
of Hadji gave him a high position, as not many
could boast of having travelled to Mecca; and from
a poor man he gradually placed himself at the
head of a strong faction, whose efforts had well-
nigh dethroned the reigning sovereign.

"Opportunity alone was wanted, on the part of
the Hadji, to act on the offensive, which he had not
long to wait for, having rendered himself amena-
ble to punishment on the evening preceding the
day appointed for his trial. The Hadji held a
council of his friends, and having through treachery obtained the Sultan's seal to a document,
authorising him to put to death both the Pangerans, he soon obtained assistance, and, arriving at
two in the morning, proceeded to the attack.

" Arrived at the houses of the Pangerans, which
adjoined, they planted cannon at all corners, then
surrounding and making holes in the roofs, kept
up a constant fire on the inmates, which was returned with much spirit. Such was the cowardly
disposition of the Pangerans' friends, that they
feared to attempt a rescue, and so gallantly was
the house of Muda Hassim defended, to which

Budreddin and his family had retreated, that noon, the following day, found both Pangerans much wounded, but still fighting. After a council of war, it was agreed that the house must soon fall, therefore despatching a favourite domestic named Jaffa, with his signet ring, to give to Rajah Brooke, and beg him to avenge their death, Muda Hassim, collecting his own and his brother's family round a barrel of powder, and commending themselves to the Lord of Hosts, fired a pistol, and committed thirty-five souls into eternity.

"The explosion had scarcely taken place, when a re-action occurred among the citizens of Brunè, and Hadji Samun scarcely escaped with a few followers to the Nambacos river, where he was discomfited a short time after by Captain Mundy, in H.M.S. Iris, and his forts destroyed." Such was the Pangeran Suliman's tale.

Jaffa reached H.M.S. Hazard at a moment when her captain was stepping into his gig on his way to Brunè (which was only twelve miles distant), a letter purporting to be from the Sultan asking him to visit having arrived.

Jaffa's tale was soon told, and the Hazard sailed immediately in search of the admiral, who, arriving shortly after, destroyed the forts and took possession of the royal city, and there offered terms to the absent Sultan, who, though known to be an imbecile, is looked upon with extraordinary awe and majesty by his subjects, by whom he is thought to be in the keeping of divine power, the Pangeran Moormëen, the prime minister, expressing himself to the effect that the Sultan's body was sacred and beyond the reach of harm.

From the above it may not appear extraordinary that the Sultan should feel a little uneasiness regarding the return of the refractory Hadji.

Arrived at Brunè, his Highness Omar Ali received Captain Heath with strong demonstrations of joy at the prompt way in which he had acted, and a conference ensued, in which it transpired that Hadji Samun had married the daughter of the Nakhoda, *i. e.* "gentleman," Rahsid, and, with his adherents, was living at the Nakhoda's expense. The question of British interference was a delicate one, as the home despatches forbade it; while the speech, on taking possession of Labuan, might be construed by the Malay into a right of protection from the enemies of the Sultan.

After some preamble it was agreed that the court writer should indite a declaration, and the Nakhoda sign it in presence of witnesses on both sides, the Sultan not appearing.

Entering the court-house with the prime minister, Pangeran Moormëen, Captain Heath called for Nakhoda Rahsid, who protested against the truth of the charges laid against his son-in-law, stating his behaviour since his return to have been decorous in the extreme, and his return, caused by almost starvation ; and promising to become security for his good behaviour in future, he affixed his mark to the following statement.

" Whereas, this is a writing of agreement between Captain Heath and Nakhoda Rahsid.

" If Hadji Samun, or Hadji Mohammed, or Li Asmad, or Stamid, or Sikendal, make disturbances in the city of Brunè upon any pretence whatsoever, or stir up others by slanderous words, I, Nakhoda Rahsid, will bear the penalty.

" Signatures,

" PANGERAN MOORMEEN, { Bintang Chinese merchant.

" Lieutenants HEARD and HERVEY,

" And all the Rajahs (of the blood),

" And all the Pangerans (princes),

" And all the Orangkajas (governors),

" And all the Nakhodas (gentlemen),

" And all the people."

Thus the Hadji remained in Brunè.

CHAPTER XIX.

MANNERS AND CUSTOMS OF THE BORNEO MALA

The Malays a proud Race. — Their Character. — Descripti
Borneo.—Its Products.—Household Furniture.—Dress o
Malays. — Their Indolence. — Arabic the character of
Writing.—Learning.—Marriage.—Mode of Burial.—Religi
Orang Caya, or Superintendant of a District.

THE Malays in general are a proud race;
much more so than those who remain at home
the descendants of the conquerors of Borneo.
immense island is almost environed by Ma
while the interior is still in the hands of
Aborigines, who constantly make war upon
another. The pride of the Malay is to be trace
the very sands he walks upon; head erect, the
of the foot never shows in the print. Ragged
dirty as he may be, he is still a Malay and Mol
medan; and consequently, far in advance o
Christians and followers of other prophets. On
Chinese he looks with the most sovereign conte
In temper, the Malay is sulky; in character

is treacherous, zealous, suspicious, and indolent. But Bornese habits have been materially changed of late years; formerly the Sultans were sea-kings, whose wealth and power lay in the number of their fleet and fighting men. Their possessions were frontiered by a fierce race of Dyaks, or other Aborigines, with whom they were continually at war. A partial truce with their unquiet neighbours would be taken advantage of by the Sultan; who, at the head of a chosen number of followers, would put to sea, and declare war with the world afloat; surrounding the enemy in such numbers, that a merchant vessel (and even a Spanish frigate and gun-boat on one occasion) had no chance whatever. But English arms have at last nearly cleared the seas of these pirates, and policy has settled the disputes on shore, so that now they till the ground, and labour honestly for their bread, and have seldom recourse to arms, except in civil war, or secret murder; neither of which are uncommon. Formerly a piece of ground was cleared, and the crop having been taken, it was allowed to rest for seven years, when it would again be cleared and cultivated; but now that they are obliged to provide for themselves, the ground has a heavier demand made on it.

Borneo is productive of gold, diamonds, crystal, copper, iron, loadstone, tin, and antimony; diamonds in alluvial soil, and deposits near the base of mountains, also in sandstone, and the sand mountains of Ponteanak, (a Dutch settlement) and Banjan-Massing.

Gold is found, in grains, in alluvial soil, and in the sands of the rivers; also in the mines of Salak, Sukadon, Tampazook, Matam, and many other places.

Tin is said to be found at Sarawak; copper at Mandore, in Pontianak; rock crystal, called water diamond, at Sulo and Kaman; loadstone at Pulo Bongorong. But none of these mines are worked by Malays. Chinese emigrants from Canton, have in many instances made a fine harvest, but at great risk from their treacherous neighbours.

Nature has been bountiful to this indolent race, fruits of all kinds to be found within the tropics, grow wild, as also sago, pepper, and tobacco, which form articles of trade; vegetables are very inferior for want of cultivation, as is also the sugar cane.

They exercise no trades except those of boat-builders, and a few blacksmiths, or armourers.

The women can sew, but there is no spinning wheel, or other household instrument in Borneo.

The seas abound in fish, which form the principal animal food. Rice is the staple, while curries of fowls, eggs, or vegetables are much in use. The flesh of animals, or as we call it butcher's meat, is seldom used, excepting dried deer's flesh, which is esteemed a luxury. Sweetmeats are much in demand, made of coarse sugar, from the scarcely cultivated sugar-cane, and rice fried in cocoa-nut oil. Fish is preferred salt, and of a high flavour. They have ducks, which they keep for their eggs; and also bullocks and goats; but as Mohammedans, no pigs.

Their drinks are either plain water, or sherbet, rice-water, and cocoa-nut milk. Tea and spirits are neither made, nor amongst these orthodox Mussulmen allowed.

The house is raised about six feet from the water or ground, consisting of four or six rooms, lofty, thatched, and matted. The flooring is of split palm trees, the round part uppermost, which throws off the dirt, and consequently keeps the room moderately clean. Those of the Pangerans are matted, but the furniture is very scanty indeed, as the natives all squat on their hams, or mats; each mat is supplied with a pillow. Around the sides are arranged the krisses, spears, shields, &c., but no other ornaments, and few household utensils; fingers being a prior invention to forks and spoons, they keep up the older custom sanctioned by the wisdom of their ancestors.

The Malay is a fop in his dress, *sans doute*, as the gayer the colour, the more it is preferred. The dress consists of a short, peculiarly-made jacket, and loose inexpressibles, fastened by a red sash, in which is stuck the invariable kris. On the head is a turban, all these are of colours to please the wearer. There is no linen or flannel, and no shoes; but on the fingers are generally some two or three rings, roughly made of silver or gold, having a diamond, or a species of vegetable ivory, found in about one cocoa nut out of four thousand. The above is the dress of the better classes, while a turban and inexpressibles, and sometimes merely a cloth round the loins, is deemed sufficient for the generality of the sovereign people. As a mark of beauty, the enamel is filed from the teeth, which are then dyed black, as it is unfit for men to have white teeth like dogs. The women have but one article of dress, consisting of a flowing robe, reaching from above the waist to the feet; they use much gold in their hair, and on their arms and legs, and, if rich, are almost covered with it. The robe is of a bright colour. Children under ten are seldom clothed.

I have before said, that the Malay is extremely indolent; he smokes and chews betel-nut perpetually, and, unless actually obliged, he will not work; it therefore constantly happens that men get into debt, for which the law demands a self sale, for years or months, according to the sum owed, a species of slavery from which the debtor, when once bound, if it be for any large amount, seldom escapes; wives, children, and all follow. He is quite at home in his canoe, standing up in, and managing the smallest craft, in the most masterly manner. Boys, scarcely able to walk, are seen paddling about the water-streets of Brunè.

The Arabic is the character used in writing, the Malays having none of their own; and the number in Borneo who can both read and write well is considerable, though I do not think the Sultan can do either; but his chancellor manages that for him. There are some learned and travelled men in Brunè, who, as good Mohammedans, have made the pilgrimage to Mecca. These are the teachers, and the Koran the lesson.

Marriage is performed much in the same manner as in most eastern countries. At twelve, the girls are shut up, and only seen by the members of the family. A young man wanting a wife, mentions it to his parents, who go and pay a round of visits and, having chosen him one, a day is fixed on which the ceremony is performed, and they become man and wife.

Their tombs, even those of the Sultans, are plain. The body is buried with the feet towards Mecca, generally on the side of a hill, over which a square stone pile is erected, in size according to the rank of the deceased, but without dates or inscriptions of any kind.

The language is curious and easy, a sentence consists of four words, seldom more, the plural is signified by repeating the single number; verbs have no conjugations: in counting they count to ten, as satu, one; dua, two; ten is sapulo, or one ten; then eleven is sablas; duablas, &c., to twenty, thirty; duapuloh, tiga putoh, &c.

The Sultan besides in regal state, is in a religious point of view the head of his people, he is always surrounded by bearers of different devices of honour, and seldom left without one or more Pangerans (prince) attending on him. Beyond this there is not much state. At his court any subject can enter the council-chamber, first performing the salam as he seats himself on his hams, provided he wears his kris. The Koran and ancient usages guide as laws, but power of life and death is in the hands of all Rajahs, and most Pangerans, which renders life unsafe. His majesty is very poor, while many of his subjects, and particularly one, Merah Moormëen, are very rich.

Each district is under the superintendance of a head man, called Orang Caya, literally "a rich man." In Thibet the title of Orang Cay is given to high

nobles, like Ricos hombres in Spain. The Orang
Caya collects the revenues and brings them himself
to the Sultan : they consist generally of pepper and
sago, and are apparently small. A party of fishermen in Labuan told me they would pay the Sultan
for the right of fishing, were it not in our possession,
a picul of pepper yearly (one hundred and twenty
pounds). Pangerans are seldom Orang Cayas, but
have sometimes more than one district under them,
and are called Rajahs. Great respect is demanded
by Pangerans, while little or none is shewn to
Orang Cayas.

CHAPTER XX.

SEARCH FOR COAL.

Shape of the Island of Labuan.—Map of it.—Description.—
Search for Coal.—Appearance of the Island.—Its Products.
—Illness of the Exploring Party. — Coal discovered.— Its
Quality and Quantity.

THE island of Labuan, as it appears on the map,
is in shape, as near as possible, an isosceles triangle.
At its base, which is to the south, is Victoria Bay,
forming a good harbour, with about six or seven fathoms of water, with good anchorage, (the name Labuan means "anchorage" in the Malay language,)
and a harbour of refuge in the north-east monsoon.
On the west side of it is Point Hamilton, beyond
which is the China river, an arm of the sea extending about three or four miles inland, when it
is terminated by a mangrove swamp; beyond this
is the point of Kinnan-San, the south-west angle
of the island. The west coast is dangerous to near
in a boat on account of the surf; the anchorage
(not safe) is in twelve fathoms all along it. To

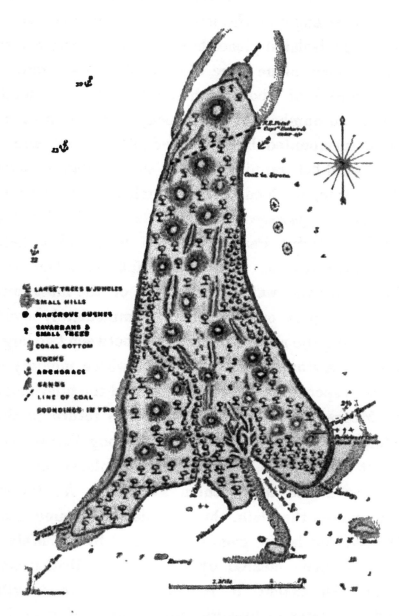

LARGE TREES & JUNGLES
SMALL HILLS
MANGROVE BUSHES
SAVANNAHS &
SMALL TREES
CORAL BOTTOM
ROCKS
ANCHORAGE
SANDS
LINE OF COAL
SOUNDINGS IN FMS

CHART OF THE ISLAND OF LABUAN.

the east of Victoria Bay is Point Pasley, the
south-east angle of the island.   This promised coal,
but a few isolated pieces here and there, below high
water mark, alone were discovered.   Near here is
a waterfall of about eighteen feet from a small
river, and numbers of little rocky points with sandy
bays, surmounted by pines and other trees, and a
long sand-flat running out for some distance; over
it the tide, at flood, boils in such a manner as to
render the passage extremely dangerous.   To the
north of Point Pasley, about a mile and a half,
is Tanjong-Tarras, with a waterfall, at which the
Malay prahus water; it is one of the most picturesque spots on the island.   Immediately over,
and facing the rising sun, on a cliff, between two large
trees, is a stone tomb to a Hadji, whose memory is
much respected, he having performed the pilgrimage
to Mecca, and died shortly after his return in the
odour of sanctity.   Between Tanjong-Tarras and
Point Pasley, are several watering-places, but requiring art to make them available, . At Pasley
commences the plain, the only piece of ground near
the sea that is free from jungle; said by the Malays
to have been cleared by some former British set-
tlers.   In extent it is half a mile in length,
and a quarter in breadth, with a burn of very indifferent water running through what has all the
appearance of being an artificial channel, the work

of the unknown British, before mentioned. Near here coal was expected to be found, but very minute particles only were discovered.

A party of three, consisting of Assistant-Surgeon Joliffe, and Midshipman Morgan, of H.M.S. Iris, and myself, soon after the taking possession of the island, sallied forth to explore the southern base, and ascertain its probable productions and search for coal. We started at Tanjong-Tarras and proceeded westward, examining each tree and flower as we came across one; until having passed three mangrove swamps, and finding ourselves on the confines of a fourth on the west coast of the island, we deemed it advisable to prepare for the night; darkness was already setting in, and return was out of the question. Our pic-nic was not an agreeable one; we cut down some boughs, collected leaves, and gained the summit of a hill, when we doled out a small quantity of brandy; and cold and wet through to the skin, lay down as close together as we could to profit by each other's warmth, but were unable to sleep from the annoyance of gnats and musquitoes.

At daylight, wet, cold, and uncomfortable, we breakfasted off a small piece of biscuit and the remnant of the contents of our flask, and set out to return, taking a direction a little more to the north than we came by, and crossing the China river

by a fallen tree, we reached a mangrove swamp
on the eastern side, to the north of Tanjong-Tarras,
about noon, just as the flood tide made, and experienced the dangers of it, being obliged to run
for our lives.

The following are the observations I made. The
country appears a succession of small hills, varying
from one hundred to one hundred and fifty feet in
height, crowned with trees; many of them had
fallen in different places, which, with the under-
wood or jungle, makes walking very difficult. At a
distance of about two miles from Tanjong Tarras,
we opened a large savannah, clear of wood, very
damp under foot, but apparently excellent pasturage.
Another hill was followed by another savannah, and
so on to the Mangrove swamp, which reached down
to the sea : the waters of the China river were fresh
and over my head in depth, as I proved by jumping
in. To the west of this river the water is of a
whitish colour from the soil being of a light-coloured clay, which may be very valuable hereafter for
brick-making and pottery ; to the east it is of iron-
red, the soil also being of a red and dark colour.
The rivulets are, many of them, dried up in the
hot season, but the soil seems rich in the extreme.
Among the trees are pine, dammer, or pitch, teak,
fir, cedar, iron wood, enormous upas,* India rub-

* The sap of this tree runs like milk, and thickens into a sub-

ber, gutta percha in large quantities, and a few
camphor trees. On some of the smaller of these I
counted upwards of twelve kinds of parasite, or air
plants, and the roots are here and there surrounded by clusters of the pitcher plant, from which I
drank the water, with a strong flavour of Crema
Tartar, but very refreshing. The only fruits that I
came across were jack-fruit and wild almond; but
flowers are numerous and beautiful, lilies of many
varieties, creepers, wild honeysuckle, and others,
"the fairest that may feast the bee," of whose
names I am ignorant, but the all-useful bamboo
unfortunately is not there. Bees are in profusion,
as are the birds, some of them of beautiful plumage, but no songsters; amongst others, snipes,
pigeons, jungle and water fowls. The Lemur or
flying squirrels are in great numbers and variety,
with myriads of monkeys, some wild bullocks
(whose ancestors have escaped from wrecks), wild
hogs, deer (but not many, and very wild), lizards of
different kinds, from an inch to a fathom long, alli-
gators, quanas, and turtle. Snakes do not abound,
but there are a few, and, among others, the boa-
constrictor, and a very beautiful species, something
like the whip snake, of a green colour and perfectly

stance like India-rubber, but is *not* of the deadly poisonous nature
commonly supposed. I have often had some poured into my
hand, without the slightest bad consequences ensuing from it.

harmless, that I have had playing about my arm constantly. The sea abounds with the finest fish, and oysters cover the rocks; shells are in great variety. About one hundred and fifty Malays visit the island, fifty of whom are beeswax hunters, and the rest fishermen; half of these latter haunt the creeks, and the rest the China river. They are very civil and useful.

Here I wish I could say that the effects of this trip terminated with me; but having shortly before recovered from a fever, on its breaking out again, with renewed violence, Captain Gordon, myself, and many of the crew were attacked by it. The captain died, and filled the second grave in the island (the Hadji's, above mentioned, being the first), and Sergeant Oburn, of the marines, the third, from the same complaint, but, after two relapses, I managed to recover, though it was not until the 31st of January, 1847, that the state of my health enabled me to agree with Lieut. Heath to try the northern end of the island, and see whether any available coal-field existed on it or not.

We landed together on the N.E. point, a spot where Captain Bethune had noticed an outcrop of coal, only discernible at low water. We followed its strike, and by digging in its direction soon proved it to be a vein running W.S.W. with a dip of twenty degrees northward; but about twenty yards from the outcrop we lost all trace of it under a high rock. In the hopes of finding the vein in another direction, a shaft was dug to the S.W. of the outcrop, passing through three feet of sand, then ten feet of blue clay, but we only found minute particles of coal, nodules, and iron pyrites. Two days having been thus occupied, owing to the unfavourable state of the weather, our search was discontinued for several days, as we had nearly nine miles to proceed by boats to reach the N.E. point from the plain; but on the 8th of February, we again went to work with a compass and entered the jungle, intending to examine all the ravines and beds of streams for particles of coal; and at a distance of about a mile and a quarter from the beach we discovered an open bed of it, the strike of which corresponded with the outcrop, we therefore struck out in an E.N.E. direction, and came to four different fields of coal in successive ravines, each time sending one of the boat's crew who accompanied us to follow out the stream, which mostly ran from south to north, while the ridges of the hills were something near E.N.E. and W.S.W. After leaving the last of these beds, still continuing on the E.N.E. direction, we reached the beach at about fifty or sixty feet from the outcrop, thus proving the conjunction of these fields.

On the 9th we again started, and passing the

before discovered fields, endeavoured to cross the
island in W.S.W. direction, but owing to the
extreme thickness of the jungle we found, as
the small pieces of coal in the streams had led us to
expect, that we were to the northward.

Letters from the Sultan of Borneo, of an important nature,* requiring the presence of Lieutenant
Heath, he proceeded in H. M. S. Wolf, leaving me
in charge of the island with a party of marines and
seamen, living in tents on the plain; but owing to
some rumours of pirates, I could not leave the protection of the flagstaff, and it was not until the end
of the month, on the return of Lieutenant Heath,
we were able again to proceed. Landing on the
opposite side of the island we struck immediately
into the jungle, and whenever we met with a stream
searched up and down for small pieces of coal; and
when any were found we knew we were to the northward, and proceeding up the stream soon came on a
bed. Whenever unable to find any we travelled
north, often with the same success, and thus traced
the E.N.W. and W.S.W. line from one side of the
island to the other, and notwithstanding the difficulties of the jungle we came upon considerable quantities of iron and sandstones of every hue.

The nearest exposed portion is by measure three
hundred yards from the beach to which we cut a

* Vide *supra*.

road, and on one of the only two bays which afford
shelter and anchorage for vessels.

About five hundred yards from this beach we cut
another shaft through a bed of coal, the dip of which
was about twenty-two degrees to the northward, the
shaft was ten feet deep at right angles with the dip,
and not with the horizon, thus :—

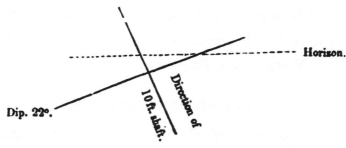

The quality has been tested and pronounced excellent. From the foregoing, it will be seen that
any quantity of coal may be had without the trouble,
intricacy, and expense of mining operations, inasmuch as it lies above high water-mark; and some
of it at a distance of only three hundred yards
from a beach where there is good anchorage for
ships—labour, cheap and abundant, can be had from
China to dig on the spot an article which, up to this
time whenever used in those waters, has been imported from Newcastle.

While the last shaft was in process some heavy
rain fell. One day on going there I found a large
boa constrictor gorged with a bird of the kite tribe
in its throat and drowned: wishing to shew it I had

it taken out and left under a tree, while the boat's crew went to the beach to their midday meal. On our return the boa was nearly devoured by a huge alligator, who stood as if inclined to dispute our passage, but not being hungry he thought better of it, and retired much to the satisfaction of all parties.

The following paragraph, in the main correct, I observed in the Singapore Free Press, copied partly into the Mark Lane Express.

LABUAN—COAL DISCOVERIES.

By the arrival of H. M. S. Wolf, we have received intelligence from Labuan down to the 20th of March. The Columbine, brig-of-war, relieved the Wolf.

Whilst the Wolf was stationed at Labuan, advantage was taken by her Commander (Lieutenant Heath, R. N.) and Lieutenant F. E. Forbes, R. N., to ascertain something relative to the products of the island. Their researches have been successful in discovering a large seam of coal, commencing at what may be termed Captain Bethune's out-crop, and extending across the island in the directions E. N. E. and W. S. W. The thickness of the seam was ascertained to be ten feet one inch ; the dip 22° N. N. W., and the extent about one and three-quarter miles. A path has been cut to the nearest portion of the seam, which is stated to be three hundred and thirty-four yards from the beach, and distant about eight miles from Point Pasley. But what is not a little satisfactory is the circumstance of the seam being found near a bay where there is good anchorage. This bay, and also that known as Victoria, are the only bays the island possesses. Much care was bestowed in ascertaining the direction of the seam of coal, which was observed at seven different places, beside the portion already mentioned as exposed on the beach, all having the same dip and nearly a similar degree of thickness. The depth of water in the bay will allow of steamers of moderate draught of water to proceed close in shore; supposing the average thickness to be about two-thirds of that ascertained, the seam of coal in the bay would yield nearly seven hundred tons, which might, we are assured, be worked by the least experienced persons. Several trials were made of the coal: it is generally reported that the heat and flame were equal to Newcastle coal, but was consumed in less time. Lieutenants Heath and Forbes, to whose assiduity and perseverance we are mainly indebted for tracing the seam, convey two casks of the coal taken from Labuan for the inspection of the naval commander-in-chief at Penang. We may remark that the direction of the coal on the is land of Labuan, is nearly at right angles to that found on the mainland of Borneo Proper.

Situated near the bay above-mentioned was a great number of camphor trees which are described as being of the first kind. There were also found large quantities of iron in its native state.

We learn that the natives residing at Labuan are committing great havoc amongst "the giants of the forest." Every description of tree is cut down for fire-wood, including some of the fine and valuable camphor trees. Considering that Europeans are not permitted to land, we think the natives ought, at least, to be interdicted wilful destruction of the crown's "woods and forests"—the camphor, caoutchouc and dammer trees are alike the victims of the flames. And the Times in a city article, September 28, 1847, bears the following testimony :—"The advices from Labuan and Borneo are still of an encouraging character. It appears that the coal of Labuan has been well tried, and pronounced of an excellent quality; it is also not only in large quantities, but conveniently situated for working. Bruné and Sarawak are stated to be perfectly quiet, and commerce is steadily progressing. The Sultan of Borneo has executed a deed authorizing the working of the coal-mines on the coast. Mr. Brooke, it is said, will arrive on a visit to England by the present mail."

Since writing the above, the following paragraph appeared in the Daily News, November 23: "At Labuan, great progress was being made in working the extensive seams of coal. Chinese coolies from Singapore were employed in the operation under the direction of Mr. Mills."

APPENDIX.

THE EIGHTEEN PROVINCES OF CHINA PROPER, WITH THE LATITUDES AND LONGITUDES OF THE CAPITALS, OFFICIAL APPOINTMENTS, SALARIES, ETC.

CHINA Proper is divided into eighteen provinces, each of which is under the guidance of a governor and proper officers, the most convenient mode of illustrating whom and their offices, will be to give the following account of those of the Province of Kwang-tung, or Canton, and an abbreviation of those of the others.

1. Keying. Governor-general of the provinces of Kwang-tung and Kwang-si, and imperial commissioner, charged with the management of foreign affairs at the five ports of Canton-foo, Amoy-been, Fuh-chau-fou, Ningpo-fou, and Shanghae-heen, has a salary of 15,000 taels. Under his government are 38,194,552 souls, or for Kwang-tung, 27,610,123, and Kwang-si, 10,584,429. Canton, the capital, is situated in lat. 23° 10′ N., and long. 3° 31′ W. of Pekin, called Kwang-chou-foo. (His title is Tsung-tung, or " governor," of Leang-Kwang, or the two Kwangs.)

2. The Foo-yuen, or " Lieutenant-governor," has a salary of 13,000 taels.

3. The Te-tuh, " Commander-in-chief of the military forces," called also Luh-lŭ-Te-tuh. Salary 5,000 taels.

4. The Te-tuh, or "Commander-in-chief of the naval forces," called also Shuy-tsze-Te-tuh, or "Son of the water, Te-tŭh." Salary 5,000 taels.

5. Tsiang-kiung, "General of the Manchou garrison." Salary 8,000 taels.

6. Piéching-sze, "Treasurer, commissioner of finance, and superintendent of the territorial department." Salary 8,000 taels.

7. Ngancha-sze, "Criminal judge, commissioner of justice." Salary 4,900 taels.

8. Hioh-tai, "Literary chancellor." Salary 2,000 taels.

9. Liang-tau, "Commissary-general, or grain commissioner."

10. Yen-yun-sze, "Commissioner of salt."

11. Grand-hoppo, Hae-kwan, "Commissioner of customs."

12. Chifu of Kwan-chou-fu, "Prefect of Canton." His functions correspond nearly to those of mayor in European cities.

13. Kwang-hu, "Commander of the militia (native Chinese) and armed police of Canton."

14.⎫
15.⎭ Che-heen, or ⎧"Magistrate of the district of Nauhoi."
          ⎩"Magistrate of the district of Pwanyü."

16. Sub-magistrate of Nanhoe.

17. Magistrate of the district of Heang-shou.

18. Assistant to prefect of Canton.

19. Sub-magistrate of Heang-su.

These are merely the officers of the city of Canton and its environs.

Chi-le is the most northern of these provinces, the capital of which is Pih-kin, or Pekin, meaning literally, "northern capital." Pekin is not only capital of the province of Chi-le, but also of the whole empire. It is situate in lat. 40°, and is the seat of the central government, as well as the residence of the sovereign, Taou-Kwang, a son of the late emperor, Kea-King, who succeeded his father, Aug. 24th, 1821. His succession was owing, it is said, to his having saved his father's life in an attack made by some insurgents on the palace of Yuen-min-yuen. He was born on the 12th of September, 1782. He has been twice married; the late empress died in 1831, and the present succeeded on the 10th of September, 1834. His family is said to consist of six children, four sons and two daughters, the younger of whom, Yih-tsung, the son of a Manchou concubine, was adopted in 1845, under the name of Tun-Kwang-Wang, by the Emperor's brother, Tun-Tsin-Wang, who was childless. The Emperor has another brother, Hwang-Keung-Wang-Meen-hin (Meen is the significant name as a kinsman of the Emperor, or yellow girdle). In succession the Emperor has choice among his sons, no son of a Chinese (concubine or not) can succeed; and in Tartars legitimacy is preferable and requisite, but primogeniture not necessary.

THE EMPEROR'S MINISTERS (RESIDENT AT PEKIN) ARE AS FOLLOWS :—

THE TSUNG-JIN-FU,

Or "Officers for the control of the imperial household," are six in number, viz. :—

President, or Tsung-ling, one; Tsung-ching, two; Tsung-Jin, two; Fu-ching, one; Treasurers, two.

THE NUY-KO, or Cabinet.

Ta-heo-tsze, three; Hie-pan-ta-heo-tsze, two; Heo-tsze, ten.

THE CHUNG-SHOO-KO, or Herald's Office.

Keun-ke-ta-chin, "Privy Council," selected from all the higher stations, without any rule as to rank or number.

HAN-LIN-YUEN, or *Imperial College*.

Presidents, two—called Chang-yuen-heo-sze.

It includes the office of Ke-kew-choo, for recording the emperor's daily words and actions, the chief officers of which office are also chief of the college.

LEW-POO, or *Six Supreme Tribunals*.

1. Le-pŭ, or "Civil Office," composed of Presidents, or Shang-shoo, two; Vice-Presidents, or Shelang, four.
2. Hoo-poo, "Board of Revenue," Superintendent, one; Presidents, two; Vice-Presidents, four; Lords of the three treasuries, or Kwan-le-san-kwo, two.
3. Li-pŭ, "Board of Rites," Presidents, two; Vice-Presidents, four.
4. Ya-pu, "Board of Music," Superintendents, two.
5. Ping-pu, "Board of War," Presidents, two, and all Governor-generals; Vice-Presidents, four, and all Foo-yuens.
6. Hing-pu, "Board of Punishments," Presidents, two; Vice-Presidents, four.

THE BOARD OF WORKS.

Kung-pu, "Board of Works," Superintendent, one; Presidents, two; Vice-Presidents, four.

Kae-laow-ya-mun, "Office for the superintendence of streets and roads in and about Pekin, under the Kung-pŭ.

OTHER PUBLIC OFFICES.

1. *Le-fan-yuen*, "Foreign and Colonial," Superintendent, one; Presidents, two; Vice-Presidents, two; Superintendent Vice-President, one.

2. *Foo-cha-yuen*, "Censorate," Chief censors, or Foo-yu-she, two; Chief censors of the left. Governor-generals of provinces, Chief censors of the right. Secondary censors, or *Foo-too-yu-shee*, three; of the left. Foo-yuens are secondary censors of the right.

3. *Lew-ko*, "Censors of the tribunals and offices at Pekin." Officers called Kei-sze-chung, Censors of the provinces, and also of the tribunals and offices at Pekin, called Taou-keen-chayu-che.

4. *Chen-sze-foo*, for preparing public documents, and examining in history and general literature, under the Presidents of the Han-lin-yuen. Members called Chen-sze and Chaou-chen-sye.

5. *Woo-king-po-sze*, in the Han-lin-yuen, are descendants of Confucius, Mencius, and their most distinguished disciples.

6. *The Tung-ching-sze-sze*, for receiving memorials, &c., if not secret and sealed, from officers in the provinces, correcting them and forwarding them to the cabinet, Tun-ching-sye-sye, two.

7. *The Ta-le-sze*, a criminal office, or tribunal, secondary to, but independent of the Hing-po, for trying criminals in certain cases. Two officers, called Kings; two officers, called Shaou-kings.

8. *The Tae-chang-sze*, for attending to the appointed sacrifices, and other rites, at the public altars and temples of Pekin. Superintendents, two; Kings, two; Shaou-kings, two.

9. *Kwang-luh-sze*, for providing food, &c., at the imperial entertainment, as well as victims, &c., at the public sacrifices. Superintendent, one; Kings, two; Shaou-kings, two.

10. *Tae-puh-sze*, "imperial stud." Presidents, two.

11. *Hung-lo-sze*, "sacrificial court." Superintendent, one; presidents, two.

12. *Kwo-tsze-keen*, a college for the instruction of Manchou, Mongol, and Chinese literature, particularly the former. One superintendent, and two officers, called Tse-tsen; three professors, a Manchou, a Mongol, and a Chinese.

13. *Kin-tsei-keen*, astronomical board. Superintendent, one; presidents, two.

14. *Tae-e-yuen*, grand Medical Hall. Superintendent, one; president, one.

15. *Lwan-e-wei*, imperial carriages, banners, canopies, &c. Superintendent, one; Tartar presidents, two; Chinese president, one.

The privy council is generally divided between the Chinese and Tartars, as also most of the above offices in them, are one hundred and four places, filled by eighty-two different persons, of whom, in 1845, thirty-seven were Manchous; nine Mongols; thirty-six Chinese.

High rank in the army appears exclusive to the Chinese, and almost so to the Mongols. One, commander-in-chief of the guards, a Manchou; two, general of the left, Manchou; three, general of the right, Manchou.

Tu-tung, or "Generals of the eight banners," all Manchous; Tu-tu-tungs, of the eight banners.

Pekin is in lat. 40° N., long. 2°, of Greenwich 110° E.; its local officers are, superintendent of the city; Yin, or "mayor;" Tetuh, or "commander-in-chief of the city guards;" Foo-tu-Tung, or "lieutenant-general," two.

The population of Chi-le is about 40,000,000.

The capital, next to Pekin, is Paou-ling-Foo, lat. 38° 53 'N., long. 0° 52' W. Governed by a Tsung-tuh, governor-general of Chi-le and its rivers, whose salary is 16,000 taels.

The following officers belong to the general class of each province, viz. :—Tetuh, or " commander-in-chief," salary, 9,000 taels; Pooching-sze, " treasurer," salary about 9000 taels; Ancha-sze, "judge," salary 8000 taels; chancellor, salary 4000 taels.

They will not be repeated, there are, besides, in Chi-le director of the Gabelle at Tien-tsin, salt commissioner at Tientsin.

The Tsung-tŭh, or governor-general of Leang-Keang, has under him two provinces ; viz., Keang-tsu and Kiang-se. Capital of Keang-tsu is Nankin, or Keang-ning-Foo, lat. 32° 4', long. 2° 18' E. Residence of the governor-general, whose salary is 24,000 taels. Keang-tsu has a population of 54,494,641. Principal officers, Fou-yuen, lieutenant-governor, resident at Soo-chow-Fu ; salary 12,000 taels. Governor of the rivers of Keangnan, 8,000 taels. Governor of inland transport, on the grand canal, 9,500 taels. Chitsau, grain commissioner, salt commissioner, at each Nankin and Luchau.

PROVINCE OF NANGHUI.

Capital, Ganking-Fŭ, lat. 30° 37', long. 0° 35' E.; residence of the Foo-yuen, or " lieutenant-governor," whose salary is 10,000 taels ; has a population of 49,201,992.

PROVINCE OF KIANGSE.

Capital, Nan-chang-Fŭ, lat. 28° 37', long. 0° 36' W ; residence of a Foo-yuen, with a salary of 10,000 taels. Has a population of 43,814,866. Te-tuh's office, filled by the Foo-yuen, grain commissioner, salt commissioner, prefect of Kwang-sin-Fu.

Tsung-tuh, or "governor-general of Min-Chĕ," has under him Fuh-keen and Che-kiang provinces.

PROVINCE OF FUH-KĔEN.

Capital Fuh-chau, residence of the governor-general, lat. 26° 2′, long. 3° 0′ E.; whose salary is 18,000 taels. Has a population of 22,699,460, including Formosa.

Foo-Yuen, 13,000. Te-tuh-shuy-sze, "Naval commander-in-chief." Grain commissioner. Salt commissioner. Prefect of Fuh-chau. General of the garrison at Fuh-chau, and superintendent at the ports of Fuh-keen, salary 4,600 taels. Intendant of council at Tae-wan, in Formosa.

PROVINCE OF CHE-KIANG.

Capital Hang-chow-Fŭ, lat. 30° 20′, long. 3° 39′ East, residence of a Foo-yuen; salary 10,000 taels. Has a population of 37,809,765. Tsung-Keung, or General of the garrison of Han-chow-foo, and Commander of the Manchou troops. Naval commander-in-chief. Salt and grain commissioners. Prefect of Ningpo, Fuh, &c.

Tsung-tuh, or Governor-general of Hoo-Kwang, of Leang-Hoo, or Hoo-Hoo, has under him Hoo-pih, and Hoo-nan, or N. and S. Hoo.

PROVINCE OF HOO-PĬH.

Capital Woo-chang-Fu, lat. 30° 34′. long. 2° 15′ W. Residence of the governor-general, whose salary is 15,000 taels. Population 39,412,940. Foo-Yuen, 10,000. Tsung-Keung, or " General of King-chou-Fuh." Grain and salt commissioners.

PROVINCE OF HOO-NAN.

Capital Chang-sha-Fuh, lat. 28° 12′, long. 5°, 41′ W. Residence of a Foo-Yuen, salary 10,000 taels. Population 26,859,608. Grain and salt commissioners.

PROVINCE OF SHAN-TUNG.

Capital Tsi-nan-fŭ, lat. 36° 44′, long. 0° 39′ E. Residence of a Foo-Yuen, salary 15,000 taels. No-Tsung-Tuh, office of Te-tuh, filled by Foo-Yuen. Population 41,700,621. Governor of the rivers of Shan-tung and Honan. Residence Tseung-Fŭ, salary 11,000 taels. Intendant of the water transport. Grain and salt commissioners.

PROVINCE OF HONAN.

Capital Kae-fung-Fu, lat. 34° 52′, long: 1°, 53′ W. Residence of a Foo-Yuen, with a salary of 15,000 taels. (No Tsung-tŭh). Population 33,173,526. Office of Te-tuh filled by Foo-Yuen. Grain and salt commissioners.

PROVINCE OF SHANSE.

Capital Tae-Yuen-Fu, lat. 37° 53′, long. 5° 56′ W. Residence of a Fu-Yuen, salary 10,000 taels. No Tsung-tŭh. Office of Te-tŭh filled by Foo-yuen. Population 20,166,071.

PROVINCE OF SHENSI.

Capital Legan-Fu, lat. 34° 15′, long. 70° 34′ W. Residence of a Foo-yuen, salary 12,000 taels. Population 14,698,449. Te-tuh, or "Commander of the forces in

Koo-yuen and its dependencies;" Tseang-keun, or "General of the forces of Legan-Fu," and "Commander of the Manchou." Grain and salt commissioners.

Tsung-tuh, or "Governor-general of Shen-Kan," *i. e.* Shensi, and

PROVINCE OF KAN SUH.

Capital Lan-chow-Fŭ, lat. 36° 8', long. 12° 33' W. Residence of the governor-general. Salary, 20,000 taels. Population 21,878,100. Tseang-Keang, of Ning-hea-Fŭ. Salt commissioner. Te-tuh, or "Commander-in-chief of the forces in Anse; Governor of the Mongols of Tsing-Hae."

PROVINCE OF SYE-CHUEN.

Capital, Chin-too-Foo, lat. 30° 40', long. 12° 18' W. Residence of a Tsung-tuh, salary 13,000 taels. No Foo-Yuen. Population 30,867,375.

Tseang-Keun of Ching-too-Foo.

Tsung-tuh of Leang-Kwang, or the two Kwang, has under him Kwang-tung, already described, and

PROVINCE OF KWANG-SE.

Capital, Kwei-lue-Foo, lat. 25° 13', long. 6° 14' W. Residence of a Foo-Yuen, salary 10,000 taels. Population 10,584,429.

Tsung-tuú of Yunk-wai, has under him Kwei-Chow, and

PROVINCE OF YUNNAN.

Capital, Yunnan-Foo, lat. 25° 6', long. 13° 36' W. Residence of a Tsung-tuh, salary 20,000 taels. Foo-Yuen 10,000 taels. Population 8,008,300.

PROVINCE OF KWEI-CHOW.

Capital, Kwei-Yang-fu, lat. 26° 30′, long. 9° 52′. Residence of a Foo-Yuen, salary 10,000 taels. Population 7,615,025.

APPENDIX, No. II.

POPULATION OF CHINA PROPER.

Provinces.	1847.	1813.
Chi-le	40,000,000	27,990,874
Kiang-tsu	54,494,641	37,843,501
Gan-Hwug	49,201,992	34,168,059
Keang-se	43,814,866	30,426,999
Fuh-Kien	22,699,460	14,777,410
Che-Kiang	37,809,765	26,256,784
Hoo-pih	39,412,940	27,370,098
Hoo-Nan	33,173,526	18,652,507
Shan-tung	41,700,621	28,958,764
Ho-nan	33,173,526	23,037,171
Shan-se	20,166,072	14,004,210
Shen-se	14,698,449	10,207,256
Kan-suh	21,878,190	15,193,125
Sye-Chuen	30,867,375	21,435,678
Kwang-tung	27,610,123	19,174,030
Kwang-se	10,584,429	7,313,895
Yun-nan	8,008,300	5,561,320
Kwei-Chou	7,615,025	5,288,219
	536,909,300	367,680,100

LIST OF OFFICERS.

PROVINCIAL.	LOCAL.
Tsung-tŭh, " Governor-general."	Military officers
Foo-Yuen, " Lieutenant-Governor."	of various
Loo-Luh-te-tŭh, " Com.-in-chief."	ranks.
Shuy-sze-te-tŭh, "Naval Com.-in-chief."	Chee-foo, " Ma-
Hae-Kwan-Keen-tuh, " Customs."	gistrate."
Poo-chingsze, " Treasurer."	Che-Hien, "Ma-
Ancha-sze, " Judge."	gistrate," and
Leang-loo-chow, "Grain commissioner."	under-officers
Yen-Yun-sze, " Salt commissioner."	answering to
Literary Chancellor.	nearly all em-
Tsiang-kiung, " General-in-chief."	ployed in En-
Foo-tu-tung Manchou, } General.	glish cities,
Foo-tu-tung, Chinese }	towns, coun-
	ties, &c.

APPENDIX No. III.

COMPARISON OF MILITARY RANK.

CHINESE AND ENGLISH.

Foo-tung and Tseang-Kiung of the Eight banners	General.
Foo-tung and Tsung-ping . . .	Lieut.-general.
Foo-tseang	Colonel.
Tsan-Tseang	Sub-Col.
Yew-Kweih	Lieut.-Col.
Foo-tsze	Major.
Show-pei	Captain.
Tsëen-tsung	Lieutenant.
Po-tsung	Sub-Lieut.
Wae-Wei	Sergeant.
Gih-wae-wae·wei	Sub-Sergeant.

APPENDIX No. IV.

THE TWENTY-EIGHT DYNASTIES OF CHINA.

Name.	Sovereigns.	Years of Reign.	Commencing.
1. Mythological	3	81,600	B. C.
2. Wu-ti	8	647	2,852
3. Hia	17	439	2,205
4. Shang	28	644	1,766
5. Chau	35	873	1,122
6. Tsin	1	3	249
7. After Tsin	2	44	246
8. Han	14	226	202
9. Eastern Han	12	196	A. D. 25
10. After Han	2	44	221
11. Tsin	4	52	265
12. Eastern Tsin	11	103	317
13. North Sung	8	59	420
14. Tsi	5	23	479
15. Liang	4	55	502
16. Chin	5	32	557
17. Sui	4	31	589
18. Tang	20	287	620
19. After Liang	2	16	907
20. After Tang	4	13	929
21. After Tsin	2	11	936
22. After Han	2	4	947
23. After Chau	3	9	951
24. Sung	9	157	960
25. Southern Sung	9	153	1127
26. Yuen	9	88	1280
27. Ming	16	276	1368
28. Ta-Tsing the present dynasty }		201	1644

The present dynasty, Manchou Tartars class only twelve sovereigns, including Taow-kwang, the present Emperor. Six have sat on the throne of China, of whom Sun-chi was the first: prior to Sun-chi, two Emperors, Tien-ming, and Tien-Tsung, or Tsung-teh, reigned over small portions of conquered Chinese territory, besides Manchuria. The first four Emperors being Emperors of Manchuria only, before whose time the Manchou race was unknown. The Chinese give it a fabulous, but not distant origin; but it is believed that they spring from the Tongouse tribes, from the banks of the Amor. After Sunchi, who reigned eighteen years, succeeded Kang-He, who reigned sixty-one years; Yum-chim thirteen years; Kien-lung sixty years; Kia-king twenty-five years. Taw-kwan, still reigning, twenty-five years.

APPENDIX, No. V.

CHRONOLOGY OF CHINA.

THE CYCLE OF SIXTY YEARS FROM 1847.

1847. Ting-wei.	1856. King-Shin.	1865. Yĭh-chòu.
1848. Mow-shin.	1857. Ting-szé.	1866. Ting-Yin.
1849. Kè-yèw.	1858. Mow-Woò.	1867. Tingmau.
1850. Kăng-sŭh.	1859. Ké Wei.	1868. Mow-shin.
1851. Sin-haé.	1860. Kang-shin.	1869. Ké-sze.
1852. Tin-Tszè.	1861. Sin-Yeu.	1870. Kang-Woo.
1853. Kwei-choù.	1862. Tin-Sŭh.	1871. Sin Wei.
1854. Keă-Yîn.	1863. Kwei Hae.	1872. Jin Shin.
1855. Yĭh-màou.	1864. Kă-tsze.	1873. Kwei Yeu.

1874. Kea-Suh.	1885. Yih Yeu.	1896. King-Shin.
1875. Yih-Hae.	1886. Pin Seu.	1897. Ting Yeu.
1876. Ping-tsze.	1887. Ting-hae.	1898. Mou Suh.
1877. Ting-chow.	1888. Mow tae.	1899. Ke hae.
1878. Mow-Yin.	1889. Ke chou.	1900. Kang tsze.
1879. Ke-mou.	1890. Kang-Yin.	1901. Sin chou.
1880. Kang-shin.	1891. Sin Maou.	1902. Jin Yin.
1881. Sin-tse.	1892. Jin Shin.	1903. Kwei Mau.
1882. Jin-Woo.	1893. Kwei Sze.	1904. Kea Shin.
1883. Kwei wei.	1894. Kea Woo.	1905. Yeh Sze.
1884. Kea Shin.	1895. Yih wei.	1906. Ping-Woo.

APPENDIX, No. VI.

OFFICIAL RETURNS OF THE TRADE WITH VARIOUS PORTS OF CHINA.

MR. DAVIS (NOW SIR JOHN) TO THE EARL OF ABERDEEN.

(Extract.)   Victoria, Hong-Kong, August 8, 1845.

I have the honour to inclose a detailed report from Mr. Consul Alcock, concerning the trade of Foo-chow-foo, and its prospects as a place of European commerce.

This report is divided into four heads.

1st. The existing native trade, population, resources, and demand for foreign goods.

2nd. The restrictions and prohibitions affecting trade, among which opium certainly cannot be included, as it enjoys unlimited toleration.

3rd. Capital and currency, under the second of which bank notes are largely in use.

4th. The production of tea for European markets, and the means of traffic with the black tea districts.

REPORT ON THE EXISTING TRADE AT THE PORT OF FOO-CHOW, AND ITS CAPABILITIES AS A PLACE FOR EUROPEAN COMMERCE.

1st. *The existing Native Trade, Population, Resources, and Demand for Foreign Goods.*

The wide and discursive nature of this inquiry, and the numerous ramifications it presents, have, together, formed one of its chief difficulties. The sources from which information has been derived, have been proportionably numerous, and as might be expected, not unfrequently very contradictory data have been the result. A short visit to Foo-chow, recently made by a British merchant, for the purpose of ascertaining what demand and resources might be counted upon, came very opportunely, enabling me to bring together a number of Chinese traders and others, in pursuit of their own interests and curiosity, and to gather from their unconstrained remarks and inquiries, means of testing the accuracy of previous information, and arriving, I believe, at a fair conclusion.

Foo-chow-foo, although a provincial city, the seat of local government, and of vast extent, containing a population, which, in the absence of any official data, I cannot estimate at less than half a million souls, does not appear to be considered by many of the inhabitants, a place of great trade or resort for merchants from the other provinces. The authorities, from the governor-general downwards, distinctly assert that it is a place of little trade, and decreasing in commercial importance. This, to a certain extent, has been confirmed by information derived from other sources. A trader of reputed substance and respectability affirmed, in conversations, that the trade of the port had considerably decreased during the last few years, which he attributed to the " drain of capital, in the best of times not very plentiful, caused by the opium traffic ; immense sums being expended in the purchase of the drug, to the impoverishment of the purchaser, which would otherwise have been invested in a more legitimate and profitable commerce."

Nevertheless, so much detailed information of the most circumstantial kind has been supplied as greatly to qualify this statement. Whatever may be the truth as to the decrease of late years, I think there is proof that a brisk and very extensive trade is at the present time kept up with most of the maritime provinces, both by sea and land, and also with the towns of the interior. Among the chief of them are enumerated Keangse, Chang-chow-foo, Tseucn-chow-foo, and Fuh-ning-foo, also Loo-choo, Shanse, Shantung, Teentsin, Ningpo, and Sze-chuen.

The Ningpo trade, it may be observed, comprises the main part of the Shantung commerce. Ningpo being a port more easy of access to large vessels than Foo-chow, the Shangtung junks chiefly congregate there, and the produce is sent to Foo-chow by the smaller Ningpo craft. Thirteen junks belonging to Foo-chow carry on the direct trade to Shangtung, and are expressly kept for this trade, though on entering the port they are generally obliged to discharge half of their cargoes into lighters at the mouth of the river, in order to admit of their ascent as high as the bridge.

Each town or district sends its respective produce or manufactures to the market. The sea-board trade seems unquestionably to be the more extensive of the two, although one of the main branches of this commerce, that with Soo-chow, including all silk manufactures, has lately been changed, in consequence of the extensive depredations committed by pirates, from a maritime to an inland trade.

The chief articles of export are tea, paper, bamboo, oranges, orange-peel, sugar, sugar-candy, copper, sycee and dollars, bamboo roots and spars, together with various articles of Straits' produce, opium, and innumerable sundries. Many of these exports are of course first imported.

Rhubarb from Han-kow in the province of Sze-chuen, may be expected to form a staple article of export. The southern and more northern parts are chiefly supplied from that place.

The imports are not less various. Foo-chow is supplied with foreign goods to a large amount from Tseun-chow-foo and the port of Amoy, for which she sends sycee and specie. Opium however forms the staple article of trade, the drug being consumed in these districts to a large amount. Straits' produce, in all their variety, find a market here. Inferior Japan goods from Loo-choo, and gold employed by the Loo-choo merchants in the purchase of piece-goods British or American manufacture, are among the imports.

To every one of the places enumerated, junks take back exports in exchange for the cargoes brought, the whole trade being one of barter.

For a more explicit and detailed statement of this trade, with the estimates furnished of its value, and the number of traders, junks, and boats employed in it, I must refer to the tabular return, formed from the whole of the information obtained. By this return it will be seen that upwards of one thousand traders, and a similar number of junks and boats, are employed, independently of the traffic by land, the tonnage of the shipping averaging nearly half a million of piculs, say, 29,000 tons, and the estimated annual value of the import and return cargoes is given at 7,455,000 dollars. No doubt some considerable allowance must be made for inaccuracies, for possible errors or misstatements, yet taking the whole of the details into account, it would seem sufficiently proved that there is a very large and widely-diffused trade with the city and port of Foo-chow.

This considerable trade seems to be sound, and almost exclusively carried on by barter, that of Loo-choo in some degree excepted, either one or two junks arriving annually with tribute, cargo, and about 10,000 dollars in Japan gold, for the purpose of purchasing our manufactures. Last year they are reported to have purchased 10,000 pieces of long-cloth, brought overland from Amoy. About a hundred Loo-chooans came over in each junk, all more or less interested and engaged in trade.

The demand for Straits' produce and for British manufactured goods, is certainly considerable; nearly every third person has some article of dress from our looms about him. In a walk through the city most of the drapers' shops are observed to contain some for retail, as also goods of American manufacture. Goods of inferior manufacture seem in greatest abundance, although some of the information received represents those of superior quality to be best adapted for the market.

During Mr. Glen's hurried visit, all the Chinese traders who came, professed themselves more or less anxious to make purchases to the extent of several thousand dollars. Mr. Glen's inability to supply them, or indeed to give the market price at which he could bring the goods, prevented their sincerity from being put to the proof, not only as regarded actual purchases, but as to any definite orders for quantities or qualities of goods. They gave it as their general opinion that all manufactured goods would sell, chiefly however cotton fabrics, coarse long-cloths, and manufactures of superior quality. Articles of Straits' produce would also find a ready market. They further stated, that a barter trade would be most desirable, and that tea could be supplied for that purpose. For goods sold by retail, or in small quantities, however, there seems no reason to fear any want of specie at the commencement of a trade.

I inclose a return of the quotations of the market price of the articles chiefly in demand, furnished by the merchants of the place. These prices, I am informed, are calculated to yield a very handsome profit, and in the present glut of the Canton and Shanghae markets, would be realized with avidity. It is impossible to vouch for the perfect accuracy of the quotations; nevertheless, the persons furnishing them being those likely to purchase, it may fairly be assumed that they would not fix a higher value than they were prepared to give.

Mr. Glen, who seemed an intelligent merchant, well versed in business, in his hasty survey of the capabilities and wants of the port, went away with an opinion that Foo-chow-foo afforded a fair field for commercial enterprize, and that there was no want of customers for British goods, who were able and willing to pay for them in cash. To this conclusion a former despatch shews I had previously come as the result of my inquiries.

It may be surmised that the establishment of a foreign trade at Foo-chow would tend to revive the energy of its own native commerce, Foo-chow not being rich in products, and supplied even with necessaries from other provinces. Merchants frequenting the place often find some difficulty in getting returns for their goods, a defect which it is believed the appearance of foreign merchandize will amply supply.

2nd. Restrictions and Prohibitions effecting Trade.

Amongst the articles restricted or prohibited as objects of general trade, are tea, large spars for masts, salt, iron, sulphur, saltpetre, cows'-horns for powder-flasks, and lead.

Tea is only allowed to be exported in certain quantities, a rule which it is understood does not apply to the foreign trade, and an export duty of two taels per pecul is levied on shipment.

Large spars for masts, and salt, are government monopolies; and iron, sulphur, saltpetre, cows'-horns, and lead, are strictly prohibited, being entirely used by the authorities for cannon, ammunition, and accoutrements.

Although opium must be classed among the prohibited articles, so perfectly nominal and ineffective is the letter of the prohibition, it is generally inferred from the immunity the traffic enjoys, that the Chinese government is no longer opposed to its introduction. It seems very certain that the demand for this drug does at this moment, and probably may always, far exceed that for manufactured goods of every description. The total annual amount imported, I am credibly informed, is not less than 2,000,000 of dollars. A chest often realizes 800 dollars, although 680 dollars is given as a fair quotation, and at least four chests are daily retailed in the city and suburbs. Others again estimate the daily consumption at eight chests, and confidently affirm that one half of the whole population are addicted to smoking it. The use of it seems to extend to the very lowest classes; coolies, and even beggars, are in the habit of taking a pipe, though it may often be at the price of their meal of rice. They allege that having once commenced the practice, they become unable to follow their avocations if the daily stimulus be withdrawn, and this sufficiently accords with medical experience in Europe.

Foo-chow is supplied from Chinchew, both by sea and land; by the latter route chiefly, although within the last few weeks more than one opium clipper has been in the mouth of the River Min, furnishing a supply adequate to the demand. When transported overland in any large quantity, a company or caravan club together for the purpose, and travel well armed, not from any fear of the government taking legal measures against them, but on account of apprehended attacks from robbers, to whom the value of the drug forms a strong attraction. When carried in small quantities, the travellers open a chest, and distribute it throughout their luggage, for safety from plunderers and to escape attention.

Independent of the demand for the city and suburbs, it forms an article of export and traffic with the interior, although this branch of the trade chiefly goes through Tseun-chow, on account of its proximity to Chinchew, where, it is well known, several of our opium clippers are always lying.

In reference to the connivance of the authorities in this traffic, it would appear that the use of opium has become far too general a practice to admit of secrecy. It is therefore impossible that the government should not be aware of the existence of numerous smoking shops in almost every street. It is true, these establishments are described as bearing the exterior appearance of private dwellings; but they are fitted up with all the conveniences and apparatus for smoking, and are chiefly frequented by military, police, and other *employés* of the authorities.

One hundred of these resorts, I am told, may be numbered within the walls of the city: and the fact that they are very generally to be found near the precincts of the mandarins' gates, leaves no room to doubt the undisguised connivance of the authorities, and the general prevalence of a well-founded impression of immunity to all who purchase or smoke the drug.

A vague report that occasionally opium has passed through the custom-house, as a medicine, has reached me, but it wants confirmation.

In reference to the whole of these details respecting the introduction and consumption of opium, notwithstanding it is a subject on which the Chinese do not like to speak openly, and only communicate freely after enjoining secrecy and feeling confident in the integrity of the party inquiring, yet all questions were answered with such readiness and apparent straightforwardness, that their statements may fairly be assumed to have been dictated by a candid desire to tell what they knew, and for once, without evasion or circumlocution, to speak the truth.

Whatever may be the demand for foreign produce here, it may safely be inferred, I think, that opium stands at the head of the list, and at present it appears to be the chief or staple article of commerce with those points from which they derive their foreign supplies. Its use both in the city and the interior is widely spread.

3rd. *Capital and Currency.*

Houses and land appear to be considered a more advantageous investment for capital than commerce, since the person carrying on a flourishing trade generally becomes a victim to the cupidity of the mandarins, who never fail to exact large sums from the commercial community when opportunity offers.

Business is carried on by barter, ready money, and promissory notes, the latter sometimes being delivered by agents on their employers at the various cities; and it is strong evidence of the general good faith and soundness of the commerce, that the latter is considered a very good way of payment, and often accepted in preference to any other for convenience sake.

The mode in which the business and traffic of the port is carried on, throws some light upon the nature and extent of their commercial transactions. The merchants from the several places trading with Foo-chow generally accompany their goods to the market, effect their purchases and return in one season, to repeat their visit on a similar errand the following year. The chief part of the business, nevertheless, would seem to pass through the hands of a small body of merchants at Foo-chow, who in fact maintain a kind of monopoly.

Of the three modes of dealing referred to, that by barter is the most prevalent; by ready money, the least. The latter is indeed at all times a scarce article, though, if due notice be given, no great difficulty is experienced in collecting a moderate sum. For instance, to obtain from 10,000 to 20,000 dollars it is said would be the work of three or four days, and if required on the spot at once might not be procurable. Dollars and rupees pass current by weight in the port, but in the interior none but Carolus or pillar-dollars are received. Sycee and gold are used as well as dollars; of the former there is now a good stock, of the Teen Tsin paou, in the market, this being the time when the merchants from that place frequent Foo-chow for the purposes of trade.

The almost universal monetary medium of Foo-chow is paper currency consisting of bills or promissory notes, analogous, in many respects, to our country bank small note issues. There are upwards of one hundred banking establishments at Foo-chow, most of them held to be in possession of large capital. A million dollars is quoted as the maximum. Each of these establishments are banks of deposit and banks of issue, their notes bearing the seal of the firm; these are for any amount; four hundred cash being the minimum, and about 1,100 dollars the maximum. Herewith is inclosed one which has been some time in circulation. They are issued either for dollars or cash, at the option of the drawer. On presenting these bills at their respective firms, they may always be cashed at a very small discount, in which the banker's profit consists. Two cash are paid on each dollar on entering them for bills, and on drawing out the dollars again a further sum of eight cash is demanded. The mere fact of the universal prevalence of this banking system and paper currency, forms in itself very unquestionable evidence of an advanced state of commerce and finance at this port; and there is little doubt that the same advantages result from these establishments here as in Europe, by the security and increased facility they give to all commercial transactions. While in many other parts of China they still adhere to the primitive and clumsy method of making payments in bars of silver, with all the attendant inconveniences of weighing and assaying, they seem little in arrear of the monetary system of Europe at Foo-chow.

If I lay some stress on this circumstance, it is that I deem it an indication of considerable importance, one which affords proof of more enlightened views and improved capacity for commercial operations.

It seems that in small sums dollar bills are preferred to specie, not only on account of their being more portable, but the further consideration that a bill always commands a fixed price, according to the value of the dollar in the market, whereas when dollars themselves are used, account is taken of the weight of each.

No reasonable ground of doubt seems to exist, that in the case of foreign merchants receiving a number of these bills in payment of goods, he would always be enabled to cash them by taking them to their respective banks of issue to the amount of several thousand dollars.

The credit of the banking-houses is spoken of as firm. Each person, as he pays away a bill, inscribes his name or affixes his private seal on the back, so that in case of its proving to be a forged note it may be traced. These parties do not, however, become in any other way responsible, if the original issuer of the bill should prove insolvent. Such an event is not of frequent occurrence, although occasionally a firm becomes bankrupt, say one or two instances in the course of the year. These, however, would not appear to be fraudulent bankruptcies, since they generally pay fifty cents in the dollar.

Upon the whole, the information received, as to the financial transactions, and even the resources of the city and port, cannot be considered other than satisfactory and encouraging, in reference to any retail trade, even on a large scale, in foreign goods. The paper medium affords great facilities, the credit on which its currency is based seems sound, and neither dollars, sycee of the best quality, nor gold, are so absolutely deficient as the authorities may have probably been led to believe, certainly not so scarce as to offer any obstacle to the opening of a brisk ready-money trade for British goods to a considerable amount.

Large transactions, involving the disposal of a whole ship's cargo to one house, and several in succession, can only be contemplated in reference to, and in connection with, a barter trade, the chief element of which at this port must be tea, on the Chinese side.

4th. *Production of Tea for the European Markets, and means of Traffic with the Tea Districts of Fokien.*

The Bohea Hills, situated in the districts of Tsung-gan and Keen-yang, are described as a continuous range of great elevation, extending one hundred le. Many particulars respecting this district will be found in the inclosed paper, drawn up by Mr. Parkes, from information collected from the Chinese at Amoy. Perfect accuracy cannot be expected from informants who may not be familiar, from personal observation, with the details; nevertheless, the system under which the tea is gathered and sold, the limits of the Bohea district, the inadequacy of the produce of the best farms and crops to meet the demand, and the consequent deterioration of the whole produce by the admixture of leaves of inferior growth, and, finally, the nature of the route to Foo-chow, all subjects of great importance, are described with such apparent care, that I consider the statement, as a whole, worthy of attention.

Chinese have stated in conversation that the demand for the European market is trifling compared with the much larger quantities consumed by themselves; but however true this may be, if quantity merely be taken into account the tenor of the information given in this paper agrees with that obtained on the spot, and confirms an opinion given in evidence, in 1830, before a Committee of the House of Commons, by several witnesses, viz., that an increased demand of rapid growth could not easily be met by the Chinese. I believe that any increased supply would not be good tea, and deterioration of quality must almost certainly follow as a first result. Whether later this might not be remedied by the increased cultivation and production of the finer kinds of black tea, in this province or elsewhere, is a question which I will not attempt to discuss. The very large amount of the finer kinds of black tea which annually find their way into Russia would seem, however, to favour this view, since the growth is obviously not limited to this province, nor does it, indeed, seem certain that the Bohea districts are those in which the finest black tea is even produced.

The more immediate object of the present inquiry, however, has not been to determine any remote questions arising from the prospect of a decrease in the cost price, and a larger demand consequent on the opening of a new market, but to ascertain, with some approach to certainty, whether the produce of the tea districts in this province can be obtained by a short and direct route from the hills to Foo-chow, and at a cheaper rate than at Canton. The following facts I think place this beyond doubt.

The inclosed tabular form shews at one view the principal stages and the relative distances of Foo-chow and Canton from the Bohea Hills and tea districts of Fokien. The distance to Canton, upon the best information, and the evidence of those engaged in the annual journeys, is 324 leagues; to Foo-chow, 84, or little more than one-fourth.

The difficulties and dangers of the route from the tea districts to each of the two ports are not described with the same conclusive unanimity. Nevertheless, the evidence before me is sufficiently clear upon the main points.

The transit from Tsung-gan to Nan-gan-foo is by water, and upon the whole easy travelling, though during the first stage to Hokow, a distance of twenty leagues, there is a strong current, and in some places of the river there are many rocks. From Nan-gan-foo to Nan-heung, a distance of thirteen and one-third leagues through the hill districts, tea has to be carried over the mountains by coolies, which is troublesome and expensive, but it can be performed in a day. When on the other side of the hills, there is good water communication from Nan-heung-foo to Canton, 117 and 7-9th leagues. It is not the less described as a long and tedious journey.

The distance from Foo-chow to Sin-chun is given, the latter place being the emporium or central market for tea, which is brought from all the surrounding localities and districts where it is cultivated. This town is situated close to the hills where the migratory population of tea-gatherers follow their occupation during the season. To this point the farmers and merchants alike proceed, and there the purchases are made. Thus, notwithstanding there are large quantities grown in all the surrounding districts, some at a considerable distance, their produce is still taken for sale to Sin-chun, the point established by common consent and custom for the sale of the crops. It is the place of resort for purchasers from all parts of the empire, and the commercial transactions are consequently on a large scale. The sales are chiefly made in April, May, and June.

From Foo-chow to Sin-chun the route constantly ascends, and is dangerous in its whole extent, especially from Yen-ping to Këen-ning-foo. To ascend the river from twenty-five to thirty men are required to tow each boat, but labour here is the chief inconvenience; the danger to be encountered lies in the descent, owing to the rapidity of the current. Nevertheless, all the merchants send their teas by the river the cost of transport being so much less than by land, thus furnishing a sufficient comment upon exaggerated accounts of the danger and risk attending the navigation which are prevalent. In Sin-chun there are always boats for this journey habitually employed by the tea-dealers, and although to transport goods from Foo-chow to Sin-chun by river occupies fourteen days, and by land ten or twelve, to descend with the current from three to four days only are necessary; by land, the same journey to Foo-chow requires nine days. A letter from hence, it is stated, might be sent to Tsung-gan, and an answer received in ten or

eleven days. It would go overland, for which six days
are required, and return by the river probably in four. I
have been assured by one of the tea-merchants lately arrived from the Bohea Hills, and his statement has been
confirmed by others, that the rapidity of the current does
not form such a serious obstacle to the transportation of
the tea as might be anticipated from description, the navigation being well known. The loss of a boat is of rare
occurrence, and generally to be attributed to carelessness,
or the untrustworthy state of the boat employed. It is
also to be remarked, that the route to Canton is by no
means exempt from the same difficulties and dangers,
arising from similar physical causes, while the journey is so
long and tedious, that the travelling there and back, with
the settlement of the accounts arising from the transactions of each season, is looked upon as the work of a year.

The advantages in favour of Foo-chow as a tea-mart
appear still more striking upon comparison of the cost of
transport to each port.

A boat can be hired to make the voyage from Sin-chun
to Foo-chow at an average cost of 20,000 cash. As each
of these boats carry thirty loads of about 100lbs., the
charge amounts to little more than 600 cash per load, while
the transport of the same quantity to Canton is stated
to cost more than five times this amount. Each load of
tea, I have been informed, entails a further expense of
4,000 cash, to transport it by land from the district of
its growth to Sin-chun, from whence it is always sent by
river, but the assertion seems to me of doubtful accuracy
as to the amount. On further inquiry it moreover would
appear that the whole cost of transport to Foo-chow,
including carriage from the hills to Sin-chun, does not
exceed 900 cash per picul, and this last statement I believe
to be more correct.

This expense of carriage, however, be it more or less, weighs of course equally upon the teas for Canton and Foo-chow. From Sin-chun to Canton the cost of transport is variously estimated here by persons employed in the traffic, the amounts given vary as much as from six to two dollars per picul. I believe, upon a careful analysis of the whole, that three dollars will be found a near approximation to the actual expense.

It will thus be obvious that the charges of transport must form no inconsiderable proportion of the whole cost price of the lower qualities of tea to the purchasers of Canton, and if that can be diminished to so great an extent as this information would indicate, an assertion of the partner who has lately been despatched by one of the firms from the tea district to Foo-chow, to endeavour to open the market to foreign trade, may well be credited; viz., that he can afford to sell the tea at Foo-chow, which he must otherwise send to Canton, at one-fourth less than the price it would bring at the latter port. A member of another large firm, having considerable dealings in tea at Canton, states that they could sell at 20 per cent. less than at Canton. This will appear the more feasible if it be remembered that, not only does the greater expense of transport enhance the value of tea at the Canton market beyond that which it would justly bear at Foo-chow, but additional duties are imposed during the transit by the lengthened route.

On leaving Sin-chun, or the district of Tsung-gan, a duty is levied upon all tea, for whatever place or port it may be destined. This varies, according to the quality, from 5 candareens to 1 mace per picul, and is referred to by the tea-traders as a trifling tax, no other duty being levied on the route to Foo-chow.

The tariff duty of 2 taels 5 mace per 100 catties, is

imposed only on shipment at Foo-chow, as at Canton.

If this class of charges be compared with those levied on the road to Canton, it will be found that, according to the extract from the " Hoo-poo-tsih-le," published under authority by the Chinese Secretary, Mr. Gutzlaff, refering to the transit or inland duties, coarse qualities of tea pay transit duties at three additional places on the road to Canton, viz. at Kaen, Taeping, aud Pishin; and fine classes at two.

The inclosed Return will serve to shew the exact relative proportion in which the first cost of tea is enhanced to the purchasers at Canton and Foo-chow respectively, taking the original value of common and fine tea at Sin-chun at nominal prices at ten and twenty taels per picul, which is purposely assumed at a very low rate, though probably furnishing a sufficiently close approximation to their average value to the trader in the tea district. The tea which is gathered in the third and fourth moons being considered of the best quality, it is during this period that the merchants make their purchases, for which purpose they pay an annual visit to Sin-chun. Most of the tea-dealers, however, are natives of the tea-districts, and to them, therefore, the proximity of Foo-chow, I am assured by one of themselves, would offer many advantages. Still on this point I have been most anxious to obtain correct information; for in China, at least, it is not always sufficient that a change from a long-established custom should be to the advantage of the parties concerned. They not only must be convinced that such is the case, which is all that is required in most communities, but they must entertain a spontaneous desire of their own to adopt the innovation for the profitable result. English merchants appear to me to be under very erroneous impressions, especially those who have long resided at Canton, when they assert that for money the Chinese are ready to undertake anything. Long contact with Europeans seems to have imparted some of the money-seeking and money-getting qualifications of our own mercantile communities to the Chinese at that port, consequently what is asserted of them there may be true. Of the fallacy of the opinion, as relates to this province or city, I have daily and practical experience. Money seems to possess little power of inducing them to do that to which they are either not accustomed or otherwise disinclined.

It has been the more satisfactory to me, therefore, to receive very unequivocal assurance, not only of the willingness of the tea-growers and merchants to make Foo-chow their market in preference to Canton, but their eager desire to accomplish this change, in proof of which, as I have already stated, one of the partners of a firm has been sent down from the tea district, and with express instructions to endeavour to dispose of their season's tea, amounting to 1,240 chests, at this port, and to ascertain if there be any large demand, and foreign goods to exchange against their tea.

Nor is his firm the only one which seems to be attempting to make a diversion in the tea trade in favour of Foo-chow. This tea-dealer further gives it as his opinion that the tea-traders would generally take our goods to any amount for which we demanded tea, and he considers that such a barter-trade would be most desirable and profitable for both parties.

Of the diminished cost of tea by reduced duties and expense of transport, of the willingness of the tea-dealers to transfer the sale of their produce to the market nearer home, and of the practicability of the route, I think there no longer exist any reasonable grounds of doubt. These three

points established, it only remains to be shewn how great
a reduction in the cost price of our chief export from
China might thus be effected, in order to determine the probability of these advantages outweighing other and less favourable circumstances inseparably attached to the port, and
the adverse interests which must be hostile to the change.

Although easy to shew that a great difference must
result, and by what means the saving will be effected, it is
nevertheless most difficult to determine with any accuracy
the amount. Three classes of data are wanting for the
solution of the question, shewing

First. The total cost of transport and duties on tea
proceeding to Canton.

Secondly. The same in reference to Foo-chow-foo.

Thirdly, and finally. The selling price of tea *in the
trade*, that is, to the first dealers in the tea district.

The latter is the more necessary, since, no doubt, in
passing from the farmers and cultivators to the traders,
and thence into the hands of the Canton merchants and
monopolists, a considerable charge is grafted on the cost
price of Sin-chun, in addition to the expense of transport
and payments for duties, for the advantage of the intermediate dealer and the Canton hong merchants, whose profits
on the transaction must thus be realized, and they are
probably not small.

A British merchant, purchasing tea at Foo-chow, might,
I think, readily come in direct relation either with the
first producer, or, at furthest, one intermediate dealer;
the whole of the profits of the third party, and the difference of cost of transport and duties levied in the longer
and shorter routes would thus be saved to the foreign purchaser. Whether this be 25 per cent., as asserted by the
working partners of the firm already alluded to in the tea
districts, or more or less, it would seem unquestionable

that the saving must be large, so considerable, indeed, as to offer a premium of unusual magnitude upon all transactions for the purchase of teas at this port, even if it offered no prospect of a further profit upon the barter of British goods against tea, to which a new market would be opened.

The sale-price of teas in the interior is a great desideratum; but for the present it has proved unattainable. Upon further investigation, I came to the conclusion that although a Chinese of average intelligence and honesty might have been found to proceed to Sin-chun, unless he had some knowledge of the trade and qualities of tea, the thousand circumstances that influence its real value, the price demanded, and the market price obtained, the result would, I fear, have proved nugatory. Indeed, with the attendant circumstantiality of samples and prices, the information might have served only the more seriously to mislead whoever reasoned upon them.

Nothing can exceed the jealousy of the few tea-dealers within reach, or the reluctance manifested by them to admit of any uninitiated person, Chinese or European, into the price secrets of their dealings, as indeed might very readily have been expected.

Another difficulty arises from the universal practice here of all traders and shopkeepers demanding, in the first instance, an exaggerated price for their goods, so different from, and so variously disproportioned to, the sum which in the end they are prepared to take, that the first demands furnish no kind of criterion for the value of the commodity, or the real market price. Thus, although I forward herewith a box containing samples of tea, with the prices annexed, as demanded at Foo-chow-foo of a Chinese, not known nor suspected, I believe, to have any dealings in communication with the English,

I look upon these prices as little better than mere random demands for a bidding. The price at which a chest or chop of tea may be purchased here can only be ascertained by a merchant on the spot, prepared to enter into a *bonâ fide* transaction. Still, notwithstanding the absence of such data, the certainty of a large diminution in the first cost of tea at Foo-chow-foo seems to me fully and satisfactorily established.

It may not be a necessary consequence from these premises, that a large and prosperous exchange of British goods and tea will take place at Foo-chow. It is easy to foresee, notwithstanding the elements of success enumerated, that many other conditions are necessary to ensure so great and startling a change in all the arrangements, monetary and personal, of the trading community,—changes affecting in a vital degree the interests of large bodies of Europeans in different parts of the world, and of the Chinese of the two provinces in which the ports of Canton and Foo-chow are situated. Something, no doubt, will depend upon the Chinese in the tea districts and at Foo-chow,—something, too, on the steps taken to resist it by the Canton hongs and traders; but much more, I conceive, upon the British merchants—the initiative rests with them. On them, too, fall the first inconveniences,—the changing of establishments and the risk. It will be essential that any house entering into the tea trade here should have its own experienced tea-taster on the spot, without which there would be doubtful security for the quality purchased. The tea-traders themselves have been the first to make the suggestion. These circumstances appear to me to offer the most serious obstacles.

I must believe, from all the information to which I have had access, that the entrance to the river, and its navigation to Pagoda Island, to an experienced pilot, offers no insurmountable difficulty, no danger, which is not equalled by the physical peculiarities of many other flourishing ports in different parts of the world.

The bad approach and the troublesome navigation are doubtless disadvantages, together with the long prevalence of the north-east monsoon, and the want of a good harbour off the mouth in the south-west: these are unquestionably grave and serious drawbacks, but no more. So also in reference to the difficulty and danger attending the transport of goods by river, to and from the interior, and more especially cargoes of tea, it is made light of by those most familiar with the intricacies of the navigation; and the tea-dealers, I am led to believe, are quite prepared, by the intervention of houses in Foo-chow, or otherwise, to conclude bargains in tea, with the condition annexed, of delivering them at a fixed price, at their own risk and cost, either at the anchorage off Pagoda Island or any other part of the river where it may best suit a ship of burden to lie for her cargo.

Some advantages might probably be derived from the publication, by authority, as I believe has already been suggested by Mr. Lay, of some plain sailing directions, in reference to the approach and entrance of the Min, drawn up by Captain Collinson, from his surveys.

I confess the possibility of misunderstandings and collisions, with a large population, such as Foo-chow possesses, in which there are of course many ill-disposed persons, and where all, by the ignorance engendered by their isolation and exemption from the personal effects of the late war, are prone to an arrogant and offensive assumption of superiority, if not a right to insult, seems to me not the least of the impediments adverse to the opening trade.

I have little faith either in the power or hearty good-will of the authorities to repress or punish insult or violence offered to a British subject; and any untoward occurrence arising from these causes might very seriously retard the best directed efforts to establish friendly and commercial relations. It is to be hoped, however, that firmness and moderation may suffice to avert such possible contingencies.

I have only farther to add, that passing in review and carefully weighing all that my information suggests as to the advantages and disadvantages attached to this port as a place of British trade, more especially for the barter of manufactured goods with tea—for on this depends the existence of a trade of any importance—I do not feel warranted in forming sanguine anticipations of a great or rapid development of foreign commerce; and I see sufficient on the adverse side to render a prediction of even ultimate prosperity hazardous. But I am bound also to state my strong conviction that Foo-chow-foo, as a port, enjoys many of the most important elements of a large and successful trade. Time alone can shew how far the advantages which it offers are counterbalanced by inseparable disadvantages, and particularly how far the former are of a nature to excite the British mercantile community to divert their capital from Canton and employ the same amount with energy and intelligence at Foo-chow-foo, for it is scarcely necessary to add that on this, after all, must depend the prospects of the port as a mart for tea and British produce.

(Signed)   RUTHERFORD ALCOCK, Consul.

Foo-chow-foo, June 16, 1845.

CONSUL THOM TO SIR JOHN DAVIES.

British Consulate, Ningpo, January 10, 1846.

SIR,—I have now the honour to wait upon your Excellency with the returns of British and foreign trade at the port of Ningpo for the year 1845. This document speaks for itself: foreign commerce does not seem destined to flourish at Ningpo.

The cause of our failure is very easily pointed out; Shanghai has drawn everything to its centre; it has flooded this market with its superabundant importations, and attracted thither the teamen who were previously inclined to prtronize this port.

Mr. Mackenzie, our only merchant, gave up his establishment here in September, and went to join his brother at Shanghai. He gave the place a very fair trial, but he could get no support: his constituents found that better sales and better purchases were to be made at Shanghai, and they naturally sent their goods and their orders where they could be realized and executed to best advantage.

Shortly after the withdrawal of Mr. Mackenzie, Mr. Davidson, a merchant established at Chusan, rented a house inside the city, and sent over an assistant with a parcel of British goods, to try with what success trade might be done at Ningpo. But, strange to say, he found the native hongs plentifully supplied with our cottons and woollens, viâ Soochow, and retailing them here at cheaper rates than he (Mr. Davidson's assistant) could afford to do, although he had brought his parcel directly from Chusan. To explain this commercial phenomenon it will be necessary to remind your Excellency that in our immense transactions at Shanghai there are two prices known in the market, viz. the cash price and the barter price. On the first opening of the port of Shanghai, some sales of our manufactures were effected for cash, but latterly everything has been done by barter. The British merchant, on bartering his cottons and woollens, gets a higher nominal price for them than he could get were he to sell them at the cash price of the day. On the other hand, the teaman or silkman just adds an equivalent to the price of his silk or tea, and so the account is balanced. As almost all the parties interested in this trade, either ship goods or get their returns in produce, or give orders for produce and pay for it in British goods, the system works well enough; the English agent sends home a better account-sales to his constituent: it is true that the invoice of produce may be a little high priced, but it is hard to distinguish the quality of tea within a tael or two per picul, or of raw silk within ten or twenty dollars per picul, whereas a difference of five cents on a yard of woollens, or ten cents on a piece of long cloths, would cause the greatest dissatisfaction at home. Thus, if a manufacturer in England were to ship a parcel of British goods to Shanghai, and to give positive instructions that his returns should be made in bills at six months' sight, the utmost that he could expect is, that his agent should go into the market, sell his goods at the cash price, take this money, buy with it a bill at the current rate of exchange, and remit it to him. But A. B.'s account sales of goods sold for cash would be very different from his neighbour C. D.'s, which had been bartered. The particulars I am now detailing are not well understood in England, and when such a circumstance happens it generally causes an unpleasant correspondence between the constituent at home and the agent out here. On the other hand, if a large English tea-dealer were to ship specie wherewith to purchase his investment, there is no doubt that a man with ready money in his hand can at all times command the best teas in the market; still, how are you to convince a constituent at home that he has got a better bargain for his dollars than his neighbour has got for his goods? Thus the system of indiscriminate barter goes on, though the rule suggested by self-interest ought to be, for the tea and silk dealers to send out cash to pay for their investments in Chinese produce, and to leave the manufacturer of British goods to ship his cottons and woollens for his own account, or get rid of them as he otherwise best might.

The Chinese who has sold his tea or silk for cash takes it to the tea or silk country, and employs it to prepare a new adventure. The Chinese who has bartered his tea or silk for British goods takes them to Soochow, and turns them into ready money there, submitting to a discount of 5, 10, or 15 per cent. as his necessities may be less or more urgent. The Soochow speculator having purchased them at a bargain, sends them over the empire; every place, and Ningpo among the rest, is inundated with them. The British merchant residing at Chusan sends goods over to Ningpo, thinking that by reason of his proximity he can place them here cheaper than by the circuitous route of Shanghai. But he is mistaken, and is taught his mistake by bitter experience. He sees (e. g.) white long cloths quoted at Shanghai at two dollars ninety cents, and he expects to get as good a price at Ningpo. He does not not consider that this two dollars ninety cents is the barter price, and that the Chinese speculator has a bonus of fifteen or even twenty per cent. to pay land-carriage, transit duties, &c., &c., and still leave him a small margin of profit. The Ningpo or Chusan merchant sees that account-sales are sent home from Shanghai at two dollars ninety cents, he does not like to send home a worse account-sales, but he wants cash, and he cannot get this: the natives are retailing at less than two dollars ninety cents; he is not authorized to take produce, so he must either submit to a sacrifice or retire before native competition. This last has been done, Mr. Davidson has withdrawn his assistant, and Ningpo is now to be supplied from Shanghai, viâ Soochow. The only consolation amidst this loss of trade that remains to us is, the fact that the transit duties at Soochow and Hangchow must be exceedingly light and reasonable upon British goods, otherwise they could not supply us so cheaply from Shanghai. This is indeed a great consolation, for the transit duties involve many difficult and delicate questions, and at one time caused me a good deal of uneasiness.

The great difference between the cash and barter prices at Shanghai reminds me of what took place at Canton in the years 1836-7, previous to Hingtai's failure, and I fear that it betokens an unhealthy state of trade in the north. Should, however, any commercial crisis take place at Shanghai from over trading, things will soon find their level again; in no respect do I think Ningpo likely to be benefitted by such an event.

About the beginning of November, Mr. Watmore, the American merchant, called in here, and proposed to the green-teamen a very extensive operation. There were at that time 5,000 chests of green teas in and about Ningpo, and he offered to buy the whole of them. The transaction would have amounted to about a lac of dollars, and might have been the making of the port of Ningpo; but the green-teamen did not understand their true interests, they asked much higher prices than they intended to take; they delayed, they higgled about trifles, and Mr. Watmore having other business to attend to, was obliged to break off the negotiation, leaving them to repent of their folly and obstinacy when too late. The teas have since been sent on to Shanghai, and the green-teamen are now closing their hong, in despair of any more customers ever coming this way again.

In now announcing to your Excellency the nullity of foreign trade at Ningpo, I have no blame whatever to throw upon the Chinese authorities. With the exception of one or two trifling disputes about iron and saltpetre, I have always found them most cordially endeavouring to extend foreign commerce.

Nay, indeed, only a short time ago I had a petition presented me from the body of. the green-teamen (with the sanction of the authorities), praying me to exert my powers and compel the English merchants to take their teas off their hands at fair prices; and on my replying that I had no such power, many of them thought (and I think to this day) that the blame rests with me for not compelling British merchants to come to this port to trade.

The reason of our bad fortune is sufficiently apparent. Buyers and sellers have alike found Shanghai to answer their purposes much better than this place; they have all gone thither, and the foreign trade of Ningpo (as naturally it should) has died of inanition.

The native trade of Ningpo has equally declined during the year 1845. The timber trade from Fokien, the rice and sugar trade from Formosa, the oil and pea trade from Shantung, the fur trade from Tartary, are all complaining of losing money. In short, an air of impoverishment seems to pervade the whole of this dictrict.

While such is the state of trade at Ningpo, the Chusan trade has declined no less and from the same reason, viz., its proximity to Shanghai.

There are two British merchants and one American merchant there (the last is, however, about to leave).

The following rough statement of the amount of their trade for the year 1845, has been furnished me by an intelligent resident, and may be relied upon as a very good approximation of the truth:—

British goods imported into Chusan in 1845	£8,640
American . . .	14,300
Total imports at Chusan in 1845 .	£22,940
Total exports from Chusan in 1845 .	£24,735

This is hardly equal to a fraction of the Shanghai trade, and is not a tithe of the trade Chusan employed in 1842-43 before Shanghai was opened. It is important to bear this fact in mind, for many persons contend that if Chusan were a British possession, it would become the seat of an immense trade. This is a mistake. Granting that even Chusan were to become a British possession to-morrow, it could not be made a more free port than it has been these last four or five years; and we see that so long as we enjoy a moderate tariff of duties, it can no more enter into competition with Shanghai, than Hong-Kong can with Canton.

When I was over at Chusan in September, I observed a great many junks at anchor in the harbour. These were principally laden with timber, rice, sugar, &c., &c., in short, they were conveying the produce of the south to the north of China. They had merely put into Chusan for a few days to purchase supplies from the natives; they took off a little opium, but hardly touched our manufactures: indeed they were already fully laden, and had no surplus funds to make fresh investments. Thus, although several hundreds of junks have anchored temporarily at Chusan during the last year, yet British trade has benefitted little or nothing thereby. The greater portion of our manufactures disposed of there have been bartered against alum with the Wenchow and Iaichow people.

Chusan, has, however, enjoyed a fair share of the opium trade. The quantity disposed of during the past year is calculated as follows, viz. :—

Bengal	. .	1,000 to 1,200 chests
Malwa	. .	2,500 to 3,000 „
Turkey	. .	150 to 300 „

This amounts to about a tenth part of the whole of the opium trade. Only a small portion of the above has found its way to Ningpo; the greater bulk of it being sold for the coast of Fokien.

It becomes an interesting question—" How will the giving up of Chusan affect the trade of Ningpo?" We see that the amount of business done at Chusan is small; and even were every dollar of it to be added to the trade of Ningpo, the sum total would be insignificant after all. Supposing that the opium ships were to shift their anchorage to Chinhai, and that the authorities here were to connive at it as openly as is the case at Shanghai, still I doubt if even this would much benefit foreign commerce at Ningpo. Allowing that the opium ships would receive a quantity of specie in exchange for their drug, and that this specie was available for investment in silks and teas, still the parties to whom these opium ships belong have already establishments to keep up at Canton, Hong-Kong, and Shanghai; they will hardly consent to keep an agent or tea-taster, &c., &c., for any trifling advantage to be obtained here, and would give orders to have the specie shipped for Hong-Kong, rather than it should be invested in produce at Ningpo. Indeed, were they willing to encourage this market, they might do so now as easily from Chusan, as at a future period, even if the ships lay at Chinhai. The authorities here have permitted foreign merchants during the last two or three months, to import goods and ship off produce in native boats, paying duty as per tariff. This is indeed a very great boon for the Chusan trade, and yet it would not appear to be attended with much advantage, for the privilege has only once been availed of by a British merchant, and thrice by an American merchant.

Having gone fully into the subject of cash and barter prices at the beginning of this letter, I beg now to wait upon your Excellency with the following statistical details, which may possibly prove useful to her Majesty's Government. When I arrived in this country early in 1834 (a few months previous to the expiring of the company's charter), British goods, Indian cotton, and Chinese produce, were selling at the following rates (I put in juxta-position the present rates, that your Excellency may see the result at a glance):—

| | Prices in dollars. | |
	1834.	1845.
Woollens (Spanish stripes) .	1.60 per yard	1.20 per yard
Long ells	9 per piece	7 per piece
Long cloths . . .	4.75 „	2.90 „
Cotton Yarn . . .	35 per picul	25 per picul
Cotton (Bombay) . .	8 taels „	6 taels „
Raw silk . . .	350 „	480 „
Tea (average price of Company's last investment .	23⅛ taels „	25 taels „

Thus, in 1834, 219 yards of woollens would procure a picul of silk, and 20 yards of woollens would procure a picul of tea. In 1845 it requires upwards of 400 yards of woollens to procure the other. In 1834, 39 pieces of long-ells would buy a picul of silk, and 3½ pieces a picul of tea.

In 1845 it would require 68 pieces and 4⅓ pieces to purchase the same.

In 1834, 74 pieces of long cloths would buy a picul of silk, and 7 pieces a picul of tea.

In 1845 it requires 165 pieces, and 12 pieces (very nearly), to do the same.

In 1834, 10 piculs of cotton yarn could buy a picul of silk, and 1 picul of cotton yarn could get $1\frac{1}{13}$ piculs of tea.

In 1845 it requires 19 piculs of cotton yarn to get a picul of silk, and $1\frac{1}{13}$ piculs of cotton yarn to get a picul of tea.

In 1834, 32 piculs of Bombay raw cotton would procure a picul of silk, and 3 piculs a picul of tea.

In 1845 it requires 55 piculs to purchase the one and 4 piculs to purchase the other.

This table will shew that since the abolition of the company's charter the prices of our productions have been gradually declining, while the prices of Chinese produce have been steadily rising. This is not selecting 1834 as a particularly good year, and 1845 as a particularly bad year, but by consulting the prices current for the last twelve years, it will be found that this rise on the one side, and fall on the other side, has been gradual and progressive. It is no answer to say, " We now import double the quantity that we did before, and therefore we can afford to sell them cheaper," for the Chinese now produce nearly double the quantity of tea that they did at the expiration of the company's charter, and yet so far from having reduced their prices they have augmented them, and I consider a tael or two a picul as a great augmentation, remembering that the general character of the present investments is very far inferior to the choice selections of the company.

The fact is the Chinese merchants combine much better than the foreign merchants, they have more patience, they are not so hard pushed, nor are they split into such a variety of parties and contending interests as the foreigners are. This will explain why the produce of their industry should rise, while ours keep falling. Another fact to be borne in mind is, that when the price of Chinese produce has once risen, it is very difficult to bring it down again. This was exemplified in 1836 ; the price of Isattee silk had hardly before that time gone above 370 or 380 dollars, but during that year, partly through speculation and partly through the operation of the company's finance committee at Canton, the price was raised to 500 dollars, and the quantity usually shipped was doubled during that year. But after 1836-37 the quantity began to fall off, though the price continued to rate much higher than in 1836, and we could not account for the paradox, that with better prices offering a smaller quantity came to market. It was found, however, that by our speculations of 1836, not only had we raised the prices upon ourselves, but also upon the native manufacturer, the producer of silk kept the vantage ground he had gained, and, as he could get these enhanced prices from the native consumer, he declined to make any abatement in favour of his foreign customers. Our manufacturers could not afford, however, to give 500 dollars a picul for raw silk, and as England was not entirely dependent on China for this article, our people went elsewhere for it.

I have called your Excellency's attention to these details for the following reason,—I observe that a strong party at home are now urging her Majesty's Government to reduce the duty on tea from 2s. 1d. to 1s. per lb., arguing that from its greater cheapness the consumption will be doubled, and that the revenue will be no loser by the reduction. This is a very plausible theory ; but I am afraid that these people, who speak so confidently, have not duly considered what would be the effects of such a reduction in this country. Is there no possibility that speculation would again be at work, that on the prospect of such a reduction taking place, large orders would be sent out by a thousand contending parties, that the prices of tea would be run up, perhaps doubled, and that the deficit in our revenue, and all the benefit intended for our people, would be transferred to the pockets of the Chinese producers? Let it be remembered that we are entirely dependent upon China for our supply of tea, there is no second market that we can go to if the supply here don't suit us. That this is no idle fear may be proved by reference to the returns of trade for 1836-37; this was a year of great speculation both with the English and Americans, and the average price of all the teas shipped off during that season was 33¾ taels per picul (nearly a half more than the company used to pay for their investments), although a large proportion of that year's teas was classified by the trade at home as " trash " and " rubbish."

Next year was a year of commercial suffering both in England and America, few competitors appeared in the market, and these with exceedingly moderate ideas, and the over-speculation of 1836-37 was retrieved by the caution of 1837-38, else there can hardly be a doubt that tea, like silk, would have·kept its high prices. It is, however, extremely likely that it would again rise, and by no means so certain that it would again come down in the event of a reduction of the duty in England, and I consider that this suggestion is worthy the attention of her Majesty's Government.

I have, &c.,

(Signed)   R. THOM.

SIR JOHN DAVIS TO THE EARL OF ABERDEEN.

(Extract.)   Victoria, Hong-Kong, April 28, 1846.

My Lord,—I have the honour to forward herewith Mr. Consul Macgregor's report and returns of the foreign trade of all flags at the port of Canton, during the year 1845, which did not arrive in time to be forwarded by the mail, which left us on the 25th.

I only this morning received from Captain Balfour at Shanghae the inclosed returns of the British and foreign trade at that port for 1845. The Consul states that he deferred them so long, " having been desirous to accompany the annual trade returns with a detailed report on the future prospects of the trade at this place," but that " the disclosures which have recently been made as to the mode in which trade has been carried on render it unadvisable in me to write anything so as to create expectations which might not be fulfilled."

He evidently alludes to the barter system under which the commerce has been conducted (partly on account of the scarcity of silver occasioned by the opium trade), and to the embarrassments occasioned by the failure of Chinese brokers. These are matters which so entirely concern the merchants themselves, that they can only be regulated by their own improved experience and better understood interests, and therefore all interference is out of the question. Some temporary check may be given to the trade, but the port of Shanghae is evidently destined to be one day the principal seat of European commerce. The British imports and exports for 1845 have each exceeded a million sterling.

The land regulations established by Captain Balfour in communication with the Intendant of Shanghae have been entirely approved by me in my reply to the Consul, and, as I there observed, will form good models for rules of a similar nature at the other ports.

CONSUL MACGREGOR TO SIR JOHN DAVIS.

Canton, April 23, 1846.

SIR,—In addition to the returns of the British trade for the past year, which I forwarded in a previous despatch, I have now the honour of transmitting to your Excellency, for the information of Her Majesty's principal Secretary of State for Foreign Affairs, the following returns illustrative of the foreign trade at this port during the same period, viz.:—

1st. A return of the trade of the United States of America.

2nd. A return of the trade of France.

3rd. A return of the trade of Holland.

4th. A return of the trade of Denmark.

5th. A return of the trade of Sweden.

6th. A return of the trade of Germany.

7th. A return of the trade under various flags.

8th. A synoptical table affording a comprehensive view of the import trade from foreign countries at this port during the past year, specifying the quantities and description of the commodities, as well as their estimated value, and distinguishing the national flags under which they were imported; and

9th. A similar table referring to the export trade at Canton during the same period.

Before entering into particulars of the above-mentioned returns, I must premise that most foreign vessels bound to China usually discharge part of their cargoes either at Hong-Kong or Macao, to wait the chance of a market at the northern ports. Such of the goods so discharged as may ultimately be directed to Canton for sale, are sent in lorchas, or other small craft, and are not included 'in the before-mentioned returns. This circumstance will, in most instances, account for the paucity of imports therein shewn, and must be borne in mind in order to prevent the real extent of foreign trade from being underrated.

The value of the commodities imported and exported has invariably been computed upon a moderate estimate according to the average prices of the year in this market. In doubtful cases, however, or where this was not practicable, for instance, in the valuation of manufactured and other articles not sold by weight, I have consulted persons conversant with such matters, although I readily admit that from unacquaintance with the particular description and quality of such goods, the valuation given may sometimes prove either above or under the mark.

I shall now proceed to take a cursory view of the trade of each of the foreign nations in succession, adding such observations as may seem to be required in further elucidation of the subject.

I have to report that the American trade last year, in point of the quantity of the goods imported and exported, considerably exceeds that of the preceding year, and that there is a corresponding increase in the amount of American shipping employed.

It would appear from these returns, that the legitimate importations (exclusive of bullion) from Great Britian, the United States, the West Coast of America, Manila, and the Eastern Archipelago, in fifty-eight American vessels of 28,613 tons, amounted to 2,478,048 dollars. Among these, fabrics of cotton were imported to the amount of 1,452,302 dollars, of which I have the satisfaction to state, a considerable part was of British manufacture, exported from Liverpool in five American vessels of 2,458 tons. Among the other American staple articles I have chiefly to note cotton, ginseng, and lead, imported to the amount of 530,954 dollars. In consequence of scarcity in the southern parts of China, rice to the amount of 195,077 dollars, was supplied by the Americans, who also imported specie from the South American ports on the Pacific to the amount of 722,253 dollars, as far as I have been able to ascertain. The total amount of importation stated at 3,200,301 dollars, does not include, however, the American trade at Macao, nor the quantities of goods proceeding from American vessels, and shipped from that place in lorchas, &c., for Canton, adding which items the American import trade in this quarter would probably not fall short of 3,500,000, dollars.

As regards the American export trade, I find that forty-three American ships of 19,269 tons, departed in the course of the last year for the United States, Calcutta, Manila, the South American ports in the Pacific, and the South Sea Islands, with commodities to the amount of 7,979,864 dollars, among which the article of tea is most conspicuous, forming an item of 6,290,254 dollars, and shewing an increase in the quantity exported of 23,456 piculs, equal to upwards of 3,000,000l.

According to their own returns made out for the season, from the 1st of July, 1844, to the 30th of June, 1845, the Americans state the exportation of tea in American ships at 20,752,558lbs. The exportation of silk fabrics of all sorts, mostly for the supply of the South American markets, is stated at 1,041,542 dollars, an amount which no doubt would be larger, but for the well-

known fact that silk piece goods (like many other articles
of small bulk and great value) are shipped off from
hence to a great extent without passing through the
Custom-house.

The American shipping also shews an increase, as will
appear by the following comparative statements, viz.:—

	Arrivals.	Departures.
1844,	57 ships of 23,273 tons.	49 ships of 21,600 tons.
1845,	83 ,, 38,658 tons.	85 ,, 37,959 tons.
Increase,	26 ships of 15,385 tons,	36 ships of 16,359 tons.

This favourable result, however, I find on examination,
is owing not so much to a corresponding increase in the
trade with the United States, as to the intermediate trade
of American vessels between Manila, Batavia, the Straits
of Malacca, the South Sea Islands, and China, besides
the coasting trade, in which about a dozen of fast-sailing
vessels were engaged in the course of the year.

The most prominent features in the trade of the Americans last year appear to have been the following: they
imported goods to a much larger amount than in the year
preceding, and even had recourse to purchases of manufactures in the British markets, in preference to availing
themselves of credits on London, in part payment of the
teas exported to the United States. Their shipping in
the China waters was more numerous than in 1844, and
had a fair share in the carriage of goods coastwise. They
sent out their own vessels to Calcutta and Bombay for
the opium they required in the China trade. They succeeded in getting the management of great part of the
continental business into their hands, which, independently of pecuniary advantages, offers the facility of em-
ploying their own drafts on London, to some extent, in
remittances for consignments received, in lieu of appearing with their bills in the market, which occasionally, and

particularly at so critical a juncture as the present, is attended with some inconvenience.

The French trade at Canton offers but little of interest to communicate. Of three French vessels of 799 tons, which arrived last year, only one entered with a cargo consisting of rice. On the other hand, three vessels of 963 tons departed for Manila, Bordeaux, and Havre, after having completed their cargoes with teas, and other China produce, to a rather greater extent than last year.

The returns will shew that the Dutch trade at Canton, as regards the imports from Java last year, has been very limited, the value of those on which duty was paid, not having exceeded 77,751 dollars. This figure does not include, however, the commodities disposed of to a much larger amount at Macao, nor those forwarded in lorchas for sale in the Canton market.

Ten Dutch ships of 3,118 tons, departed in the course of the year for Java, Manila, Amsterdam, and Rotterdam, after having completed their outward cargoes at Canton with tea, cassia, and other articles, to the amount of 635,535 dollars.

From the Consular returns communicated to me, of the combined trade of the Dutch at Macao and Canton, it appears that the total of imports amounted to 978,715 dollars, and of exports to 801,113 dollars, in twenty Dutch vessels of the burthen of 6,050 tons.

In the absence of ships, the Belgian trade suggests no other remark than that several parcels of broad cloth of Belgian manufacture were imported here from London in British vessels, and seem to have been disposed of at prices corresponding with the superior workmanship of the article.

With the exception of a Danish ship of 372 tons, which had remained over from 1844, and departed for Singapore and Copenhagen at the commencement of last

year, with a cargoe of tea, cassia, and other staple articles
of China, all the Danish vessels which arrived at Canton
in the course of the year, to the number of three of 948
tons, were employed in the carrying trade for other
nations, and departed for Singapore, Hamburg, and Lima.
The total value of exports laden at Canton, were estimated at 141,129 dollars.

The Swedish ships which arrived at Canton in the
course of the past year to the number of six, measuring
2,066 tons proceeding from Bombay, Batavia, and the
northern ports of China, were, like the Danish, almost
exclusively employed in the carrying trade. Only one
of them, the *Prius Carl*, sent out on an exploring expedition by the merchants of Stockholm, and in the cargo
of which the Swedish Government is said to have been
interested, arrived with 80 tons of iron, and 1,000 tubs of
steel, and about 1,300 bales of Bombay cotton, which two
former articles were not discharged on account of being
unsaleable here. The result of this expedition being far
from affording encouragement for sending out further supplies of Swedish produce, it is to be presumed that the
merchants of Stockholm will henceforward strictly adhere
to the only remunerating branch of their trade in these
parts, which seems to be the carrying trade, for which
their ships, built, fitted out, and sailed at a very small
expense are particularly well qualified.

The returns under the head of the German trade,
embrace collectively the trade in Austrian, Prussian,
Hanseatic, and other vessels belonging to subjects of the
Germanic Confederation.

The German trade during the year 1845, as compared
with the previous year, shews a much greater increase
than that of any other nation.

There arrived from foreign ports with cargoes, or part

thereof, two Austrian ships of 567 tons from London and Liverpool, five Hamburgh ships of 1,484 tons, from Singapore, Hamburg, and Mazatlan, one Bremen ship of 200 tons from Bremen, eight German ships, of 2,251 tons, while there departed five Hamburg, two Bremen, and two Austrian, one of the aggregate burthen of 2,571 tons, for Singapore, Manila, Hamburg, Bremen, and New York.

German vessels last year, as appears from the returns above quoted, served as carriers for British manufactured goods, to the extent of nearly one-half of their aggregate imports, for "Straits' produce," to the extent of one-fourth, leaving only another fourth for their own products and manufactures, which apparent disproportion will be sufficiently explained on referring to the introductory remarks preceding the details of the present report.

The most important article of import from Germany is undoubtedly broad cloth, and although I have no means of ascertaining the exact quantity of German woollen cloths annually sold in this market, yet from the information I have obtained, I am induced to think that the direct importation at this port may safely be estimated at 40,000 yards per annum, of the value of 60,000 dollars, besides 60,000 yards, which in the absence of a regular intercourse, but more from ignorance on the part of the German manufacturers as to the particular mode of packing the goods for China, have hitherto received their last finish in England, and arrive here as British goods in British vessels. As the advantage of German cloths, however, consists in quality, and the disadvantage in form, it must be presumed that the trade in this article (which the Chinese want, but do not manufacture themselves,) will increase, and at no distant period be carried on direct, without the instrumentality of English packers.

Nearly one-third of the exports in German vessels was carried to the United States ; the remainder for the consumption of the German market shews a great increase over the exports of the year preceding, and the German ports having both vessels to employ and manufactures to send in return for Chinese products, it must be expected that they will more and more endeavour if possible to supply their wants direct from this country.

The returns of the trade carried on with Canton under various flags, includes two Spanish vessels of 1,406 tons, arrived from Manila with rice and paddy, but which returned in ballast; one Peruvian vessel of 150 tons from Lima, with specie; and one Columbian vessel of 93 tons from Mazatlan, with cotton and specie, both of which latter vessels returned to their respective ports with cargoes of silk manufactures and China products.

The trade with the ports of South America in the Pacific, namely, Mazatlan, Callao, and Valparaiso, is of great importance, and has hitherto chiefly been carried on in British and American vessels. Of late the Hamburghers have despatched several ships to those ports with an assorted cargo, with the proceeds of which, invested in bullion or dollars, these vessels are sent to China for a return cargo, consisting in all sorts of wrought silks and other Chinese manufactures saleable in the South American markets. Independently of the two South American vessels above-mentioned, four American, one Danish, and one Swedish vessel, were engaged in this trade last year, in which British shipping had no share on account of the scarcity of vessels to which I alluded in my report on the British trade.

With reference to the two synoptical tables, it remains for me to explain that the commodities therein stated as imported in " Portuguese lorchas," proceeded almost exclusively from Macao, where these goods originally arrived in foreign vessels, and were subsequently transhipped in the roads into lorchas for this port. These goods, therefore, in so far as they have been regularly entered at the Canton custom-house, must be considered as forming part of the legitimate trade in which each of the foreign nations has to claim a share proportional to the extent of their respective commercial operations at this port. The tables above alluded to exhibit an aggregate of imports amounting to 14,062,811 dollars, and of exports 30,566,426 dollars. On comparing them with the return of imports and exports of the preceding year, the former shews a deficiency of 3,780,438 dollars, while the latter offers an increase of 5,052,477 dollars.

The first year in which the foreign nations have been enabled fully to avail themselves of the advantages secured to them by our treaties with China, has now expired, and the question would naturally suggest itself, in how far their trade, which is chiefly concentrated at Canton, has been developed, and in what degree it has interfered with our own. The several returns and tables furnished by me, and the explanatory remarks accompanying them will, I trust, tend to indicate in some measure the extent to which the Americans, our competitors in the supply of cottons, and the Germans, Dutch, and Belgians, in the supply of woollens, have carried their operations. The former, no doubt, will for some time to come remain dependent either upon our credit, or upon our manufactures, to enable them to continue as heretofore; and the latter possess, themselves, too few articles of bulk adapted for the consumption of China, to allow of a direct trade to any considerable extent, without a combination of other markets in their schemes. As for the other nations of Europe, their commercial intercourse with China, for obvious reasons, is not likely to grow into any importance, and the only advantage they may possibly be expected to derive from it, will be to become occasionally the carriers of the commodities entering into the British or the American trade. I find on inquiry into the relative state of British and foreign shipping in this district, that in 1844 (when British ships were abundant), the proportion of British tonnage to the aggregate burthen of the vessels engaged in the trade of Canton, was about 80 per centum, calculating the aggregate of tonnage both inwards and outwards; and that in 1845, when, from various causes, there was an unusual scarcity of British tonnage, while foreign vessels freely dropt in from all quarters, the proportion, in consequence thereof, declined to 65 per centum. With regard to trade, and adopting the aggregate value of imports and exports as the basis of computation, the difference between the two years is still smaller, the proportion of British to the whole of the trade at Canton in 1844 being 77 per centum, while in 1845 (when the trade of foreign nations had come into full play) it was 70 per centum; and from the facts which have come under my observation, I am inclined to think that if this mode of computation were applied to the whole of the legitimate China trade, these proportions would not be materially effected either one way or the other.

I have, &c.,

(Signed) FRANCIS C. MACGREGOR.

(Extract.)   Her Majesty's Consulate, Shanghae, March 30, 1846.

SIR,—Having been desirous to accompany the annual trade returns with a detailed report on the future prospects of the trade at this place, I have, with this view, till the present time deferred forwarding them to your Excellency: the disclosures, however, which have recently been made, as to the mode in which the trade has been carried on, render it unadvisable for me to write anything so as to create expectations which might not be fulfilled.

Notwithstanding the objections which may be raised as to the mode in which the trade has been done, it is gratifying at the end of this, the second year since this port was opened, to be able to exhibit, as these returns do, so extensive a trade, and which has sprung up under those difficulties peculiar to the opening of every new commercial mart in China ; and although the difficulties which still exist may for a time check the steady course of the trade, they cannot prevent this place being considered the maritime emporium for the north-western, central, and northern provinces of China, over which our goods can easily be conveyed by the noble internal water-communications of this country, which, commencing at this port, lead into the very heart of the empire.

I have given my particular attention to secure facilities for conducting the trade, abstaining myself from all interference with its details, and have endeavoured to prevent any meddling on the part of the Chinese authorities ; the English and Chinese merchants have therefore enjoyed free scope for their energies, and have traded how and with whom they pleased. Any obstructions which may now be felt are those attendant on the mode hitherto of conducting the commerce, and can alone be overcome by the merchants themselves, and not by government arrangements.

The site set apart for the residence of our merchants is universally allowed to be conveniently situated for conducting business with the Chinese and with our own ships, which lie at anchor opposite to and close to the buildings of the merchants; and the extent of ground, from (60) sixty to (75) seventy-five English statute acres, already rented out to the foreign community, must be admitted to be considerable in extent, affording space for dwelling-houses, gardens, places of amusement, and, above all, for extenstve warehouses for stowing merchandise.

The regulations for the land, herewith enclosed, were drawn up by his Excellency the Taoutae in communication with me, and they afford the community an opportunity for making all those arrangements requisite for the public cleanliness, police, security, and good order of their location; and it is to be hoped that the merchants will combine to carry out regulations which are calculated to secure all the advantages which could reasonably be expected.

I have, &c.,

(Signed)   G. BALFOUR,

H. B. M.'s Consul for Shanghae.

A RETURN of the Number and Tonnage of Merchant
Vessels which arrived at, and departed from, the Port
of Shanghae, during the year ending the 31st of December, 1845, distinguishing the Countries to which
they belogned, viz.:—

ARRIVED.			DEPARTED.		
Under what Colours.	Number of Vessels.	Tonnage.	Under what Colours.	Number of Vessels.	Tonnage.
British	62	15,971	British	66	16,760
American	19	6,531	American	17	5,931
Spanish	2	600	Spanish	2	600
Swedish	2	650	Swedish	2	650
Hamburg	1	324	Hamburg	1	324
Bremen	1	320	Bremen	1	320
Total	87	24,396	Total	89	24,585

Shanghae, December 31st, 1845.

G. BALFOUR,
H. B. M.'s Consul at Shanghae.

SHANGHAE LAND REGULATIONS.

KUNG MOOKEW, imperially appointed Intendant of Circuit of Soochowfoo, Sungkeangfoo, and Taetsangchow, and
superintendent of customs in the province of Keangnan.

I now take all the regulations first and last agreed upon
by us in communication together, in accordauce with the
treaty, which have already been separately published by
me, the Taoutae, and hung up at the Custom House, and
specially forward a copy thereof, requesting the Honourable Consul will examine into, translate, and publish them
generally for the information of all renters of property
north of the Yang-king-pang, that they may act in obedience thereto. Wherefore I write this, wishing the
Consul daily happiness.

KUNG MOOKEW, imperially appointed Intendant of Circuit of Soochowfoo, Sungkeangfoo, and Taetaangchow, and Superintendent of Customs in the Province of Keangnan, again issues a proclamation in accordance with the treaty.

In the year 1842, the imperial commands were received, in reply to a memorial permitting commercial intercourse being carried on at the five ports of Kwangchow, Fuhchow, Heamun, Ningpo, and Shanghae, allowing merchants and others of all nations to bring their families to reside there, and providing that the renting of the ground for the building of houses, must be deliberated upon and determined by the local authorities in communication with the Consuls, both acting in conformity with the feelings of the local inhabitants, so that mutual and perpetual harmony might be attained.

Hence it has been determined, in conformity with the feelings of the inhabitants and the circumstances of the locality of Shanghae, that the grouud north of the Yang-King-Pang and south of the Le-Kea-Chang, should be rented to English merchants, for erecting their buildings, and residing upon, and some regulations which have been agreed upon in reference thereto, and to which obedience is necessary, are hereinafter specified.

CAPTAIN BALFOUR, HER MAJESTY'S CONSUL AT
SHANGHAE.

I HAVE received the Honourable Intendant of Circuit's letter, together with the copy sent of all the regulations first and last agreed upon by us in communication together in accordance with the treaty, and I thoroughly understand them. As the regulations in question must be conductive to the good order, peace, and comfort of all the people of my nation, I, the Consul, will of course translate and publish them to all renters of property north of the Yang-King-Pang, for their obedience thereto, and I will send the Intendant of Circuit a volume of the regulations in the English character, to be placed on record. Wherefore I write this reply, wishing him daily happiness.

IT having been determined upon, according to treaty, in conformity with the feelings of the people, and the circumstances of the locality of Shanghae, that the ground north of Yang-King-Pang, and south of Le-Kea-Chang, should be rented to English merchants, for erecting their buildings, and residing upon, I now take several regulations in reference thereto, which have been agreed upon by me, the Intendant of Circuit, and the Honourable Consul, in communication together, and to which obedience is necessary, and specify them as hereinafter follows :—

REGULATION I. ON merchants renting ground, the local officers and the Consul must in communication with each other define its boundaries, clearly specify the number of Poo and Mow, and put up stone landmarks : where there are roads, or paths, these landmarks must be placed against the fence, so as not to occasion obstruction to passengers ; and upon such landmarks will be plainly engraved how many feet outwards the real boundary lies. The Chinese must report the transaction at the offices of the Intendant of Circuit, and of the Magistrate and Hae-fang of Shanghae, in order that they may address their high officers thereupon, while the merchants will report to the Consul, so that it may be put on record. The deed of the lessor renting out the land, and that of the lessee acknowledging such rent, will be executed in the form of indenture, and presented to be examined and sealed, when they will be respectively given into the possession of the several parties, in order to establish good faith, and to prevent encroachment and usurpation.

II. There was originally a large road along the bank of the river, from the Yang-King-Pang northwards, which was a towing-path for the grain junks, and which subsequently could not be kept in repair from the sinking away of the bank. Since, however, that portion is now rented out, all the renters must repair and replace this road, so that persons may pass to and fro. Its standard width must, however, be two Chang five Chih of the Canton Custom House measure, so as not only to prevent passengers from crowding and pressing one against each other, but likewise to serve as a preventive against the washing of the high tide upon the houses. After the road shall have been completed, the officers and men who urge on the grain junks, as well as respectable tradesmen, will be at liberty to walk along it; but idlers and vagrants will not be permitted to spy about there. With the exception of the merchants' own cargo and private boats, no other small boats of any description will be suffered to stop or anchor at the jetties off the merchants' private lots, lest it should lead to an opening for causes of quarrel; but the Custom House guard-boats will as usual cruize about there as occasion requires. Upon these jetties the said merchants will be permitted to erect gateways or railings, for the purpose of opening and shutting at pleasure.

III. It has been determined that four large roads, leading out to the river from east to west, should be reserved in the grounds rented by the merchants for public thoroughfares, viz. :—

> One north of the Custom House ;
> One upon the old Rope Walk ;
> One south of the Four-Lot ground ; and
> One south of the Consulate lot.

A road running from north to south was also to be reserved on the west of the former Ningpo warehouse. The standard width of these, with the exception of the Rope Walk, which was originally two Chang five Chih of the Custom House measurement in width, must be two Chang of the Government land-measure, not only to give space and room for passengers, but likewise to prevent the calamities of fire. Jetties must be publicly constructed upon the beach, where these roads go out to the river, each to be of the same width as the road to which it pertains, for the convenience of landing and shipping off. Arrangements must likewise be made for reserving two roads southward of the Custom House, on the north side of the Kwei hwapang and of Allum's Jetty, when the land shall have been rented there. Should it be necessary to make other new roads besides these, they must also be determined upon by the authorities in communication together. Should the roads, which are already rented, and the prices of which have been previously paid by merchants, become injured or destroyed, they will be repaired by the renters of the lots adjoining, and the Consul will hereafter get all the renters publicly to consult together and contribute equally towards them.

IV. Government roads have hitherto existed in the grounds at present rented by the merchants; but as numerous persons will now be passing to and fro, it is to be apprehended that disputes and brawls may take place, and it is therefore determined that another straight road, two Chang in width, shall be made for a thoroughfare to the westward of the river, and upon the small canal, commencing north, at the public road on the south side of the ice house, adjoining the military working sheds, and ending south, on the west side of the Letan (Red Temple) on the bank of the Yang-King-Pang; but the ground must be definitely rented, and the road completed, and measures must be taken by the authorities in communication with each other, to ascertain clearly what roads ought to be changed, when notice will be given by proclamation; and passengers must not be obstructed before the new road shall have been completed.

On the south side of the military working sheds, leading eastward to the jetty, at the Towpa Too Ferry, there has hitherto been a public road, which also must be made two Chang wide for the convenience of passengers.

V. In the lots rented by the merchants there have originally been Chinese people's graves; these the renters must not trample down nor destroy. Should cases happen where the graves require repair, the Chinese will be at liberty to acquaint the renters thereof, and repair them themselves.

The established periods for sacrificing and sweeping at the tombs are seven days before and eight days after (total, fifteen days), at the Tsing Ming term, about April 5th; at the summer solstice, one day; five days before and after the 15th of the seventh month; five days before and after the 1st of the tenth month; and five days before and after the winter solstice. The renters must not offer - them any hindrance, which would offend their feelings; nor may the individuals who sweep and sacrifice cut down trees, nor dig away earth for laying it on their graves from any spots distant from the said graves.

The total number of graves in the lots, as well as the family names to which they belong, must be distinctly entered into a list, and henceforth they must not again enter any more in the said lots. Should any Chinese, who are owners of the graves, wish to remove them and inter the bodies elsewhere, they will be at liberty to follow their own convenience.

VI. The periods at which merchants rent ground being various, some early, and others late, a merchant must, after he shall have settled the price of his ground, make such known to the neighbouring renters, in presence of whom, with the Weiyuens, Tepaou, and an officer of the Consulate, the boundaries will be publicly defined, so as to avoid confusion and mistake.

VII. Some of the merchants in renting land have paid equal deposit money and yearly rent, others a high deposit and a low rent, making uniformity hitherto impossible. They must now increase the deposit money at the rate of ten thousand cash for every one thousand cash of annual rent reduced, and over and above the sum thus added to the deposit money, pay a fixed annual rent of fifteen hundred cash for every mow of ground.

VIII. As regards the receiving of the annual rents by the Chinese: Every merchant that has negotiated for the rent of land must first reckon up the rent due for the odd days of the current year's rent, and pay it off with the deposit money, when the deed of the lessee acknowledging the rent, and that of the lessor renting out the land, will be drawn up, sealed, and delivered, after which, the period of paying the annual rent will be definitely fixed for the 15th day of the twelfth month of each Chinese year; on which day the next ensuing year's rent will be paid in full by the renter. When the time for receiving the rents arrives, the Superintendent of Customs will address the Consul ten days before the day fixed, who will tell all the renters to pay their amounts on that day, into the hands of the government banking-house; that establishment will give receipts to the renters, and then pay out the sums to the owners of the ground, upon authority of their rent-books, clearly inserting therein the payments made, so that the books may be ready for examination and comparison, and false and fraudulent claims prevented.

Should a renter pass the period fixed, and not pay his rent, the Consul will deal with such according to such of his country's laws as relate to rent defaulters.

IX. After merchants shall have rented land and built thereon, the merchant on his part alone on reporting the same may cease to rent his ground, when the deposit money will be restored to him, but the original owners will not be permitted at pleasure to cease renting it to him, still less may they make any further increase in the terms of the rent. Should any merchant not wishing to reside upon the lot rented by him, transfer the whole to another party, or should he take his land and sublet parts of it to others, the rent of such land (with the exception of the sale or the rent of the house newly built thereupon, and the expenses of filling up and adding of earth, &c., which he will negotiate for himself,) may only be transferred at its original rate, upon which no increase may be made, so as to prevent persons trading in the rent of land for the sake of gain, which would give the Chinese occasion for complaint. In either of the above cases, a report must be made to the Consul, who will address the local officers, and they will together place it on record.

X. After merchants shall have rented land they may build houses for the residence of their own families and dependents, and the storing of lawful merchandise; they may erect churches, hospitals, charitable institutions, schools, and houses of concourse : they may likewise cultivate flowers, plant trees, and make places of amusement. But they must not store contraband goods, nor fire off muskets or guns at unseasonable periods; still. less may they fire balls, or shoot arrows, or act in such a disorderly manner as may endanger or injure people, to the terror of the inhabitants.

XI. Should any persons die, the merchants will be at liberty to convey and inter them according to the funeral rites of their country, within the boundaries of the merchants' burying-ground. And the Chinese people must not offer any obstruction, nor may they destroy and break up the graves.

XII. Merchants renting ground, as also those renting buildings, within the boundaries to the north of the Yang-King-Pang, must, in concert together, build and repair the stone and wooden bridges, keep in order and cleanse the streets and roads, put up and light street lamps, establish fire engines, plant trees to protect the roads, open ditches to drain off the water, and hire watchmen. The Consul will be requested by the various renters to urge the propriety of assembling together and publicly consulting about and contributing towards the necessary expenses incurred thereon. The hire of the watchmen will be equitably settled by the merchants with the people, while the names and surnames of such watchmen will be reported by the Tepaou and Seaoukea to the local officers for examination. The regulations regarding the watchmen will be laid down, and the head men to be especially responsible for them appointed by the authorities in communication together. Should gamblers, drunkards, and vagabonds commit disturbances, and injure or annoy the merchants, the Consul will address the local officers, who will adjudicate such cases according to law, as a warning to all. If any barriers be hereafter erected, they must he determined upon and defined by the authorities in communication together, according to the circumstances of the ground: and after they shall have been erected, the periods of opening and shutting them will be made known in a proclamation, and likewise publicly notified in English by the Consul. They must be such as are convenient to both parties.

XIII. The value of the houses and land on the south side of the new Custom House being higher than that of those on the north side, in order minutely to ascertain what the amount of such value ought to be, it will be necessary, as in the Regulations for levying duty upon a valuation, for the local authorities and Consul, in communication together, to appoint four or five honest and upright Chinese and English merchants, to take the prices of the houses, the rent of the ground, the expenses of removal, and the labour of raising ground, and make an honest and equitable valuation thereof, so as to maintain justice and fairness.

XIV. If individuals belonging to other nations should wish to rent ground and build houses, or rent houses for residence or storage of goods, within the boundaries of the ground north of the Yang-King-Pang, set apart to be rented to English merchants, distinct application must first be made to the English Consul, to know whether such can be acceded to, so as to prevent misunderstandings.

XV. The merchants who now repair hither being more numerous than formerly, and there being still persons who have not yet settled for lots of ground, measures must therefore be taken by the authorities in communication together for successively renting additional land to them whereon to build houses and reside. The native inhabitants of the said quarter must not rent to each other, nor may they again build houses there for the purpose of renting to Chinese merchants; and hereafter when English merchants rent land, the number of mow must be defined: each family may not have more than ten mow, so as to prevent those who first arrive from possessing broad large lots, while those who come subsequently have small and narrow ones. After land has been settled for, the not building houses suitable for residence and storage of goods thereon will be a contravention of the treaty, and it will then be proper for the local authorities and Consul, in communication together, to examine into the matter, and take such land, and allot it to some other party to rent.

XVI. Within the boundaries of the ground north of the Yang-King-Pang, the several renters may publicly build a market-place, that Chinese may carry daily necessaries thither and vend them. Its position, and all rules for the management thereof, must be determined by the local authorities and Consul in communication together. Merchants must not build such on their own account, nor may they build houses for renting to, or for the use of, Chinese. Should the several renters hereafter wish to set up head boatmen, or head coolies, they must request the Consul in communication with the local authorities, to determine upon the necessary regulations, and appoint them within the North Hwangpoo division.

XVII. Should any persons open shops for vending eatables or drinkables, &c., within the boundaries determined upon, or for the purpose of hiring out to foreigners to lodge or temporarily reside in, the Consul must first give them a licence, for the purpose of exercising scrutiny, after which they will be permitted to establish them. If they disobey, or are guilty of irregularities, then a prohibition will be laid upon them.

XVIII. Within the boundaries above determined upon, inflammable buildings must not be erected, such as straw sheds, bamboo houses, wooden houses, and such like. Merchandise likely to endanger or injure individuals must not be stored up, such as gunpowder, saltpetre, sulphur, large quantities of spirits, and such like.   The public must not be encroached upon nor obstructed, as by erecting scaffoldings for the purpose of building, causing eaves of houses to project, and heaping up goods for any length of time upon them and such like; and individuals must not be inconvenienced, as by the heaping up of filth, running out of gutters on the roads, causelessly creating noise or disturbance, or such like.   The object of all this is to render houses and property insurable, and to afford lasting peace and comfort to the mercantile community.   If gunpowder, saltpetre, sulphur, spirits, and such like articles, be brought to Shanghae, a place must be fixed upon by the authorities, in communication together, within the boundaries, and yet distant from the dwellings and warehouses, for the storage thereof, and to prevent carelessness.

XIX. All who rent ground and build houses, or who let out houses and hire dwelling or warehouses, must annually, on the 15th day of the 12th month, report the number of mow which they rent, the number of rooms which they have built, and the person to whom they have rented them during the past year, to the Cousul, who will communicate the same to the local authorities, to be placed on record for reference.   If there be any sub-letting, or letting parts of houses, or transfers of land, such must also, as they occur, be reported, to be placed on record.

XX. The original cost, and subsequent expenses for repair of the roads, jetties, and now-to-be-erected gateways, must all be made up from the contributions of the renters who have first arrived here, and who live in their vicinity.   Individuals who may hereafter successively arrive, as well as the renters who have not at present contributed, must all likewise subscribe their proportion, to make up the deficiency, so that the use of them may be available to the public, and that wrangling may be prevented ; and the several contributors will request the Consul to appoint three upright merchants to deliberate upon and determine the amount to be subscribed by them. If there be yet a deficiency, the contributors may also publicly resolve to levy a portion upon goods landed and shipped, which will go to make up the deficiency. In either case, however, they must wait until they have reported it to the Consul, and obtained his decision, when they will act in obedience to it. The receipt, care, expenditure and accounts of the funds, will be altogether superintended by the contributors.

XXI. Individuals belonging to other nations renting ground, building houses, renting dwelling-houses, or renting warehouses for storage of goods, or temporarily residing within the boundaries of the ground north of the Yang-King-Pang, set apart to be rented to English merchants, must all, in the same manner as the English people, obey all these Regulations, so that peace and harmony may be perpetuated.

XXII. Hereafter, in all these matters newly determined upon, in accordance with Treaty, should any corrections be requisite, or should it be necessary to determine upon further Regulations, or should the meaning not be clear, or should new forms be required, the same must always be consulted upon and settled by the authorities in communication together. If the community publicly decide upon any matter, as soon as it shall have been reported to the Consul, and determined upon by him and the local authorities in communication together, it can then be carried out in obedience thereto.

XXIII. Hereafter, should the English Consul discover any breach of the Regulations above laid down, or should any merchants or others lodge information thereof, or should the local Authorities address the Consul thereon, the Consul must in every case examine in what way it is a breach of the Regulations, and whether it requires punishment or not; and he will adjudicate and punish the same in one and the same way as for a breach of the Treaty and Regulations.

Dated Taoukwang, 25th year, 11th month, 1st day.
November 29th, 1845.

(True Translation.)

W. A. MEDHURST,
Interpreter, Shanghae Consulate.

COMPARATIVE VIEW of BRITISH TRADE at the FIVE PORTS of CHINA during the Year 1845.

Ports of Trade.	Tonnage.	Imports.	Tonnage.	Exports.
		£		£
Canton . .	86,087	2,321,692	98,277	4,492,370
Amoy . .	6,655	147,494	6,655	15,478
Foochowfoo .	765	*43,981	765	*40,293
Ningpo . .	1,926	10,398	1,926	17,495
Shanghae . .	15,971	1,082,207	16,760	1,259,091
Total . .	111,404	3,605,772	124,383	5,824,727

Victoria, April 28th, 1846.

CONSUL THOM TO SIR JOHN DAVIS.

(Extract.)   Ningpo, August 10, 1846.

In my despatch of July 31st last year, handing returns of trade till 30th June, 1845, I stated that certain teas had been shipped from this port for Hong Kong, which had been there characterised as "trash and rubbish," and quite unfit for either the English or American markets. I remarked at the same time that I thought that this was

* The Consul's Returns contain on both sides (Imports and Exports) the value of a Cargo which was not unladen, amounting to £28,166. This was deducted.

in a great measure the result of prejudice, and that I thought the Ningpo teas had not had fair play. That I was perfectly correct in my surmise is confirmed by the accompanying copy of a letter from Mr. Aspinall, tea-taster to Messrs. M'Kenzie Brothers, by which your Excellency will see " that the Ningpo teas in arriving at Liverpool got a fair character, and sold at remunerating prices." Your Excellency will therefore agree with me in an observation which I previously made, " that there is no just and sufficient reason why good tea may not be shipped from Ningpo as well as from any other port in China." Indeed, considering the shock that commercial credit has lately sustained at Shanghae, I am of opinion that if one or two rich and powerful houses, with all their apparatus of tea-tasters, ready-money, &c., were to establish here just now, a very excellent tea-trade might even yet be done at Ningpo. Since the evacuation of Chusan, one merchant (Mr. Waterhouse) has determined to try this port, and I am not altogether without hopes that he will partially succeed.

In my despatch of January 10, handing returns of trade for the half-year ending December 31, 1845, I ventured an opinion, that if the duty on tea were to be reduced in England, it could not fail to augment the price of the article in this country ; and that the benefit intended for our own people, as well as the loss accruing to the British revenue, would be transferred to the pockets of the Chinese tea-growers. This opinion has been completely confirmed by every intelligent practical British merchant with whom I have conversed on the subject since writing that letter. Even without any such diminution of duty on tea at home, it is manifest to every one that the price of tea is rising relatively as the price of our products keeps falling. Good Congo, for example, which the Company used to buy at 28 and 29 taels, are now eagerly bought at upwards of 40 taels. This is caused by the daily increasing scarcity of silver. Formerly cotton (a great article of import from India) used to be sold at ten days' cash, and opium (as your Excellency is aware) was only given in exchange for sycee. Now, however, both are bartered for produce, and very large barter transactions in the latter article take place at Shanghae especially. Thus, while in former times the entire tea-market was divided between the Honourable East India Company and a few American traders, we have now the British merchants encumbered with large stocks of manufactures which they are anxious to get rid of on any terms; the American merchants, whose native manufactures have increased much within the last dozen years; the India merchants, or country trade, whose supply of cotton has very much increased since the abolition of the Hon. East India Company's charter; and lastly, the opium merchants (as stated above) competing in the same market for the same articles, tea and silk; and under these circumstances can it be matter of astonishment if the prices of these articles should rise? Such being the actual state of our market, if a reduction were now to take place in the duty on teas, can any one doubt from the extensive orders for the articles that would attend such a reduction, from the increased number of speculators in the market, and from the competition that this would give rise to, that the price of teas would be pushed up still higher? And any merchant who has had dealings with the Chinese, cannot be ignorant of the fact, that having once given him a high price for his produce, it is a very hard thing indeed to get him to accept of a lower price afterwards.

Moreover, I do not think that there is any foundation for expecting a very much increased consumption of tea in England, even if the duty were to be reduced one-half. Take, for example, the United States, the people of which are similar to our own people in tastes, and who enjoy pretty much the same average amount of comforts which are the lot of the natives of Great Britain. We find that the United States, with a population of 18,000,000 of souls, consume only about 18,000,000 of pounds of tea, paying a comparative light duty ; while the 27,000,000 of the British Islands take off about 40,000,000 of pounds of tea, after paying a comparatively heavy duty! and there is no country in the world where the consumption of tea is anything in the same proportion. Still further, if with a duty of 2*s*. 1*d*. per lb. staring them in the face, we cannot prevent people shipping inferior teas from this country, which on getting to England are properly called " trash and rubbish," how much more of still inferior teas must we expect, were the duties to be reduced one-half? For these and other cogent reasons I most earnestly pray Her Majesty's Government to pause, and not to give ear to fallacious statements, however flattering they may appear, in a question where millions of the national revenue are at stake ?

THE END.

LONDON:
Printed by S. & J. BENTLEY, WILSON, and FLEY,
Bangor House, Shoe Lane.

LONDON:
Printed by S. & J. BENTLEY, WILSON, and FLEY,
Bangor House, Shoe Lane.